THE CHALLENGE OF AGING

Other Books by John A. B. McLeish

A CANADIAN FOR ALL SEASONS: The John E. Robbins Story

THE ULYSSEAN ADULT: *Creativity in the Middle and Later Years*

SEPTEMBER GALE: *The Life of Arthur Lismer*

THE FAIRFIELD JOURNAL

NOT WITHOUT BEAUTY (Poetry)

JOHN A. B. McLEISH

THE CHALLENGE OF AGING

Ulyssean Paths to Creative Living

1983
Douglas and McIntyre
Vancouver and Toronto

Douglas & McIntyre Ltd.
1615 Venables Street
Vancouver, British Columbia

Canadian Cataloguing in Publication Data
McLeish, John A. B., date
    The challenge of aging

Bibliography: p.
Includes index.
ISBN 0-88894-363-6

1. Aging - Psychological aspects.   2. Creative ability.
3. Rejuvenation. I. Title.

HQ1061.M34   305.2'6   C82-094563-3

Designed by Michael Solomon
Printed and bound in Canada

To the members of
The Ulyssean Society
and
to those Ulyssean men
and women, unknown to the
world, but known to the
readers of this book,
whose lives have helped
to light the windows
of the world.

CONTENTS

FOREWORD

When *The Ulyssean Adult* appeared in 1976, it represented a protest and a lonely voice against the myths of aging and the steady denigration of older adults in North American society, and elsewhere. It was not only that the society did not believe in the capacities and still-unused resources of men and women in their later years, but great numbers of these did not believe in themselves. The foreword of *The Ulyssean Adult* quoted a prominent publisher friend of the author and other hitherto productive adults like him as looking forward with dread to what they conceived to be the unredeemable decline of physical, mental, and creative powers.

In contrast to these very negative views, I noted at that time the phenomenon of what I called "The Ulyssean Adults," adopting the name from Ulysses, the legendary Greek explorer and hero, whose final voyages took place in his late years. These Ulyssean adults were men and women, aged from 50-plus to 80-plus years, appearing in my seminar and personal circles who refused to accept the myths and labels of aging, and used their later and very late years to continue to seek, to learn, to produce, and to create.

During the subsequent six years, signs have appeared of some modest change in public opinion away from simply depreciating older adulthood, and especially there seems to be some quickening of interest among media people and politicians. Much of this early change of climate seems to have come from consciousness of the increased numbers, and hence the increased voting and buying power, of the older population. Much also may have come from the new influence of books like *The Ulyssean Adult*, numbers of which are listed in the revised bibliography—books that treat the later years with new respect, wisdom, wit, and hope.

However, *The Ulyssean Adult* and the present revised edition, *The Challenge of Aging*, still appear unique in three respects: their *systematic* attacks on the myths of aging; their emphasis on sustained creative powers in the later years; and their identification and description of what are now becoming widely known as "Ulyssean people."

In fact, most of the gains made in appreciation of older adulthood may still be illusory, since so-called "senior citizens" and "golden agers" continue to be patronized and referred to as a population to be treated as declining or exhausted in powers, and to be regarded as dependents rather than accepted as equals and superiors. Thus, statements such as those made by *The Ulyssean Adult* and *The Challenge of Aging* have yet to be heard and understood by great numbers of people, and these books continue to have significant roles.

Just as the inspiration of *The Ulyssean Adult* came largely from my own seminars and personal circles in the ten years and more before 1976, so the ideas of *The Challenge of Aging* have been tested many times in circles amounting to many hundreds of adults during the past six years. Many fresh insights have been added; a substantial amount of wholly new writing has been done; and the extensive bibliography of the first book has been heavily revised to provide for more than 70 new references.

In addition, since a new Ulyssean Society has been born in the years between, a comprehensive description of the Society and its work has been included in the Afterword to serve as a model and incentive to groups elsewhere who might wish to form a chapter of the Ulyssean movement.

Therefore, the Creed of the Society, which is also included in the Afterword, is perhaps a fitting close to this Foreword:

As a Companion of THE ULYSSEAN SOCIETY I am committed to the noble concept and the provable fact that men and women in the middle and later years can, if they choose to do so, richly maintain the powers to learn, produce, and create until the very last day of the life journey.

John A. B. McLeish
May 1, 1983

ACKNOWLEDGEMENTS

I am grateful for permission to reproduce brief passages of text from the following copyrighted works: THE DIVINE COMEDY by Dante Alighieri, trans. by Charles S. Singleton, Ballingen Series LXXX, vol. 1, Inferno (copyright© 1970 by Princeton University Press). Reprinted by permission of Princeton University Press. JOURNALS: VENTURESOME YEARS by David E. Lilienthal. Copyright 1966 by Harper and Row Publishers, Inc. PASSPORTS AT SEVENTY by Ethel Sabin Smith. Copyright 1961 by W. W. Norton and Company. CREATIVITY AND ITS CULTIVATION by H. H. Anderson. Copyright 1959 at Harper and Row Publishers, Inc. TOWARD A PSYCHOLOGY OF BEING by Abraham H. Maslow. Published by D. Van Nostrand Reinhold© 1968 Litton Educational Publications, Inc. THE CREATIVE EXPERIENCE by Stanley Rosner and Lawrence E. Abt, The Viking Press© 1970 by The Viking Press. THE GHOST IN THE MACHINE by Arthur Koestler. Copyright© 1968 by Arthur Koestler. Reprinted with permission of Macmillan Publishing Company, Inc. THE NEW YEARS, A NEW MIDDLE AGE by Anne W. Simon. Copyright© 1967, 1968, by Anne W. Simon. Reprinted by permission of Alfred A. Knopf, Inc. IDENTITY AND ANXIETY by M. Stein, A. J. Vidich, and D. M. White. Copyright© 1960 by The Free Press, a corporation. CHILDHOOD AND SOCIETY by E. H. Erickson. Copyright 1950 by W. W. Norton and Company, Inc. Interview with H. L. Klemme in The New York Times, July, 1971,© by The New York Times Company. Reprinted by permission. Headings with text abridged and adapted from MOTIVATION AND PERSONALITY, 2nd Edition, by Abraham H. Maslow. Copyright 1954 by Harper and Row, Publishers, Inc. Copyright© 1970 by Abraham H. Maslow. By permission of the publishers. Chart Rating Life Changes by Thomas Holmes. Reprinted by permission from TIME, The Weekly Newsmagazine; Copyright Time Inc. SOCIOLOGY OF MENTAL DISORDER by Roger Bastide, translated by Jean McNeil. Reprinted by permission of Routledge and Kegan Paul Ltd. DON'T GIVE UP AN AGING PARENT by Lawrence Galton.© 1975 by Lawrence Galton. Used by permission of Crown Publishers, Inc. ADULT LEARNING by E. L. Thorndike, published by Adult Education Association of U.S.A., 1928. Review of ALFRED BINET by R. D. Tuddenham,

Science, March 15, 1974, p. 183. PSYCHOLOGY OF ADULTS by
Irving Lorge, published by Adult Education Association of U.S.A.,
1964. SEA QUEST: GLOBAL BLUE-WATER ADVENTURING
IN SMALL CRAFT by Charles A. Borden, published by Macrae
Smith Company, 1967. THE DELIGHTS OF GROWING OLD by
Maurice Goudeket, published by Farrar, Straus and Giroux, 1966.
THE ARTIST IN HIS STUDIO, by Alexander Liberman, The Vi-
king Press,© 1960 by the Viking Press. Interview with Clementine
Hunter by Mary Gibson in Family Circle, August, 1973. CY-
CLOPEDIC SURVEY OF CHAMBER MUSIC, Edited by Walter W.
Cobbett.© Oxford University Press 1963 by permission of the Oxford
University Press, Oxford. HARRY S. TRUMAN by Margaret Tru-
man, published by William Morrow and Company Inc.© 1973. TWO
STORIES AND A MEMORY by Guiseppe Di Lampedusa, translated
by Archibald Colquhoun© 1962 by William Collins, Sons and Com-
pany, Limited and Pantheon Books, Inc. Reprinted by permission of
Pantheon Books, Inc. APPLIED IMAGINATION by Alex Osborn,
published by Charles Scribner's Sons, 1953.

In addition, I wish to express my warm appreciation to J. V.
O'Brien and Carl M. Yelland of The Ulyssean Society for their untiring
interest and work in furthering the publication of The Challenge of
Aging, together with the sustained assistance in this of the Steering
Committee of the Society, of the author's consulting colleague Dr. Fos-
ter Vernon, and very notably of Dr. Harold Bohne of Toronto.

I feel a special debt of gratitude to my editor Betty Jane Corson, and
to Patsy Aldana and Kelly Mitchell at Douglas & McIntyre.

I also wish to thank a number of friends and colleagues for their un-
failing help and encouragement in the extended task of producing this
book. These include especially my distinguished colleague Dr. J. Roby
Kidd, Myra and Daniel Krangle, Warren S. Jevons, Associate Director
of the University of Toronto School of Continuing Studies, Professor
Cope Schwenger, Ajmal Ali Khan, Armando E. Nizzoli, Sydney J.
O'Neil, Vera Rosberg, Roman Poplawski, Michel Brykert, Helen
Brunton, Eileen Ellis, Fern Gordon, Barbara Byam, and former Ambassador John E. Robbins.

Professor Franklin Morris Berry, Director of the Institute of Gerontology, California School of Professional Psychology, Fresno, California, and Dr. Virginia L. Boyack, Vice-President, Life Planning and
Educational Development, California Federal, Los Angeles, have been
untiring in their support of this publication. Further stimulus and encouragement were provided by such other American friends as Mrs.
Marty Wilson of Bellevue, Washington; Professor Dorothy H. Coons
of the University of Michigan Institute of Gerontology; Professor
Susan Ritchie, Director of the Kent State University Gerontology Center; and Jacqueline T. Sunderland, Director, National Center on the

Arts and Aging, Washington, D.C. The enthusiasm of Craig Chambers of Rancho Bernardo, San Diego, California, contributed to the original formation of The Ulyssean Society, and has extended to the publication of *The Challenge of Aging*.

Warm thanks are also due to Catherine Cain, Librarian of the Yorkville Library, Toronto, and her staff, as well as to a previous head librarian, Marjorie Grey; and to the reference staff of the library of the Ontario Institute for Studies in Education, Toronto.

If I were to add a further dedication to this book, it would be to my sister, Margaret McLeish Varey of Montreal, and to my nephews, James Richard Varey of Montreal and John Allan Varey of Burlington, Ontario.

"It is a rule of life that when one door closes, another door always opens. Let us not, therefore, mourn so much for the losses behind the closed door that we miss the opportunities waiting for us beyond the newly opened door."

André Gide

I

THE UNREALIZED POTENTIALS
OF ADULTHOOD

T HE CENTURY of adult self-fulfillment"—this is the proud title that might have been given to the twentieth century in Western society. And in spite of terrible wars and human deprivations, it is true that our social system, now approaching the year 2000, has made great gains in providing some of the means to actualize human potential. Great gains—but also great failures, the greatest of which has been the throwing away of the rich unused resources available in multitudes of men and women in their later adult maturity.

How is this possible in a society that has had the imagination to provide networks of services and inventions which directly or indirectly support and encourage adult personal growth and learning? Technological progress has made possible a popular low-cost culture— paperback books, stereo sets, long-playing records and cassettes, the transistor radio, and television with many high-grade as well as low-grade programs. Government aid has made possible thousands of public libraries, thousands also of adult education courses, night schools, colleges and universities, and pension and medical support schemes. Medical research has made possible an extension of life by over 20 years for the average citizen (more so in the case of women). Thus the adult in 1983 has gained almost another life of mature activity from the adult life of 1883.

The noted gerontologist Bernice Neugarten is even able to apply the term "young-old adult" to those adults in the age range 55-75 whom she describes as "relatively free from traditional social responsibilities of work and family . . . relatively healthy, relatively well-off, and politically active. We predict that these characteristics will become increasingly salient by the year 2000." The rather rare usage, "salient," means "conspicuous"; Neugarten's statement is a prophecy, in a book of the future: *Aging into the 21st Century*. Taken with the seemingly affirmative gains of the society, already cited, the picture seems to be one of glowing optimism.

If so, it is optimism for the future. For the *existing* scene in North American society a tragic contrast exists between the inherent potentials of men and women in their middle and later years and the technological and social benefits conferred by the environment, on the one hand, and the actual realization of those potentials, on the other hand, in terms of what Abraham Maslow called, "self-actualized adulthood." Once again, as innumerable times before in history, we are confronted with the power of obsessive ideas, of life deforming myths, in governing or misgoverning human development.

Seven great myths about aging still dominate whole aspects of our society and the minds of probably most adults, young and old. These are the myths: that, if you only live long enough, you will likely become senile; that in the later 50s and thereafter, sexual pleasure and practice virtually cease (or should cease!); that in the later years you will become more rigid in thought, more intolerant in attitude; that learning powers decline throughout later middle age (if not before) and radically fall off by late age; that creativity is likewise a steadily declining curve from the 30s on; that time for the creative life is typically exhausted (the "I-always-meant-to" syndrome); and that energy, physical and psychic, is exhausted, too.

Since great folk attitudes, whatever their source, saturate society and govern its practices, it is no surprise to find the rich promise of middle and later adulthood in our time unfulfilled. Thus, we have the phenomenon of millions of older adults, still competent, highly experienced, well equipped with creative potential, designated as "senior citizens" and "golden-agers," literally, not merely figuratively, "put out to pasture," "put on the shelf," and other obliging metaphors of the prevailing social attitudes. In North America, at least, an incessant propaganda pours from advertisers and commentators, from all forms of the media, on the health, vivacity, strength, and upsurging activities of youth and younger-age adults. So far as older adults appear, they appear either as social problems for discussion ("What shall we do with our aging population?") or as members of an exhausted generation rather than vigorous confrères in the situation comedies, eternal soap operas, and later night movies. The advertising commercials that saturate the media are just beginning to acknowledge the presence of older adults, worked in among endless reminders of the joys and physical needs of youth, as a late conversion to a steadily growing consumer market of later-age people.

It is true that the media, the commentators, and the politicians dwell also upon certain major problems of the young: notably such issues as drugs, abortion, and unemployment. But both youth and its problems are redeemed in the eyes of these people by a virtue that they deny the older adults—potentiality. Meanwhile youth and younger adults are presented with images confirming what it can mean to be old, ill, and alone in a throwaway society—to be caught in a succession of poverties: poverty of financial means (two-thirds of widowed women in Canada and the United States, aged 60 and over, live, e.g., below the poverty line), poverty of energy and achievement, poverty of motivation, and saddest of all, poverty of hope and love.

It is true that many younger adults feel for a time a certain indignation and compassion for the neglect of the human needs and conceivable aspirations of older adults. But usually this passes. Young adults must get on with their own lives. Somewhere in their thinking recurs the determination to, at the least, avoid entrapment in nursing homes, which are the cages of old and alienated "senior citizens." Yet inevitably, because they are fellow voyagers with older men and women on the great human highway, younger people do not cease to observe. Consciously or unconsciously, they are always monitoring the scene, recording what older people are like, mentally trying on certain identities they see among older adults. They look with a certain fascinated curiosity at these people, who are quite diverse in backgrounds and in the varieties of success or failure with which they seem to handle their exacting roles on the stage of later life.

Some of these "ambassadors" from the "growing old" country are, in fact, prestigious and affluent. One would expect prestige and wealth to be two sure ramparts against the hardships and sorrows of age. Yet "the man who has everything" may in fact have missed the greatest gift of all—the ability to live creatively, lovingly, and serenely through the later years. Frustrated and embittered millionaires are well known to priests and journalists; while everyone knows penniless old men and women, racked with illness, whose timeless and cheerful spirits and productivity within their own small worlds astonish and reinvigorate the younger people around them.

At all events, wherever these people go, they are observed. The aging and the old may be neglected and patronized, but they will nonetheless be observed. They represent a country privately dreaded by much of society, not for its strength but for its weakness, and not for its potential but for its supposedly interminable decline into exhaustion and death. It is the country largely assumed to be one of non-roles and non-creativity—the country of Non.

If you are young, sensitive, and observant, and secretly curious about how adults negotiate the process of aging, as has been the case with dozens of students in my seminars, you are certain to meet frequently at least these three envoys:

1. The first is the older adult to whom life always seems to have happened, rather than he happening to it, to paraphrase Erik Erikson. His lifestyle might be described as consisting of Total Expectedness. He has indeed nearly run the race and nearly finished the course; but the race has always been run on the safe and well-pounded track of routine, without the runner's even taking an occasional sortie into the enchanting but possibly dangerous countryside extending outside the track. When the chips were down—and the chips were down periodically during his early and prime years—he did what was expected of him.

This type of later adult is very often a "good" person, both with and without the quotation marks, but his or her life has consisted of negatives: Don't rock the boat, don't step outside the limit; don't get involved; don't explore yourself too much; don't disturb your years with dreams because dreams may let you down.

Many of these adults are the unknown citizens of whom W. H. Auden wrote: "Was he free? Was he happy? The question is absurd. Had anything been wrong, we should certainly have heard." In fact, as they have done all their lives, they continue to preserve a passive spectator role. Often warmly attached to the domestic scene, they are especially desolate in the later years if death or the mandates of the holy "nuclear" family leave them bereft and lonely.

2. The second envoy to come under the young adult's scrutiny may at first seem more heartening. Here is a person who at least seems to have gone through some attempts at the identification of self. He is not afraid to speak of early abortive efforts at creativity outside the expected lifestyle and career, and to talk of unrealized dreams or of untried opportunities. This individual is at least aware that in his life certain vistas, certain experiences that might have brought him closer to fulfillment, have been missed.

Thus, this older adult could well appreciate a forgotten story told by Albert Edward Wiggam in his *Marks of an Educated Man*. One summer night, to the home of a bored and disappointed man in his later middle years comes a visitor who enchants him with his wisdom, wit, and loving-kindness and also with his tales of travel, adventures, remarkable friends, books read and written and lovely deeds performed for and by others. When at length the disappointed man emerges from the spell long enough to ask the visitor who he is, he replies, "I am the man you might have been."

This second envoy is also much more aware of his own identity than the first. Through the years he has made brief sorties into the domains of unorthodox ideas, magical concepts, and across class and ethnic barriers marked "Out of Bounds." All of this has given him a certain aura that attracts younger adults.

Still, there is an air of pathos and defeat about this possible model. When all is said and done, he does not feel himself to be the man "he might have been," which is to his credit. But the disaster is that he clearly feels that the whole game is over. What can you do, he thinks, with the later years, with the zest of youth faded, the neuron system closing down, and creativity a hill city left behind with the lights receding?

3. The third representative seems at first glance to be the kind of older adult with whom one can at least join in a joyful expedition in the often forbidding country of the later years. This is the adult who has been consummately successful in his chosen field. The sight of such

success in a world filled with half-successes and outright failures is often stimulating and reassuring to the success-oriented young.

Then, with a chill of recognition, the younger observer and would-be disciple notes that many of these individuals have opted out of "the creativity game." These are sophisticated people, the smart ones, the people with the answers. Some have read Harvey Lehman's book, *Age and Achievement*, in which the peak of creative powers is placed in the 30s; or they have heard dozens of similar comments over the past 20 years. Besides, they, too, are infected by "the manifest condition": Isn't it *manifest* that most later adults, notably from the mid-60s on, have ceased to be creative? Thus, for even these debonair performers of yesterday, there are no new worlds to conquer because life itself and the old wives' tales of the folk culture have conquered them.

The form of "disgust and despair" that fills the lives of many of these older adults, though less corrosive and heartbreaking then that of non-achievers, is real and poignant enough. If you are a life-lover and something of a Faust who wishes to play many parts on the stage of what Kim's lama called "this great and terrible world," the objective is noble, and there is never enough time to realize it. A dozen lifetimes are not enough.

But in any case, this particular kind of disgust and despair does not take its most debilitating form from the brevity of life. Rather it comes from the conviction that, even with the precious time that is left, little or nothing can be done of any creative significance. If one can believe this—millions do—and make a way of life out of it in later adulthood, then indeed there is no place to go but down. The sadness of this descent can be seen even in apparently exuberant figures among this third group of older adults whose inner pessimism seeps into and sours their late-life style.

Thus our society slopes downward in the great human "life cycle," as it is brutally named, to a dark valley in some ways more fearful than the Psalmist's valley of the shadow of death. And this fact is known to the young, at least as a "gut feeling;" and as a depressingly imminent state to those adults who are themselves already on the brink of old age.

It is at this point, however, that a remarkable fourth protagonist appears upon the stage. He brings light with him, the light of creativity retained or regained, and the surging joy of human powers confidently held and used.

This is the exciting later adult personality whom I have chosen to call "the Ulyssean Adult."

The title comes, of course, from Ulysses, the Latin name for Odysseus, the adventurous King of Ithaca and hero of Greek legend who would have been about 50 when the great series of adventures described in *The Odyssey* was coming to an end, and perhaps close to 70 when he began his last adventures. Nonetheless, so open and resilient was his mind to experience, and so dauntless and questing his spirit, that Tennyson chose Ulysses as the subject of a poem dedicated to the thesis that only death can end the creative searching of such a man—and possibly not even death.

Tennyson had been an absorbed student of *The Odyssey* for years, and the portrait he paints of the classic hero is a projection of the authentic traits of Ulysses with which he had long been familiar. However, his portrait also owes a heavy debt to Dante's conception of Ulysses in late life in the wonderful Twenty-sixth Canto of his *Inferno*. In Dante's version, Ulysses, already a man in full maturity when he returned from ten years of adventures after the fall of Troy, makes the decision in late life to yet again

> . . .put forth on the deep open sea with one vessel only and with that small company which had not deserted me. . . .I and my companions were old and slow when we came to that narrow outlet where Hercules set up his markers, that men should not pass beyond. . . ."Oh brothers," I said, "who through a hundred thousand dangers have reached the west, choose not to deny experience, following the sun, of the world that has no people. Consider your origin: you were not made to live as brutes, but to pursue virtue and knowledge." With this little speech I made my companions so keen for the voyage that then I could hardly have held them back. And turning our stern to the morning, we made of our oars wings for the mad flight, always gaining on the left. . .

Tennyson's poem shows Ulysses a number of years after his return from his Mediterranean wanderings, during which time he has ruled his little kingdom of Ithaca. But he is dissatisfied with routines of kingship that could be done as well or better by his son, Telemachus. Ulysses has, in fact, been living for some years the life of Total Expectedness. This does not satisfy his restless, searching mind and spirit.

He is grateful for his past experiences:

> I am a part of all that I have met

but they have all been preparations for yet more adventures and discoveries:

> Yet all experience is an arch wherethro'
> Gleams that untravell'd world, whose margin fades
> For ever and for ever when I move. . .

The quest of adventure, mystery, and beauty has been the compelling motive of his entire life. But for all his joy and love of life, Ulysses is too much a realist not to know that although the years have given much, they have also taken their inescapable toll. Still, he calls his comrades around him, and summons them to join him in adventures in which the will is the critical element—the will to search, to discover, to accomplish dreams—in the continuing creativity of their later years:

> Come, my friends,
> 'Tis not too late to seek a newer world.
> Push off, and sitting well in order smite
> The sounding furrows; for my purpose holds
> To sail beyond the sunset, and the baths
> Of all the western stars, until I die.
> It may be that the gulfs will wash us down:
> It may be we shall touch the Happy Isles,
> And see the great Achilles, whom we knew.
> Tho' much is taken, much abides; and tho'
> We are not now that strength which in old days
> Moved earth and heaven; that which we are, we are;
> One equal temper of heroic hearts,
> Made weak by time and fate, but strong in will
> To strive, to seek, to find, and not to yield.

About 2,600 years separates the two great poems in which Ulysses appears as the central figure; yet both remain among the deathless poetry of the human race, not merely because of their craftsmanship, but because Ulysses himself is of enduring fascination to people of all centuries.

Ulysses has become, through this immense span of human time, an heroic, semi-mythical figure, but he is not a god. He is not a freak or a mutation, but intensely human: a man who symbolizes the aspirations of men—notably, of course, in his confrontation of time and fate. Yet this confrontation is without bravado. Ulysses turns it into a quest and makes it a part of the human condition.

Ulysses thought and behaved as he did because of the kind of man he was, not because he was a king in Ithaca living among gods and heroes. The time in which he played out his intrepid and beautiful life was seemingly very different from our own—light-years seem to separate the world of the barque on the wine-dark sea from our society. But the Ulyssean adult can still be found in every stratum and ethnic group in our world of the late twentieth century.

What qualities especially identify the Ulyssean person? Perhaps the most remarkable is the governing sense of quest. Ulysses has for centuries been synonymous with the restless search for travel and adventure—even to those millions who may know little of the classic. This identification with Ulysses still exists in spite of the homogenized modern education to which many younger adults have been exposed. Otherwise the story of Ulysses would not have been chosen as the subject of a hugely successful Hollywood film.

Courage is the most striking quality Ulysses manifested in his search for new experience. He is famous, it is true, for other characteristics: shrewdness and cunning, resourcefulness, loyalty to comrades, and all-too-human capacity for cruel revenge upon those who have hurt him or his family or who have endangered his honor. But his courage is so strong a feature of his nature that when it is combined with his sense of quest and his frequent loneliness and hardships, the result is a person not only heroic but movingly human—perhaps throughout history and legend the most human and heartwarming of all heroes.

Therefore, in our own time, a later-life man or woman who maintains the questing spirit, and who does so with courage and resourcefulness in a wide variety of circumstances, public or solitary, many of them terribly, even tragically adverse, may well be described as Ulyssean. It is not the time or the location but the quality of the life being lived that creates the Ulyssean adult.

The essential quality of that life is creative, and it appears in two major sorts of later-life creators. One, which for the sake of convenience might be termed *Ulyssean One*, is the man or woman who begins new creative enterprises, small or large, in later years. The other, which might be called *Ulyssean Two*, is the older adult who does not strike out on new paths and creative territories but who remains creatively productive within his or her own familiar arena of life and work from later middle age into the very late years.

The working designations, Ulysseans One and Two, are not to be taken as indicating respective grades of merit. Both are equally fine in their enactment of the drama of continuing creativity in the later years. However, although both kinds of Ulyssean adults are equal in merit and in beauty, there is a special excitement to Ulysseans One because of their quality of unexpectedness. These are best illustrated by a few actual profiles of people, in this case obviously attractive to me, but whose number could be supplemented by hundreds of others.

Edith Hamilton, whose paperback books, *The Greek Way, The Roman Way, Mythology*, and others are found throughout the world, had no thought of developing a career as a popular writer when, nearly 60, she retired as headmistress of the Bryn Mawr School for Girls. Returning to the old family home on the New England coast, she began a life of charming domestic retirement. She played expertly the roles of good sister, good aunt, delightful friend, preparer of meals, member of the community, and watcher of tides and seasons. She also told and retold stories and legends from the classical period so vividly that her friends urged her to start writing them down. For some years she resisted, refusing to believe that a wider audience existed, and insisting she was not a writer. Finally, under persuasion, she sat down and began the book that was to become *The Greek Way*, and a bestseller. Other publications followed. Yet all through her long later life, and in spite of this dramatic new venture, she maintained her other roles. She never lost her love of life. At the age of 90, having decided to visit Europe again after 25 years, she was amused to hear that her sister had remarked to a friend how glad she was that Edith would have a last chance to make that tour. Edith Hamilton then revisited Europe on *four* annual tours accompanied by her close (and much younger) friend and later biographer Doris Read. At 91, Hamilton received the freedom of the city of Athens in a moving ceremony in one of the great theaters. She described this as the proudest moment of her life. Hers was the unusual case of the Ulyssean One adult who actually touched the borders of the heroic legend itself.

Ulyssean One adults, in fact, turn up with remarkable frequency in the writing world, often as novelists, performing a totally new role after most of a lifetime spent in other pursuits. Thomas Costain was a prominent editor and a dedicated reader of history for years before he began at 55 writing a series of immensely successful novels. Costain had had at least an association with writing, but Cervantes, who began to write *Don Quixote* when he was almost 60, had been a professional soldier. Lloyd C. Douglas was 50 and a noted preacher in Montreal when he began *Magnificent Obsession*. The story was peddled among a dozen editors before becoming one of the most successful bestsellers of the century. At 72, Douglas produced the famous novel, *The Robe*. Wilder Penfield was world-famous as a brain surgeon when, in his 60s, he picked up an old story his mother had always hoped to write, and transformed her notes and ideas into the radically different plot and milieu of the fine novel, *No Other Gods*. Penfield followed it six years later with another novel, *The Torch*.

In all these cases, the factor of unexpectedness is constant. No one expected the editor, the soldier, the preacher, the brain surgeon to break out into the new adventure of writing a novel, which even as a physical exercise is strenuous and demanding—and to do so in their later years.

The reverse process is found in the late life of the French novelist, Lou Andréas-Salomé, which is recorded in a few pages by Simone de Beauvoir. Andréas-Salomé entered the world and the thought of Sigmund Freud at age 50; was in her 60s when she became a practicing professional psychotherapist; awakened late to physical participation in sex and carried it on for years, transferring this to loving platonic friendships with men in her very late years. Harassed by terrible physical illnesses and by the terrors of the Nazi occupation of France, she nevertheless sought to open up new channels of thought and action for herself not only in psychoanalysis but in philosophy, in the improvement of the human condition, and through tender friendships with a wide circle of all sorts of people. She experienced the full assault of the world on her body, mind, and spirit; yet her life was lovely at the close, still seeking enrichment in new interests, still unembittered. The life of this Ulyssean One, in fact, demonstrates that in spite of everything, life is always conquered by the unembittered.

Benjamin Spock, in his late 60s, was an internationally famous pediatrician—wealthy, medically orthodox, the foster father, in effect, of millions of American and Canadian 'Spock babies.' There was no apparent evidence of Ulysseanism in his late life, except perhaps in his devotion to intelligent play and recreation. Then the terrible Vietnam War escalated—no more terrible, in fact, than a hundred wars before it, and far surpassed by the obscene tragedy of World War One. But television delivered the conflict daily into the kitchens and living rooms of the American people, and the tens of thousands of young Americans who enlisted and died seemed uselessly sucked in by a quagmire. Public revulsion grew, but American patriotic sentiment was still strong, and Benjamin Spock's totally unexpected appearance as leader of the anti-war forces took courage and imagination. A widespread outcry arose against him; the federal government pursued him into the courts; he found himself often cold-shouldered and scowled at in airports and on streets. But the Ulyssean adventure was a success: Spock's courage was matched by his shrewdness, and he knew that he spoke for the forces of life and sanity. Furthermore, his leadership on Vietnam was simply the beginning of a second unexpected Ulyssean career in civil rights.

In his fine book, *Starting Over*, Damon Stetson describes the thoughts and actions of a midlife adult at the point where he turns from one secure and successful career and seeks a second or third one. The case in point is that of David E. Lilienthal, who by the time he was 50 had become successively chairman of the Tennessee Valley Authority and the United States Atomic Energy Commission. At this point he sought "a newer world." In volume three of his *Journals*, called significantly *Venturesome Years*, Lilienthal writes:

> At this time I was neither young nor old. . .I had to make a choice. . . .I could choose to play it safe. I could choose to live on my past accomplishments, doing what I knew I could do. That would have been easy—but personally disastrous. That course I rejected. . . .I chose instead to take on ventures new and untried, to do things I did not know I could do, to try once again to find that venturesome and affirmative life that I had always lived before, the kind of life in which in earlier years I found myself truly functioning.

The words could almost be a paraphrase of those of Dante's Ulysses. Lilienthal traveled for a time, rested, thought much, then entered a new world of action as a managerial and industrial consultant privately dedicated to helping improve the life of ordinary people of all races around the globe. In doing so, he obviously made great use of past expertise—but so did Ulysses, and so do all who venture on new enterprises in their middle and later years, even if only to use their accumulated resources from the bank of faith, hope, and courage.

Sometimes adversity, not success, is the force that drives the Ulysseans One into wholly unexpected ventures. Misfortune also presents one with choices: either to accept defeat quietly or to launch out into new creative planning and action, hoping for the best. Ralph Knode's case, also cited by Stetson, is a vivid illustration of this. Knode was born into an affluent Philadelphia family and, following college and service in the air force, married and became a successful salesman with a cement company. He had an expensive home and a portfolio of stocks started for him in his youth by his family, and seemed set in the pattern of that fortunate minority who are "comfortably fixed" for life.

Ralph Knode, however, had a severe drinking problem, to some extent the result of work for which he was emotionally unsuited. As is often the case, the two problems, the alcoholism and the work, interacted upon one another. The company placed him in office work, which he found boring. He had reached a kind of moment of truth; fortunately he had the support of an understanding wife. He made a radical decision, a Ulyssean One decision: with recollections of a boyhood trip to Wyoming, Knode decided to explore a wholly new world. For a year he worked as a ranch hand, a grueling year of hard physical work. Then he and his wife bought a small ranch, then a much larger one. Six years later, in 1970, although he still had heavy debts incurred by purchasing the ranches, Knode had conquered his problem with alcohol. He owned over 2,000 acres and a very large herd of Black Angus cattle. Ralph, his wife, and their three children were united in a life that offered more isolation than eastern city routines, but had the compensation of being home on the range. For *unexpectedness*, it would be hard to imagine a more dramatic change of career. Perhaps those who seek the path of Ulyssean One would do well to remember Charles Luckman's dictum when he abandoned the presidency of Lever Brothers to return to his profession of 20 years back (architecture): You don't have to prove anything to your friends, and you shouldn't disturb yourself about your enemies.

Sometimes Ulyssean changes in middle and later life lead to not only second and third but even fourth careers. The Canadian educator and facilitator of cultural growth, John Everett Robbins, was 50 and had been a prominent civil servant in Ottawa for 20 years when he had the opportunity to help launch the *Encyclopedia Canadiana* as its editor-in-chief. The challenge was exciting, but the venture involved giving up the usual securities of civil service life, not least the pension arrangements. Robbins took the plunge, however, producing over five years the ten-volume publication that was hailed as a major contribution to Canada's sense of identity. What next? Robbins could have stayed on with the encyclopedia, but for so innovative a person the zest was gone. He soon took on the presidency of a small college in western Canada which during the ensuing decade he transformed into a university. When he resigned in 1969, it was a gutsy decision because his term had three years to run and he had no immediate prospects. In fact, he was soon considering a post as coordinator of campus contacts for the program of external aid. But before he could begin his work he was offered, in midsummer of 1969, the job of first Canadian ambassador to the Holy See. After his three-year tour, which Robbins and his wife described as "beautiful," he came home to Ottawa, where at 71 he deeply involved himself in the work of World Federalism and other "passionate causes."

A child of fortune? Perhaps, to a degree. But Robbins was always ready to take the Ulyssean decision: to seek a newer world where the creativity he felt to be an integral part of his life could have free play, even at the risk of occasionally astonishing friends and baffling enemies with unexpectedness.

Men who retire, and women who embark on enterprises outside the home in middle and later adulthood, are often glowing examples of Ulysseans One. One example is a New York State Commissioner of Education who, on retiring at 65 in the 1950s, announced to his startled friends that he had always wanted to be a lawyer. He thereupon enrolled in the Albany Law School, graduating at 69 and arguing cases for years, including situations where he appeared before his successors as Commissioners of Education! A recent Canadian counterpart is the Ontario medical executive, Glenn Sawyer, who at 65, in the fall of 1974, enrolled in law studies at the University of Western Ontario, graduated in 1977, and now practices medico-legal work in Toronto.

Still another Ulyssean undergraduate was Harry Craimer of Montreal, who gave up the active management of his accountancy firm in 1974 to enroll at McGill University in the East Asian Studies program, taking courses in Chinese language and history, Japanese literature, and comparative economic systems.

An even more striking case of the Ulyssean student is E. Lyall Nelson of Montreal, a former banker who retired after 44 years and began B.A. studies at Concordia University which he had intended to pursue almost a lifetime before. Nelson entered in 1971, graduated in 1974 after taking 20 courses in three years, and then enrolled in M.A. studies.

Yet Craimer, Sawyer, and Nelson are mere youths compared to 90-year-old Mal Wickham, described in April, 1975, as "the oldest student at the University of Wisconsin." Wickham, we are told, returned to college studies after a career that included 40 years of farming. He *jogged* to his classes.

Enormous numbers of women now return to a former vocation after 15 or 20 years of married life. Increasingly, of course, they combine both work and marriage from the honeymoon on. But the Ulyssean element enters with the re-entry of women of quite advanced years to career or educational ventures, or with those of middle years who, feeling themselves no longer growing as persons, strike out on new paths with the inevitable hazards of possible failure. Barbara Powell O'Neill in her stimulating book, *Careers for Women after Marriage and Children*, "for the woman who wants individual self-fulfillment as well as marriage," cites Ruth K. Caress of East Meadow, Long Island, as an example of this.

Ruth Caress had reached the age of about 40 with an early college education, an able and understanding husband, a family of three children, a number of worthwhile community voluntary activities, and an attractive home. Her expression, however, of certain personal problems she was experiencing as an individual could serve as the classic stereotype of the unrealized woman in her middle years. In her interviews with O'Neill these phrases occur: "Despite all this. . .a deep sense of personal frustration. . .a sense of being without any personal identification. . .Deriving little or no gratification from the shape of my life. . ." (This syndrome could, of course, be matched by many thousands of men also, about whom L. E. Sissman writes, "Men past forty/Get up nights, And look out/at City Lights. . .")

Caress tells us that her early academic record had been mediocre; she had been long away from studies; if she went back, she would have to accept teachers who were younger than herself. Nonetheless, she decided to take the plunge and enroll in a school of social work. In spite of the hard work and anxieties of this late studentship, it was a success; there were also pleasant surprises. For example: "The kudos from teachers and supervisors were rebuilding a self-esteem badly battered by years of intellectual stagnation." She became a caseworker for a family service organization, thus pursuing a creative Ulyssean search for a richer personal identity.

Often with women as with men, the Ulyssean One adventure is something that astonishes not only one's friends but oneself. The Canadian columnist True Davidson in 1968 entered upon the extraordinary odyssey at age 66, of becoming mayor of one of Ontario's large surburban cities, East York. When she retired from the post in 1972, it was not because she felt herself too old but because she felt the urge for other ventures—writing a column for a Toronto daily paper was one. A characteristic of many Ulysseans is that they do not plan their moves as though these were chessboard strategies; they seek experience as "an arch wherethro'/Gleams that untravell'd world, whose margin fades/For ever and ever" as they move. The mayoralty of a large city was not part of Davidson's long-range calculations at, say, age 60, but her Ulyssean spirit made her ready for it.

An outstanding case of how the Ulyssean One experience can be thrust upon somebody essentially ready for it is seen in the later life of the French writer and mystic, Gabrielle Bossis. This remarkable woman was born in Nantes in 1874 and died on June 9, 1950. She was the daughter of wealthy parents, a charming, high-spirited girl whose mystical nature was long concealed by her participation in all the social and artistic activities of her class. She rejected the chance to become a nun, thus seeming in the church's eyes to choose the world; yet she refused offers of marriage that might have separated her from her hidden vocation. Bossis undertook "quite late in life," according to her translator, Evelyn Brown, the writing of religious plays, which she also often acted in and produced. She traveled extensively, not only because of her plays, but seemingly because of her *joie de vivre* and deep interest in people and their situations.

The Ulyssean adventure that marked an extraordinary development of her life occurred at age 62. Bossis began to keep an intimate personal journal of a type she could not possibly have anticipated in earlier years, and which is wholly original. It began with her trip to Canada on the *Ile de France*, continued through her cross-Canada tour, and ended shortly before her death. It was almost wholly devoted to a series of dialogues with a mysterious inner voice that Evelyn Brown remarks, Gabrielle Bossis "felt with awe, though sometimes with anxious questionings, to be the voice of Christ." The journal was written during constant travels at airports, at sea, at dozens of stops throughout France, Europe, and North Africa. Bossis was not a recluse. She had inherited money and was intensely life-loving; she had many friends and had made for herself in her later years a successful career in her own sphere of play-acting, writing, and producing. Still, the journal, which she kept for 13 years, was an intensely private thing; she never attempted to exploit the experience of the Dialogue for personal gain or power. It was published anonymously very late in her life; some years after her death, Bossis was revealed as the writer in the edition produced by Daniel-Rops as *Lui et Moi (He and I)*. The news of its authorship astounded her friends.

The secret journal was the Ulyssean adventure of Bossis's later years; to read it is to encounter a loving, creative, and Ulyssean spirit.

As we have said, the man or woman in later adulthood who does not suddenly convert to new careers and enterprises but who remains richly productive within the sphere of creativity where he or she has long performed is a Ulyssean Two. Interestingly, Ulysses himself was really a Ulyssean Two. His essential role, imposed upon him in *The Odyssey* by apprenticeship to the gods, was that of skilled captain-adventurer—his obligations as a king were both essential and incidental to his great role. The excitement of his epic voyage in late life through the Gates of Hercules was not that he embarked upon a wholly new career but that he resumed the life of quest, risk, and discovery when he found himself drying up and losing his sense of self-significance. To be a Ulyssean Two, one must obviously be more than a repeater of the routine. There must be creative action, not merely continued motion. While the dramatic and unexpected change in lifestyle and/or career that marks Ulysseans One makes the adventure and creativity of their later lives stand out unmistakably, the picture is less clear with the other Ulysseans. Here the whole question of what is creative living and doing arises much more urgently.

The word "routine," says the *Concise Oxford Dictionary*, means "the unvarying performance of certain acts." It has, interestingly, nothing whatever to do with the quality of the performance itself. A successful and aging comedian on national television may continue to delight viewers with comedy styles and laugh-inducers, which he shrewdly repeats for the fortieth year; a preacher may continue to console or inspire congregations with repeated or revamped sermons that guarantee his acceptability; a homemaker may make the same marvelous pies and present the same appetizing menu on the supper table through years of family life; and a politician may continue to be re-elected election after election by uttering the same clichés. Such habitual performances can be admirable in themselves—but they are not Ulyssean.

In all lifestyles, including those of Ulysseans, a certain amount of routine is indispensable. It provides the settled minimum order of daily living that frees mind and body for higher activities. But when the routine *becomes* the lifestyle, when the lives of men and women operate only within a circular track of unexamined attitudes, unimproved skills, and numbing rituals, then the creative spirit enters into a long catalepsy. This is the situation that led Whitehead to compare much of middle age to a highway clogged with cars, each moving at the sluggish pace dictated by the stupefying conformity of all. At the worst, the years of routine may create a personality insensitive or hostile to even promising change, made rigid by the drying-out of laughter and hope, and warmed by the memories of past achievements and redundant honors.

The word "still" can be deadly when applied to men and women caught in the nets of dull, unliberating routines: "Do you mean to say that Thorold is still in that job at Gray and Company?"; but it glows with life and energy when it describes the continuation of creative achievement into the later and often very late years. Alfred North Whitehead was still so filled with the fires of thought that he published his four major works after the age of 65; Balanchine still choreographed brilliant ballets as he crossed his 70th birthday; Edison was still inventing with rich imagination in his late 70s and early 80s; William Butler Yeats took what runners call his "second wind" after a stormy and troubled middle age, and still produced nobly and beautifully until his death at 74; Buckminster Fuller's mind and hand still teem with innovation at 85 as they did at 60.

In the lives of all Ulysseans Two the sense of quest and wonder is strong, undiminished by age. This persists in spite of enormous handicaps. Consider, for example, Handel's crushing debts, Wagner's neuroses, César Franck's almost constant neglect by the musical public, Holst's loss of most of the public he had temporarily gained with *The Planets*. The quality of intense humanness was also characteristic of these men: Whatever they were, they were real, not plastic, people. This human reality ranged all the way from Haydn's great sweetness of nature and affection to Wagner's assortment of hatreds, the most repulsive of which was his macabre anti-Semitism. No one can pretend that all the Ulysseans are "nice" people. Chou En-lai's nature was clearly both tough and cruel, yet he would certainly qualify as a Ulyssean Two.

The world of painting seems to swarm with these Ulysseans Two. Reading, for example, Alexander Liberman's book, *The Artist in His Studio*, which consists of Liberman's interviews with nearly 40 noted European artists of our time, is an invigorating experience. "Our time" begins with Cézanne, Renoir, Monet, and Bonnard, and concludes with a group of artists elderly in years but still fully generative: for example, Dubuffet, Ernst Richier, Bazaine, Giacometti, Hartung, and Manessier. The first astounding fact to emerge about these Ulysseans is their longevity; the next is their vitality. All but six reached age 70; eighteen lived to age 80, and half of those to beyond 85. Liberman began his odyssey among these painters and sculptors just after World War Two, and longevity was the least of his interests. In fact, to the absorbed reader it plays a secondary role to the élan, the joy in the wonder and beauty of the world which continues to characterize what are, after all, very elderly men.

At a great age, and ill, the Romanian sculptor, Constantin Brancusi, tells Liberman that he is still working on the concept of the bird—that in fact what he seeks is the meaning of flight. Georges Rouault remarks that one must be humble and not think that one knows; that everything must be begun again; that, after all, he has waited until age 70 before going to Italy! And Alberto Giacometti, whose passionate creativity finally exhausted him at 65, says that he has been 50,000 times to the Louvre, copying everything in drawing, "trying to understand."

Unlike Pablo Picasso, who continued to produce lavishly into his 90s, and who felt compelled to strip himself of any possessive hand, even the hand of love, few of these Ulyssean Two artists kept burning their bridges behind them. Nevertheless, they have found "that untravell'd world" in the inexhaustible continuity of their creative lives. Thus Georges Braque, who in the 1930s began his hundreds of paintings of noble and exquisite birds, is able to tell Liberman that the mystery of his great painting, *Grand Oiseau*, is beyond words—a symbol of an ever-more mysterious cosmos. And this magnificent old Ulyssean at 78 remarks wistfully to Liberman that he needs another storey for his house to shelter his accumulating canvases!

Perhaps there is both a physical and an emotional release in painting and sculpting that promotes the Ulyssean adventure, much as with other arts, especially the so-called executant arts. Conductors of orchestras are often Ulyssean figures. Arturo Toscanini continued to conduct with power until close to his death at age 90; he was not only emotionally intensely alive, but according to his masseur had much of the skin texture and the suppleness of an athletic young man. On the other hand, Otto Klemperer, who died at 85, conducted from a chair, having survived in the course of 25 years a terrible accident, a brain tumor, and severe burns. Stravinsky was still conducting and composing in his

80s: a frail, pixie-like man whose varied facial expressions so distracted his youthful biographer, Robert Craft, at their first meeting that Craft could hardly concentrate on the maestro's words. (Stravinsky was in his late 60s before Craft even met him.) His rich, often corrosive, sense of humor was the verification of David Raff's definition: "humor is a form of courage."

There are also many Ulysseans among concert pianists and other musicians. When I was a boy the story was widespread that Paderewski had to stop playing in his early 60s because of stiffened fingers, and it fortified the legend that this was the natural fate of solo instrument performers. But Arther Rubinstein's playing in creative style at over 90, and Horowitz's triumphant return to the concert stage at 72, demonstrates that the world of the Ulysseans is available to musical artists. The list of fine public performers in their later years is long and includes such names as Segovia, Montoya, Bachaus, Casadesus, Menuhin, and Isaac Stern. To these can be added the remarkable jazz virtuosi: for example, Ellington, Count Basie, Eubie Blake, and Louis Armstrong. It was Armstrong's heart that did him in at age 70—there was nothing wrong with his fingers and his spirit. His death after a brilliant all-night private performance during convalescence was classically Ulyssean. Stephane Grappelli at nearly 80 continues to enchant audiences across the world with his gifts as a jazz virtuoso of the violin.

Just as in music a great deal of attention has been given to the phenomenon of young geniuses, so in poetry a persistent myth exists that poetry is a young person's game—that the poetic fires die down as the poet enters middle age, and disappear as he or she crosses into the late years. Yet the domain of poetry is filled with Ulyssean figures. It is well known that Thomas Hardy turned away forever from the novel at about age 50 and steadily produced poetry of the first order until his death at 85. What is one to do with the astounding productivity, undimmed in quality, of Robert Frost? And the wonderful later poems of Saint-John Perse, Edith Sitwell, T. S. Eliot, Paul Valéry, Boris Pasternak, Giuseppe Ungaretti, Wallace Stevens, and Eugenio Montale?

Ulysseans both in and outside the arts are mold-breakers of conventional folk myths and pieties. Thus, Pablo Casals, Zoltan Kodály, Justice William O. Douglas, John R. Mott, and Avery Brundage all at an advanced age married young women, and these unions turned out to be loving and enduring. Men and women supposed to be ready chronologically for retirement homes, or at the very least for settling into the safe routines of later middle age, encircle the globe in small craft or set off on humanitarian missions among people of other cultures and tongues half a world away. And older adults who tenaciously love such sports as running, skiing, and fencing (among many others) prove in their Ulyssean way that "athlete" is not, as popular usage mistakenly supposes, a word always linked with young performers, but that in fact the *Concise Oxford Dictionary* is perfectly correct in defining it as a "competitor in physical exercises; robust, vigorous man" (to which, of course, we add "woman"). It is the Ulysseans who remind us that we must refer to so-and-so as "a fine athlete" without raising in our minds the eternal concept of youth.

Likewise, Ulyssean people in politics and statecraft break the mold that stamps elderly arrivals to positions of power as being typically "caretaker" figures. John XXIII was 78 by the time he reached the papacy of the Roman Catholic Church, an institution that until recently had the courage and wisdom to ignore artificial retirement thresholds. (Even now the defined or implicit limit is placed at a generous age 75, which nonetheless means that Angelo Roncalli would never have become pope at all.) Roncalli was a short, obese, unhandsome, people-loving prelate who remarked wryly on his election that he could not be called "a television pope." Except to the informed, who were few, he seemed to be a typical career churchman whose slow rise to the Curia after an early election as bishop had been marked by years spent on the half-forgotten peripheries of power: at 78, a useful "caretaker pope." Yet when this jolly, seeming nonentity found himself at the controls of a remarkable instrument called Papal Infallibility, he set in motion one of the most extraordinary enterprises in the church's history: Vatican Council II—a Ulyssean adventure. When he died at 83 his death was felt to be premature! A light, visible to men and women of every race and faith, had gone out. So you can never tell with the "caretaker people": they may be Ulysseans Two who are at last ready for the great voyage.

Most Ulysseans are not involved, however, in enterprises that catch the eye and the ear of the world. For many men and women in middle and later adulthood who feel a certain stirring or potentiality for the Ulyssean life but who still hesitate, there may seem as much discourgement as incentive in reviewing a cavalcade of famous Ulyssean people. "These are, after all, geniuses or individuals with some kind of spectacular talent," they will say. "The life arenas they work or have worked in are in themselves of heroic dimensions, with all too little reference to the equipment and potentialities of those (like us) who don't happen to move on those Olympian heights."

There is some truth in this, but fortunately not much. (This is why in later chapters you will find cameos of many private people, not celebrities.) There are, of course, creators among the Ulysseans who are almost demigods, who seem to illustrate vividly Karl Barth's definition of man as "the being who dwells on the border between heaven and earth." Michelangelo is an example who leaps to mind. Yet when one studies the many-sided portrait of Michelangelo that is presented in, for instance, Professor Robert J. Clements' biography, his genius is seen to be only an element in his Ulysseanism. Although it may seem incredible at first sight, the *dimension* of his talent is clearly irrelevant to the splendour of his later Ulyssean life.

On the other hand, there are two qualities in Michelangelo's late years that are most moving and which most fire one's imagination: his strength of will and his summoning-up of what Kipling calls, "heart and bone and sinew" for herculean tasks in spite of all kinds of fears and sorrows—these qualities are accessible in some degree to every adult who turns his face toward the Ulyssean trails.

Without them, the trails cannot be entered or the journeys completed. For many older adults in modern Western society with a great deal of free time, perhaps not affluent but not impoverished, probably not radiantly healthy but not in bad health either, it is a fact that even the writing and mailing of letters can seem a major undertaking. All the more so the labor of writing a lengthy appeal to an editor, keeping a journal, organizing easel and paints and a painting trip, sitting down to study the first elements of a foreign language, even just the physical chore of writing down a short story or a small play, let alone trying to get it published or performed, composing some poems, good or bad, or writing up or sketching out designs for new programs or buildings or enterprises—in a word, all the physical and mental effort involved in any creative exercise. Any and all of them seem too much: "We are past all that."

For all of us who have been in that state, the performances of certain "great" Ulysseans are instructive. True, they have or have had unusually powerful motivations or have long conditioned themselves to methods or patterns of work they can continue into even very late adulthood. Still, they, too, have the same physical equipment as other men and women (some, like Prescott, Pasteur, and Parkman worked under crippling, almost immobilizing disabilities), and in their later years are just as subject to the hazards of fatigue and debility.

Considering this, some of their applications of will and physical effort make one want to take stock of one's own days, schedules, and habits. A photograph exists of the 81-year-old Leo Tolstoy bent over his desk writing, and it gives one pause to realize that ten years earlier he had just completed *Resurrection*, writing all of its 200,000 words by hand. Victor Hugo, too, who had carted the mammoth growing manuscript of *Les Misérables* in and out of France for 20 years on his various escapes and hurried journeys, and had written it all by hand, also wrote out the huge *Toilers of the Sea* when he produced it at age 63. Voltaire's marvelous satire, *Candide*, which he wrote at 64, was far shorter; nonetheless, it required a major expenditure of concentrated will and sheer physical effort. Thomas Mann had the consolation, if one can call it that, of the typewriter. Still, the three major novels he published after age 70 (*Dr. Faustus; The Holy Sinner;* and the largely rewritten *Confessions of Felix Krull, Confidence Man*) comprise in all about a half-million words. Much the same nerving of will and physical effort is seen in productivity after age 60 of such women writers as Colette, Pearl S. Buck, and Katherine Anne Porter.

Companion adventures illustrate the same point. Will Durant's monumental *History of Civilization* comprises in all ten volumes of about 300,000 words each: Three of these (*The Age of Faith, The Renaissance,* and *The Reformation*) were composed and written out or typed by Durant after age 58, the third at 65: Durant followed these with five more volumes written in collaboration with his wife Ariel, from age 69 to 89. William L. Shirer was in his mid-50s, and long removed from the success of his *Berlin Diary,* when he produced the huge *Rise and Fall of the Third Reich,* evidently written over three years in the privacy of a hotel suite. Shirer then followed this with a work of equal size and importance in his mid-60s, *The Decline and Fall of the Third Republic.* Jacques Maritain was 70 when he involved himself in the labor of committing about 120,000 words to paper in *Creative Intuition* in Art and Poetry, and André Maurois was 78 when he prepared his 200,000-word biography of Balzac.

The labor of writing these books, wholly aside from the output of creative imagination required, suggests that another characteristic of Ulyssean people is that they do not brood in advance about the physical demands of their various enterprises but simply move ahead. They so absorb themselves in the adventure at hand that, so far as possible, they put out of their minds preconceptions of the arduous chores of planning, writing, typing, shutting themselves off from social pleasures, and so on. Least of all do they fret about whether they will live to complete their task.

In an utterly different world—a world very close to that of the original Ulysses—the same qualities of exertion of will and of physical energy further illustrate the Ulyssean life. Francis Chichester's name became a household word in the 1960s. What everyone neglected to mention about him was the point superbly made by J. R. L. Anderson in his book, *The Ulyssean Factor:* that in 1960, at age 59, in his first transatlantic race, Chichester changed sail 118 times in 40 days, in addition to endlessly trimming the sails of his *Gipsy Moth III.* He did this, moreover, under the handicaps of poor eyesight, of sometimes wretched health, and often in pitching seas. When he was 70 Chichester set out on still another transatlantic race, alone again, knowing that the illness that had pursued him for years was at last to bring him down. In fact, he had to turn back, but this took nothing from the indomitability of his spirit and will, and the nobility of the effort. Chichester was sailing, Anderson suggests, not to discover and explore anything *except himself.* And in fact, in our time, when nearly all the physical world is known, the search for the self constitutes the greatest Ulyssean adventure.

Most Ulyssean achievements are highly personal affairs and often they occur in settings that seem quite comfortable and almost effete. In

1959 Ethel Sabin Smith, an American prose poet and philosopher, when nearly 70 took a round-the-world journey by freighter, and not merely described the trip in a subsequent book but analyzed what this strange Ulyssean act meant to her and could mean to others. Since the cargo ships she chose usually had good cabins, good food, good service, and pleasant crews, in what ways was the adventure Ulyssean? For one thing, because in spite of the comparative comforts of travel, the voyage itself had certain hazards for what is usually called an "elderly" person, hazards both psychological and physical. Obviously, as she was steaming from Hong Kong to Singapore on a slow cargo boat without a doctor, the only woman passenger aboard—and aged 70 at that—physical crises could occur. But more real was the emotional wrench in leaving familiar scenes and friends and the comfortable routines of predictable days for months of unknown experiences, however compensated one might feel by new experiences and personal growth.

For another thing, the adventure was Ulyssean because of Ethel Sabin Smith's own attitude. She found, not surprisingly, that not all older adults who set out on voyages are Ulysseans, and she makes the point, without any thought of Ulysses or reference to him, that the traveler must have, or must develop, attitudes of quest and receptivity to change. Thus, writing of her own circumnavigation of the globe, cargo-ship style (*Passports at Seventy*), she says:

> One may take a world cruise to escape from confining demands of established habits, to broaden one's physical horizon; but it takes more than steamship tickets and baggage labels, landing passes and inoculations, to release one's mind and spirit from custom. One must be able to brace oneself against mighty winds and let them sweep through one's mind; be able to face contrary opinions and beliefs when they crest and come hissing toward one; exult when, like driving rain, unexpected facts drench one. The traveler unable to endure buffeting remains below, so to speak, in the cabin of his mind, untouched, unchanged.

Openness of mind, sensitivity to the need for new ways and new experiences; resourcefulness, courage, curiosity and a continuing sense of wonder at the kaleidoscopic beauty and mystery of the world and the cosmos; acceptance of the fact of aging but not being intimidated by it; and consciousness of the quest for the self—these are clearly some of the significant traits identifiable in the personalities of Ulyssean adults of widely differing eras and places. Equally clearly, the title "Ulyssean" is potentially available to all older adults.

The Ulyssean response at many intersections in the life journey is not only active but creative. How to choose well among the many options that open to the seeker adult, or to make some of those options possible—this is one of the qualities of creative adulthood. But creativity has many qualities, as will be seen in the next chapter.

2

CREATIVITY IN ADULTS:
WHAT IT IS, WHAT IT COULD BE

E VERY adult, whatever his or her roles in life, gives thought at some time to whether he or she is "creative"—and in what, and in what degree. All 'experimenters"—from the very young business- or working man trying privately to make up a new song on his guitar to the middle-aged amateur gardener contemplating new flower-bed arrangements and plants, to the lonely widow trying her hand for the first time with oil paints—encounter the question: "How creative am I?"

This special fascination with the concept of creativity results from its identification with personal uniqueness. Each of us is a unique being: unique because of our genes, and unique because of the nature of our millions of psychosocial intersections during our lifetime (even if we were cloned, the clones would have different experiences and reactions). No one who has appeared before us or will appear after us will be exactly us; and this is made more striking when you consider that every day of the thousands of days of our life is also in certain ways unique. Yet this conviction of personal uniqueness can be dimmed and lost in the course of the life drama; that is why the subject of creativity is so important for us to explore.

If you ask, as I have frequently asked in my public university seminars, a large group of adults of all ages and many backgrounds and vocations what they conceive "creativity" or "the creative process" to be, the richness of the returns after only a quarter-hour for reflection is striking. I now have hundreds of these definitions, and I cite a few chosen for their being representative of different approaches.

"Creativity" or "the creative process" is seen as:

The application of imaginative innovation to any activity.

Releasing the mind to new approaches and methods of problem-solving.

Expanding one's perception. Awareness.

Generating new ideas.

Inner expression evolving from environment and hereditary characteristics, after a period of germination, combining motivation and desire.

Creativity is the actuality of being.

Creativity denotes openness to growth in all its dimensions; the ability to freely play with a large number of options; to remain open to being surprised, to surprising oneself.

My life is a creative process. We are all unfolding creatively or destructively. Creativity is the ability to draw from our outside experiences and mix these with the right amount of our inner feelings and subconscious lucidness to execute something totally wonderful and unexpected.

Seeing possibilities in all things and all people. Turning potential disaster into success. Playful thinking, playing with words, ideas.

A mysterious process whereby experience, knowledge, the resources of the unconscious, and a high degree of desire to achieve a particular end, suddenly culminate in a satisfactory, possibly unique result.

It must be emphasized that these definitions, chosen from many equally stimulating, were produced upon immediate request, without notice, from men and women of all ages and occupations who had appeared for their first class in a creativity-learning seminar. It is extremely interesting to compare them with definitions produced by some of the noted theorists on the creative process and how it works.

Thus, to Alex Osborn, creativity is "applied imagination"; to George Stoddard, "the urge to invent, to inquire, to perform." To Carl Rogers, it means facilitating "the emergence in action of a novel product, growing out of the uniqueness of the individual on the one hand, and the materials, events, people, or circumstances of his life on the other hand." Rogers felt that creativity meant delivering an actual product, though that product might be so unusual as reforming one's own personality through psychotherapy. Dorothy Sayers disagreed: you could be a poet without writing a poem! And Eric Fromm's numerous perceptions on creativity include the striking observation: "Creativity is the ability to see (or to be aware), and to respond."

The two roles in creativity of doing and being also turn up in Abraham Maslow's descriptions of "special talent creativity"—the creativity of the gifted inventor, scientist, poet, sculptor, architect, novelist, and so on; and then of "self-actualising creativeness," which he saw as being creative changes in the personality, and in the capacity to do anything creatively—that is, to live creatively.

One notable conference on creativity and its facilitation invited its numerous gurus to provide their personal definitions and the result was a shower of the characteristics of creative people, including: capacity to be puzzled; awareness; spontaneity;* spontaneous flexibility; divergent thinking; openness to new experiences; disregard of boundaries; abandoning; letting go; being born every day; ability to toy with the elements; relish for temporary chaos (i.e., rigid order as the enemy of the creative process); and tolerance of ambiguity (able to play with various options.)[1]

From this galaxy of concepts of creativity, both from private people and from noted theorists of the art, you can test or enhance your own personal working definition of the creative process, its demands, and its products. My own definition, to add simply one more, is as follows:

Creativity is the process by which a man or woman employs both the conscious and the unconscious domains of the mind to combine various existing materials into fresh constructions or configurations. These, in some degree, cause significant changes in the self-system of the person concerned, or significantly alter the environment surrounding him or her, whether such a change is great or small.

However, fascinating though the definition of "creativity" clearly is to many adults, there are other questions about it that grip the seeker-adult as he or she proceeds through the middle and later years. For example: Is creativity a universal human quality or a kind of divine fire found burning only in a minority of individuals gifted by fate? Is creative power dependent on one's degree of intelligence? Is the creative potential something naturally found in children, which in most people disappears in adulthood? Can it be learned, as one learns mathematics or a language? And most of all, can it be maintained throughout adulthood? Can it be lost, and if lost, can it be regained? Does it naturally decline across the life journey?

Whether or not you believe that creativity is found in some degree throughout humankind will clearly depend on your original definition. If you believe, as was long believed in European culture, that creativity is to be spoken of in terms of grandeur, as something associated with the original act of creation, a godlike quality, then you will reserve the term and your thoughts about if for the "great" creators of the arts, science, and perhaps statecraft. If, on the other hand, you believe that there is a native ingenuity latent in the human adult that is intermittently roused by the thousands of life's intersections, you will join such expert commentators as Carl Rogers, Harold Anderson, Calvin Taylor, the botanist Edmund Sinnott (who saw it in the whole of the life process), Eric Fromm, the architect Alden Dow, and Abraham Maslow in viewing it as a universal potential in enormously differing degrees.

*Silvani Arieti, in his fine study, *Creativity, the Magic Synthesis*, differentiates well between spontaneity and actual creativity. He seems to present a more difficult case in differentiating between originality and creativity!
[1]Superscript numerals refer to Chapter Notes, beginning on page 220.

Maslow was led to this conception by the logic of his view of "self-actualisation" as one of two great arenas of the creative life. His statement on this is eloquent:

One woman, uneducated, poor, a full-time housewife and mother, did none of the conventionally creative things and yet was a marvellous cook, mother, wife, and homemaker. . . .she was in all these areas original, novel, ingenious, unexpected, inventive. I just *had* to call her creative. I learned from her and others like her to think that a first-rate soup is more creative than a second-rate painting, and that generally, cooking or parenthood or making a home could be creative whereas poetry need not be; it could be uncreative.

Another of my subjects devoted herself to what had best be called social service in the broadest sense, bandaging up wounds, helping the downtrodden, not only in a personal way, but in an organizational way as well. One of her "creations" is an organization which helps many more people than she could individually.

Another was a psychiatrist, a "pure" clinician who never wrote anything or created any theories or researches but who delighted in his everyday job of helping people to create themselves. This man approached each patient as if he were the only one in the world, without jargon, expectations, or presuppositions, with innocence and naiveté and yet with great wisdom, in a Taoistic fashion. Each patient was a unique human being and therefore a completely new problem to be understood and solved in a completely novel way. His great success even with very difficult cases validated his "creative" (rather than stereotyped or orthodox) way of doing things.

Maslow's condescension to "second-rate painting" was unnecessary to his very strong argument for the universality and catholicity of the creative potential—and in any case, his other definition of "special talent" creativity completes the picture. A lovely quatrain by W. B. Yeats on the relationship between the creative potential and the human self making its way across the life journey adds resonance to this point of view:

> The friends that have it I do wrong
> Whenever I remake a song,
> Should know what issue is at stake:
> It is myself that I remake.

How far is intelligence a factor in creativity? Many of us would accept J. W. Haefele's dictum (1962): "A creator must be intelligent, but even a highly intelligent person is not necessarily creative"—yet even this seems too bold a statement, considering how enormous is the range

of possible creative episodes and arenas, and how complex is the definition of intelligence.*

So far as creativity is seen as problem-solving, the mental or cognitive function is obviously important. However, even here the fascinating question arises as to whether some forms of intelligence are not actual blocks to creative achievement. This question emerges in the
scenes described by Edward de Bono (1967) where so-called "vertical
thinkers," as he calls the people highly programmed into exactly logical thinking, are frequently blocked from creative solutions that they
might reach through "lateral" thinking—that is, thinking in a new
key, imaginative abandoning of old routines, and rigid protocols.
Jerome Bruner has written helpfully about the importance of
guessing—although even here the phrase that immediately turns up is
"intelligent guessing." And Simone de Beauvoir with her usual flair, in
writing about creativity, intelligence, and the arts, makes the persuasive argument that there is an indispensable link between warm sexual
feeling and creativity, thus making it fair to ask whether the cold intelligence, however "high," is not often an inhibitor of creativity.

"Divergent thinking," that is, thinking when the mind is construc-
tively at play with fresh, unexpected approaches, is considered by the
British psychologist H. J. Butcher, a most perceptive student of the
subject, as possibly a different form of intelligence, or at least a different ability, from the sort of intelligence called upon for convergent
thinking—that is, the processes of purely logical or tradition-trained
thought. The whole debate on the roles of intelligence in creativity has
been further complicated by the left brain/right brain controversy. In
fact, the prime issue for seeker-adults in their middle and later years is
not whether intelligence is valuable in the creative process, since it is;
nor whether they have sufficient intelligence to create well, since they
have; nor whether their cognitive powers will remain with rich fire-
power to and through their very late years, since this they can almost
certainly ensure (see Chapter 5).

A more pressing issue is to recognize that when a man or woman is
engaged in creative action, large or small, two "kingdoms of the mind"
are typically engaged, often simultaneously: the conscious mind and
the unconscious mind. Then to recognize that, to varying degrees, the
human adult can employ these great forces to help liberate his or her
creative potentials.

The conscious mind can be seen at work in such cases as these: recalling facts and insights from the large store of information learned deliberately and always kept on hand; taking such resources and manipu-

*When L. M. Terman reported after 34 years on the life progress of his 1,000 so-called
gifted children, he was able to show many to have been successful but (in his view) few
highly creative. However, we have much to learn yet about the manifestations of creativity in private lives and also about the validity of criteria in formally testing creative
powers.

lating them to produce fresh insights, inventions, and creative material; and exercising the tremendous function of choosing from the rich but disordered flood of materials pouring forth from the great reservoir of the unconscious mind. In fact, in a recent seminar on the creative process in Toronto, when the young black composer Edford Providence was asked what he considered the essence of the process at work, he replied almost without a pause: "Choices!"—then necessarily qualified this by noting all the other powerful components involved in the act of creation.

The working in creativity of the unconscious mind has been vividly illustrated by anecdotes from the best of sources: creative people themselves. Thus, A. E. Housman, the British poet, whose youth-filled, moving lyrics seemed to belie his outer personality of the conventional Oxbridge don, described how two stanzas of one of his best-known poems came into his head "just as they are printed while I was crossing the corner of Hampstead Heath—a third with a little coaxing after tea." The fourth he had to "turn to and compose it myself, and it was more than a twelve-month before I got it right." Nietzsche reported in *Ecce Homo* that while in Italy, walking near Genoa, all of his famous work *Thus Spake Zarathustra* came to him: to use his words, "perhaps I should rather say, *invaded me.*"

Van Gogh, in a letter to a friend, described how he tried, using his conscious mind, to force the creative process. He attempted a number of drawings of what was to be a famous painting: they all failed. Then a mysterious spring opened. The next drawings, unforced, appeared with the feeling he wanted which made them live. The modern French dramatist and filmmaker Jean Cocteau described how he was "sick and tired of writing"; he fell asleep, slept poorly, woke with a start, and as though in a trance saw played out before him three acts of the play *The Knights of the Round Table*, which he transcribed long afterward. Cocteau describes this as "a visitation." He talks about "unknown forces" working deep within us, in ultimate collaboration with events in daily life.

The same phenomenon is reported from the worlds of science and invention. An oft-recited case is that of the highly creative mathematician Henri Poincaré who, frustrated for days in attempting by conscious logic to formulate a new and revolutionary theorem, decided simply to give it up temporarily and join some geographers on a trip through the French countryside. Hours after having dismissed the conscious struggle from his mind, just as he was stepping into the holiday bus, the mysterious solution occurred to him. The anecdote is a good one because it reminds us that a good deal of toil and conscious striving often precedes the illumination. The grim logician, who will try, do or die, to force all the locks by the conscious process, and his contrasting human type, the dilettante, will often, it seems, miss their creative achievement.

The architect Ulrich Franzen describes how he builds big cardboard models, pulls them apart, puts them back, playing endlessly until mysteriously "things begin to emerge." And Franzen adds laconically, "Somehow it's unconscious." Wilder Penfield, a famous explorer of the physical brain, uses the expression, "the back of the mind." He also is fascinated by the unexpectedness of the appearance of creative ideas, the sudden breakthroughs. He describes how, during the writing of his first novel, *No Other Gods* (at age 64), "while operating. . .when things were quiet and I was closing up, these characters would come to the back of my mind and we'd talk and plan."

The unconscious process at work is very familiar also in the many unnoticed or unremarked-on episodes in the lives of private men and women. So frequent is the phenomenon of an original or creative idea flashing into the conscious mind and disappearing, usually beyond recovery unless noted down, that facilitators of the creative process advise their readers or listeners to keep a small notebook at the bedside or to carry around through the day a little note pad, or idea trap, for jotting down thoughts or impressions. Many students have known the experience of going to sleep with an unsolved exercise in science or mathematics and waking up with the solution; and in mature adult life, of having the same experience with life or career problems. The unconscious mind has been at work.

Arthur Koestler writes with great élan about three creative situations where the conscious and unconscious minds intersect, which he calls the AHA, the AH, and the HAHA experiences. For Koestler, "all creative activity is a kind of do-it-yourself therapy, an attempt to come to terms with traumatizing challenges." Life at certain points presents scientists and artists (and all of us, in our way) with certain problems that overload the circuits and force the human personality and organism to find new routes, devices, strategies, inventions. If these can be found through the conscious mind, well and good; if not, what the individual will often do is to retreat into the unconscious, that great and mysterious storehouse of memories, impressions, insights, fantasies, long since lost to the recollection of the conscious mind. Koestler calls this storehouse an "underground" where mental action takes place like games, where "hidden analogies," for example, take place "between cabbages and kings." This realm of the unconscious is not the inferno of Freud's id, although it will have its infernal fires. Rather, it is a place where rich materials exist not only to inhibit or frustrate, but on the contrary, over and over again to make creative breakthroughs possible. In fact, as seen earlier, whole products and projects of the individual's creative life may be produced from the unconscious workshop with its powers of association and fusion.

The AHA experience, familiar to gestalt psychology, is described by Robert Frost as that moment when "the box clicks shut," what Koestler calls, "the flash of illumination," the experience already described of Poincaré. The AH reaction is a moment of self-transcendence, of what Koestler compares to being "in an empty cathedral when eternity is looking through the window of time, and in which the self seems to dissolve like a grain of salt in water." This experience obviously engages the whole of one's being, not only the unconscious self; yet it is usually highly evocative—the environment of many creative motivations and inspirations.

The HAHA reaction (the term comes from Brennig James) brings in the strange creativity of humor. If the first two reactions, the AHA and the AH, work to resolve the bisociation of opposites, the AHA reaction leaves the situation comically unresolved.* The creative tension being unreasonable is exploded by laughter.

Fascinating though it may be to study the unconscious mind at work in the creative process, Ulyssean adults or soon-to-be Ulysseans who are already seeker-adults cannot be satisfied to leave "creativity" to so mysterious and automatic an operation. If this were all, individual men and women could be quite fatalistic about their creative potentials, just as they are about their inheritance of specific "talents." In fact, it seems indisputable that people have special gifts for languages, for science, for musical composition, for mechanics, and so on; and this, of course, is border country to personal creativity. Is it possible, going beyond this, to become a more creative person—that is to say, a person who, whatever his or her equipment in talents, is able steadily to grow as a creative being? For such a person, the horizons of the creative life can steadily expand; new domains appear for exploration. Yeats's line returns to us, in one of its several fertile meanings: "It is myself that I remake."

In this light, even the workings of the unconscious self that seem at first sight to be so inaccessible to the influence of the known self may grow in its contribution in enriched environments and climates. If the unconscious mind is a reservoir feeding many times the creative inspiration in a hundred fields, it seems manifest that the richer the life of thought and action in turn feeding thousands of swiftly "forgotten" data, pictures, impressions, and insights into the personal reservoir, the richer will be the creative bank to draw from.

Thus, when men and women proceeding through life choose to continually open their minds to new learning experiences, rather than to close them; choose to break old drying routines, rather than be dried by them; choose to keep the wonder-filled mind of the "OK Child" awake, rather than to let it fall asleep like Rip Van Winkle for 20 or more years; choose to let fantasy enrich their thoughts, rather than scorn anything other than "the light of common day"; choose to seek

*For example, Myron Cohen, the noted monologist, tells of two Jewish gentlemen at a newsstand. One says to the other: "Why have you got your hand in my pocket?" Says the other: "I'm looking for a match." The first: "Why didn't you ask?" The second: "I don't talk to strangers."

ways to enliven and sensitize their physical senses and their psychic inner senses; and choose to seek all the strategies they can to release their solving of problems from the grip of tired and ineffective logical rituals—when they make these choices to become more "fully human, fully alive," they also surely enrich the fluid and pulsing bank of creative options in the unconscious, and also help liberate the creative powers residing in the fully conscious, but often stubbornly anti-creative, self.

The wise acceptance of these choices, these affirmations for the creative life, might be summed up as "the creative attitude," and it is—but "attitude" is too passive a term. Seeker-adults who set as an important goal the continuing use and growth of their creative powers until the last day of their life can actually build into their functions of thought and action exercises and strategies that continually freshen and facilitate their creativity. From my own and other creativity seminars I cite a few that will serve here as symbols to make the point.

1. Heighten the sensitivity of the five physical senses. *Taste:* Describe the tastes in your personal repertoire that most please or excite you. What new tastes have you recently acquired? What tastes, never experienced, but read about or heard from travelers, or imagined, can you describe? Seek for evocation of the taste, real or imagined. *Sight:* What sights most stir or vitalize you? Take some object or person often seen: describe it or him vividly, with detail, as though never before seen. (Do not confuse 20/20 sight with "seeing"!) Search in your daily activities for sights never actualized. Learn the symbolism of physical seeing: what "ordinary" sight gives you on reflection, a transfigured vision of the object or person? E.g., a candle burning on a café table, or a lonely objector at a political convention. *Sound:* What sounds most move or intrigue you? What sounds, never physically heard, can you imagine and describe? (The sounds of a cobra; of an avalanche; of a windmill turning; of a UFO approaching.) Take five minutes in your busy day to listen, utterly, to all the sounds possible to hear, and note them down afterward. Which would you normally have missed? *Touch:* Arrange with a friend or two to identify, while blindfolded, certain objects or surfaces. Imagine, and record with imaginative words, the feel of touching various things, animals, or other human beings. *Smell:* What aromas, perfumes, or smells most arouse or please you? Describe them as carefully as possible, by analogy if necessary. What smells have the reverse effect? What aromas or fragrances evoke visions of people, scenes, or stories (e.g., woodsmoke, old books, wet wool, wild roses, dry leather)? What hitherto-unexperienced aroma would you inhale with delight, if you could? Describe it as you imagine it.

2. Heighten the sensitivity of the inner or psychic senses. (The following exercises are adapted from Michael Volin.) *Imagining Colors.* Seated cross-legged or in another position of comfortable awareness,

breathing deeply and rhythmically, close your eyes. Choose any favorite color of the spectrum, and use your entire concentration to visualize this color as clearly as possible without any mental interference. Retain the image for as long as possible. *Re-creating one's surroundings:* Seated relaxed, imagine a beautiful landscape or seascape in great detail. Imagine yourself as part of it, taking it all in through the senses. Each detail should be savored. (Volin describes the case of a survivor of the terrible captivity of the Burma Road campaign, who by perfect, brief 15 minutes daily intense imaging of his native Devonshire "was more in England than in Burma," came out of the imaginary trip to his homeland refreshed and invigorated physically and spiritually, and attributed his ultimate survival to this practice of the inner life.*) I have personal knowledge of a remarkable development of this power to image new surroundings by a Toronto man, immobilized in a nursing home, who has taught himself to "travel" from time to time, to places like Florence, Istanbul, or Hong Kong. He reads about these places first and acquires some travel folders; then he sets out on remarkable mental journeys, coming back to tell of people met, incidents experienced, scenes enjoyed. *Developing the mind's eye (the pineal gland?): Travel into the past:* Sit in a cross-legged or other relaxed position suitable for concentration, breathe rhythmically, and then imagine a beautiful scene from your past travels—a place that impressed you. Travel to this place again and again in your exercise, trying to see it better and better with mind's eye. Now think of a house you lived in ten years ago. Go through it with mind's eye, room after room, trying to see it again.† *Travel into your body:* Review, before beginning, the general structure of the body systems. Breathing deeply and rhythmically, look with your mind's eye at your diaphragm. Begin to explore your breathing process as it would look like from the inside. Become conscious of how your lungs are filled up and emptied in the process of breathing. (Volin uses this exercise as a strategy in the relief of tension. The mind's eye explores each limb and part of the body, and "whenever pockets of tension are uncovered, you can instruct your body to relax in that area".)

In *How to Meditate*, Lawrence LeShan, with his usual wisdom and grace, supplies a number of meditations designed to calm and then liberate the mind and spirit for richer reality: the Meditation of the Bubble, of the Indian Campfire, of the Thousand-Petaled Lotus, of the Safe Harbour, of the "Who Am I?"

---

*Volin (p. 212) also cites Romain Gary, in *Roots of Heaven* as describing a similar experience in concentration camp by imagining herds of elephants roaming freely over Africa. He survived to dedicate his life to saving the elephants from extinction.
†An important corollary of this is traveling backward in time in one's life, in seven-year intervals. Likewise, there is an affinity here with Lelord Kordel's delightful advice: Make yourself a mental cocktail each night before sleeping by remembering with great detail and vividness one beautiful episode from previous years.

Even where these exercises in stretching the powers of the inner or psychic self are not specifically designed to contribute to one's creativity, in fact they can be powerful allies. The point has been made of the value of higher actualization of the senses, not only in the arts, but in attacking the many problems that call for greater alertness and mobilization of mind and energy. But there is another need in the creative life to which this more conscious selfhood can contribute. This is the need for what I call "creative poise"—the need of the mind to turn off useless "brain chatter," which simply impedes creative flows, and the need of the whole person many times in creative work to be rescued from the endless trivia and interruptions of many daylight hours, the distractions that can act as "the death of a thousand cuts"! The environment of creative thought often is not merely physical (Emerson seeking a hotel for a time to write his essays) but is a temporary way of life that permits us to regain our balance, our creative poise. This is one of the meanings to be derived from Wordsworth's too-much-neglected line: "Getting and spending, we lay waste our powers."

3. Cut off, like dead tree limbs, old drying routines in doing, thinking, reading, and speaking; and open up to fresh, invigorating experiences. Certain personal routines are valuable: they save us time and free us for fresh adventures. One cannot be forever looking for a different locker at the health club, a different newsstand, or abandoning a comfortable practice like tea at a favorite hour. Some routines can help us get through crises or periods of undue turbulence. But other routines prevent us from exploring fresh trails, from seeing views and horizons that challenge and renew us. Still others lead to the wastelands of unexamined, dominating ideas that can become the barriers to innovation and creative change. (See also page 15.)

Therefore: *choose new modes of doing things*. Take new routes, however seemingly similar to your usual ones, to office, church or temple, club, or other familiar destination. Find a Skills Exchange or its equivalent and develop some hitherto unexpected craft or activity. Investigate the value of one new social movement; open a conversation with three new people a week. Try to bridge an existing silence or difficulty between yourself and a colleague, friend, relative, or enemy. Seek a new cultural group—any event will do—one you like very much in prospect and one you dislike. Walk part way into their country. Travel by a new mode. Try to break an old fear, an old phobia (the thrill, the real thrill, of unlearning what we should never have learned.) See also "60 Ways to Be Younger Than You Are" (p. 213).

And: *think and read in a new key*. Check your list of favorite authors—whom have you added lately? What other reading have you missed, buried in your science fiction or murder mysteries? Browse weekly for three hours in a good community library. Deliberately buy one journal, paper, or watch one program weekly, irritatingly opposed to your usual and comfortable points of view. Read two paperbacks by

Edward de Bono. Take a course on creative processes or "how to think." Find a book of stimulating problems and teasers (all good bookstores have them). Write your own life story up to date, as if written by another person (Nehru did it!). Keep a personal reflective journal day by day for a month (and longer, if it seems beneficial). (See also Chapter 9.)

And also: *speak your own language with new zest and grace.* Browse through a good dictionary and add three new words a week to your vocabulary. Invent a new word once a week—try fresh combinations, fresh concepts. (Friends of mine who meant to spend Thanksgiving together, and missed, and knew they would miss Christmas, made up a new holiday, "Thankchrist," and celebrated it.) Freshen your slang: "old hat" is old hat. Take the tired similes we have used for years ("as smart as a whip," "as sick as a dog," etc.) and find new images for them. Also, have fun composing new phrases to follow the much-abused word, "like": "He raced toward freedom like a . . ." (Think about it.) How easily we accept and use clichés and worn-out images. Likewise with metaphors: but with these we also enter the rich realms of fantasy.

Surprise your mind by often liberating it to fantasy. Fantasy can be for sheer exhilaration, but it can also be the avenue to practical new discoveries, as the worlds of mind-storming and Synectics know. Of course, we all dream and fantasize, but most of us forget our dreams and never utilize the creative aspect of developed fantasy. For example: Imagine that the earth faces the real possibility of total destruction by nuclear war. You have been entrusted with the command and outfitting of a small spacecraft carrying some of the species' best evidences of civilization to another planet. What would you take on board this modern space ark? Or: suppose that you could be born in another place and time, of (if you like) a different racial group, in a different vocation—what would you be and do? Don't stop with the first vague picture. Keep sharpening the focus and developing the details. Or: suppose that the situation that Alvin Silverstein thinks he sees realistically coming, occurs: that death at last is conquered on earth: what are some of the results? Or suppose that all the cats in the world suddenly disappear one day at midnight: what are the consequences? You can make up many of your own fantasy situations. As for invention: somewhere some first man or woman fantasized: "Suppose human beings could fly?" The magical word, "Suppose. . .," is the other parent of invention.

Keep awake the creative child-self in your self-system, Eric Berne's "OK-Child," and release him or her frequently for experiences of wonder and rapture, of glee, of fantastic games, of the absurd. For example: list vertically the names of ten animals and great birds, and beside it place another vertical list of the most prominent feature of each creature. Now, using double-digit numbers chosen at random, create new creatures and invent new names. Also: make up a limerick starting with one of these lines: "A gorilla sat down in a bar," or "The angriest woman in France," or "The wind blew my house to Vancouver" (there is no way that you can be pompous, adult-style, with the limerick; its pizzicato middle lines will see to that!) Or: suppose that people had tails, or four arms, or that (as E. P. Torrance delightfully suggests in one of his exercises) clouds had strings attached to them. To children these are subjects for delighted speculation; adults who retain or nourish this quality also contain in themselves one of the sacred fires of the creative process.

Adopt new, untried strategies in problem-solving that invest a problem area with a harvest of insights. Most adults have been trained to approach problems as they once were taught to attack geometry exercises: with a meticulous logic, employing available "facts" in supposedly the most logical "order." In numerous situations the problem yields to this approach; in numerous others it does not. In fact, *problem-creating* is a prime exercise of the creative mind; just as being comfortable amid temporary disorder is a mark of the creative spirit. It is astonishing that we can live so long and use so little the tools provided by our minds and our language to promote the applied imagination: combine, adapt, multipy, magnify, minify, put to other uses, eliminate, rearrange, substitute.* That is: we use them haphazardly and with minimal effect, rather than systematically for rich returns. If we used them more, the world would come alive with ideas and insights.

"Combine," Goethe wrote, "always combine"—and, in fact, *combination*, usually of hitherto strange or seemingly incompatible elements, is one of the great motors of creativity in the arts, in science, in invention, in statecraft, in interpersonal life. Everywhere we look we can see evidence of the creative power of combining things—in colors, in furniture, in music, in architecture, in everyday inventions, in town planning, in food. But typically we merely *react* to the combinations devised by others: what we need to do is to develop our own faculty of combination to envision and create new things. Nor is the creative process limited only to *combination*. As one example, take a few minutes to note down some of the creative products and situations brought into being by, of all things, *eliminating* something: a personal lifestyle transformed by what you deliberately subtract from it; a manuscript transformed by imaginative editing; a too-fussy woman's outfit or an overloaded industrial design made not only "functional" but beautiful by creative elimination. (Examples of other creative "motors" at work can be found in Chapter 9.)

One of the great blocks to creative problem-solving is the fixed or-

---

*An easy way to remember these central verbs of the creative problem-solving, idea-generating process is to use the acronym, CAMPERS, which is itself a tiny example of rearranging or reversing, since the original acronym is SCAMPER—that of Sidney Parnes and his colleagues at the Creative Education Foundation, Buffalo.

thodox concept that might best be called "the dominating idea." Powerful, driving ideas obviously have their own creative role, since they can supply the will, energy, and tenacity needed to hold on to a baffling search, and of course at times the dominating concept is, after all, the right concept. But times without number, it is not; and far more: the block that destroys the creative person's work is something within his own system of long-revered practices or views, or within his cultural taboos.

The history of cultural blocks and dominating, destructive (anti-creative) ideas is a fascinating one. If you take some time to make a list of some, you may find yourself jotting down examples ranging from the three-centuries-old custom of binding the feet of aristocratic Chinese girls to the obsession of medieval town-planning with cathedral squares, to the fatal devotion of World War One generals to the role of the horse, and the blind defence of the status-quo with which the medical establishment of Vienna and Budapest (and elsewhere) met the new antiseptic ideas of Semmelweiss. All too often we ourselves look at familiar objects, literally for years, and never see the variations possible in their designs and uses because they all seem so obvious. But seeing through or beyond the obvious is another of the great motors of the creative process.

In one of his charming books on creativity Edward de Bono invites the reader to gaze at a familiar figure: a rectangle with the horizontal sides overlapping equally. He then presents, by the simple assumption that the four sides of the figure can be moved and maneuvered, like bars or sticks, 33 variations of the original figure, in L-forms, cross-forms, etc., until it seems incredible that all these forms were actually existent within the original overlapping rectangle (which, incidentally, one might compare to the shape of a dull municipal park). De Bono devotes a whole chapter to developing and speculating about these forms and their diversity, and the many further assemblies of figures that are possible once one is freed from the grip of the taken-for-granted situation. But the essence and illumination of his argument is well summed up in these sentences:

> The pieces created for the sake of explanation or description soon come to exist on their own as separate entities. They continue to exist even when the situation out of which they arose has been forgotten. . . . In this way, entities which have been created quite arbitrarily become strengthened by their usefulness until it becomes impossible to doubt their existence. When this stage is reached, such entities may actually obstruct progress.

Not *con*vergence of the wholly familiar, but *di*vergence using unexpected approaches and capitalizing upon chance and serendipity will many times provide the key to a stubborn problem. De Bono's own useful term for this less conforming, more imaginative process is "lateral thinking," and he usefully remarks:

> Vertical thinkers take the most reasonable view of a situation, and then proceed logically and carefully to work it out. Lateral thinkers tend to explore all the different ways of looking at something, rather than accepting the most promising and proceeding from that.

What this now has to do with creativity in the middle and later years is evident enough. The creative process is a spring partly flowing or seeking to flow from the man or woman's own complex nature and circumstances; but it is much more than that. It is a process actively released by many of the strategies and experiences suggested in this chapter—the strategies of search, of stretching of mind and spirit, of maintaining wonder and fantasy, of risking and even enjoying the absurd, and of not only entertaining unusual approaches in problem-solving but actively going outside the shelter of long-familiar concepts to find them.

If adults in their middle and later years feel a "falling-off" in their creative powers, or for that matter the failure of powers to awaken, the reason will almost certainly not be some mysterious ebbing and drying up of the inherent talents, whatever they are (this is developed further in Chapter 6). The problem will be with what might be called the "enabling powers" of the creative process—the will to produce and create, personal energy both physical and psychic, and competence to avoid or remove whatever blocks may be placed in one's way by the environment or by one's emotional and cognitive systems.

An interesting illustration of some of the issues at stake here is seen in the recent later-life performance of the British woman novelist M. M. Kaye, the author of *The Far Pavilions*, an enormous narrative (about 400,000 words) of fine quality. Kaye was brought up in a family descended from and maintaining the traditions of the British Army in India, and she married an officer of the same tradition. Kaye had already written a huge and excellent novel set in British India, and had begun *The Far Pavilions* when she learned that she had cancer. This evidently slowed down her writing while she fought the disease, which she defeated after four years. She was then 68. She resumed writing and completed the novel by age 74 in 1977. Many critics and readers of the book have commented on, among other qualities, its zest and drive, the thrust and power of the plot, and the vivid characterizations.

The writing of a novel of 1,000 closely printed pages, in which the pageant of plot and subplots and dozens of characters and major episodes must move with sustained strength and insight to a satisfying climax, is an awesome task. One writer of a very large book has even remarked of it later: "My angel wrote the book!"—a perhaps poetic reference to the role of the deep or Jungian self. But it is not the angel who writes the book (or paints the painting or solves a complex mathematical problem, or whatever), but oneself: a man or woman of this or that state of health, of this age or that, and in a particular set of circumstances.

A recent photograph of the author of *The Far Pavilions* shows a very pretty, elderly Englishwoman in a charming living room; she looks as if she might be about to offer tea and chat about the local county fair. Yet this is the woman who was able to call forth the energy to write a huge novel. M. M. Kaye's performance illustrates the power of the enabling forces in creativity in addition to her basic writing talent. She possessed the will, energy, stamina, self-confidence, and devotion to the concept of the creative task, which Alfred North Whitehead once termed "the Sacred Present." However, as with all created work of whatever dimension, until it is completed and can be accepted, its importance is virtually nonexistent to anyone but oneself.

This is where self-confidence enters in. One has to believe in what one is doing, whatever the creative task, and then, even or especially if the project is likely to be a long-range one, believe that it will be completed. Since the human mind, that "lithe animal," as some yogi masters term it, finds perverse pleasure many times in running down negative paths, it may make discouraging calculations. "If this novel turns out to be 400,000 words or so, and I write at 1,000 words a day" (a kind of maximum cited by many writers), "it will take me perhaps two years to do not only the writing but the required rewriting, editing, and all the rest. And I have had cancer, so that my energy may be rather less that it was. Etc., etc." (I use M. M. Kaye here solely as a prototype, with, I am sure, her distant blessing.)

Our human style, Whitehead wrote, is to mourn the past and worry about the future, while all the time the Sacred Present is passing us by, half-used, half-enjoyed.* But this negativism and loss of confidence, if and when it occurs, is dispelled by the enabling powers of the creator-person: in this case, a woman novelist. She sets to work, sitting at her desk, and writes steadily day by day, week by week, not fretting over time lost or invisible obstacles that may lie ahead—living and working in "the Sacred Present."

All creative ventures involve, of course, the likelihood of "blocks" from time to time during the process or before setting off. The lives of noted creative people are full of references to these temporary standstills, and the subject is important enough in the theory and practice of creativity that James L. Adams was able to devote an entire book (1974) to what he calls *Conceptual Blockbusting.* Among a few of Adams's cited reasons for the occurrence of creative blocks that are rele-

*A perceptive but forgotten writer of inspirational books, Dr. Frank Crane, argued persuasively that both life and faith can be made to work in dark hours by proceeding as though, generally speaking, the desired state or condition actually exists.

vant here are: fear of taking a risk; no appetite for the necessary temporary disorder into which the creative process often brings us; judging ideas too soon instead of just going ahead and generating them; lack of challenge in the actual problem (fair enough: then one naturally turns to another!); excess of zeal and too great expectations; cultural taboos that hem us in; inability to relax into wonder and humor; and inflexible use of intellectual problem-solving strategies.

To these can be added some comments from a charming paper on "How to Unblock" by the American psychotherapist and painter, Desy Safan-Gérard. Writing from the valuable double perspectives of being both practitioner and theoretician (she has also observed the creative process in action among colleagues and clients), Safan-Gérard cites the following as causes of blocks: facing the work before you are ready, without giving ideas time to develop; being too much governed by a preconceived form when the ideas cannot be contained by it (my own pastime of writing sonnets in the traditional style confirms much of Safan-Gérard's premise here!); and setting expectations too high and evaluating too soon (note how this resonates with Adams's ideas). She notes with some amusement that when her creative subjects report on what they do when faced with a temporary block, many of them report that they first go away to find something to eat!

However, for many men and women in their middle and later years, the greatest problem in their creative progress is, not inhibiting blocks within the work in progress, but rather the lack of will and the confidence to undertake creative enterprises at all. They may believe "I'm not creative," or believe that, though creative in childhood, they no longer are in adulthood (the falsity of both these premises has been already indicated).

Or they may have accepted the terrible myths of our throwaway society and believe that from the mid-50s on, and more so in later years, their physical, mental, and creative resources are all declining. As they see it, their friendship circle, their income, and their influence in various spheres—business, family, politics—are also declining. This is the terrifying misconception out of which grows the familiar refrain of all those dear hearts who "always meant to" do the special creative task but now think they never will. Reinforcing negative phrases abound: "I haven't the energy I had when younger"; "I just couldn't carry it through"; "My life's taken a different turn"; "I actually wrote a novel at 40, never published, of course; and now. . ."

Where, then, does the energy of people like M. M. Kaye come from? I suggest, as one answer, that men and women in later maturity who may feel some decline of former physical energy have wisely learned that there is something I call "essential energy," necessary for creative and other Ulyssean ventures, which they have learned to conserve and use well. And, there is also the whole radiant resource of the psychic power, closely linked to faith and will.

However, for every adult, typically Ulyssean, who sustains or regains his or her creative powers throughout later middle age and on through the very late years, there are clearly many who have given up what they conceive to be the struggle to realize themselves. Some may indeed be living, in Thoreau's unforgettable phrase, "lives of quiet desperation," but for most the process is less dramatic and in fact different. They are not desperate (in some cases it would be better if they were, since desperation may breed action): rather, they have lost confidence in their own special talents, and beyond that, in their own unique selfhood—an attitude also conditioned and reinforced by a throwaway society, beset by the myths described in Chapter 1.

Thus, those who would turn or return to the Ulyssean concept in later life need to be concerned not only about the true nature and inborn promise of their creativity but also about the crucial connections between creativity and self-identity.

3

SELF-IDENTITY, SELF-GROWTH, SELF-ACTUALIZATION

W E BROUGHT nothing into this world, and it is certain we can carry nothing out"—so says the *Book of Common Prayer*, quoting from Paul in one of those enormous half-truths that have done so much to promote and destroy the Christian faith. In fact, we bring a great deal into this world: our genetic equipment, which is crucial, the famous "nature" of the nature-and-nurture duality out of which our lives are fashioned (the mysterious "I" completes the trinity); and our shares in the folk unconscious, from which Jung evolved most of his concepts of creativity.

And we do carry something out of the world; certainly not material possessions which, when the chips are down, matter least, but our personal "self," the great work of art upon which we have been engaged all the years of our life.

Sooner or later, from perhaps the mid-40s on, men and women become critical assessors of the validity and relevance of their lives. Disguise it as we will, we are "no longer young," we are in "our prime," then our "later prime"—the euphemisms change as the years pass. The first cool winds of the evening that is at hand begin to blow, even though the summer sun is still burning vividly in the afternoon sky.

Anne Simon writes of a new middle age that is a kind of superb central span connecting two lesser spans, young adulthood and aged adulthood, in the great bridge of the human life journey. The people of this central span are not only heavily engaged in many productive activities of their own, but are also assisting with the problems of those younger and older. Simon's book, *The New Years*, has a happy ending:

> For the first time in history and for the first time in his life, the man of middle age can comprehend the great sweep of the life span as it now stands revealed. He can order his life to suit the new facts about getting older which it has brought to light, seize its options, pioneer. . . .Independence is his passport to loving, to being loved, to being useful and needed.

The governing word throughout is "can." Simon's book is splendid because of its belief in the potentiality of adult human beings, even though she labels the twentieth century "this savage century," and sees the present multitudes of middle-agers in North America as being victims in many ways of a universal cult of youth. In short, the adult in his middle years becomes the secret watcher of the implacable clock of the life drama which measures and demythologizes his younger dreams and carries him onward to the dark outlands of a youth-dominated society.

Time Magazine, in an article still surprisingly valid after 15 years, places the happy ending at the beginning. America, we are told, has a ruling class, a "command generation": one-fifth of the whole population of the United States, or nearly 43 million people between the ages of 40 and 60: the middle-aged Americans. The first half of the article glitters with dozens of names of middle-aged celebrities; the actress Lauren Bacall adorns the cover of Time and supplies the glamorous central theme of the discussion. A compelling case is made for the undoubted power and glory of the middle years, and for the colorful and fascinating maturity that separates adult men and women from adolescents and early adults.

This euphoric presentation of middle age in our era may have contributed a new zest and confidence to many North Americans passing through the period that one British psychologist describes as that of "menopausal man."

Yet the article gives almost as much attention to the panic and melancholy that descend on great numbers of middle-agers. It is Eric Berne's "balance sheet" time, a period of agonizing reappraisal, and not only for the individual. Many marriages that were once flooded with youthful passion, or anchored in family cares and joys, suddenly seem drab and empty; it is the age of the second affair; the peak of alcoholism, of pregeriatrical drugs, of escalating cardiovascular attacks, often the result of being strait-jacketed by fate.

This conception of the middle-age crisis crosses cultural frontiers in the Western world. Thus, Dr. Martin Herbert, writing in *Strip Jack Naked* about middle-aged men in Great Britain, describes the purposelessness and grayness which many middle-agers feel during their so-called "prime" years. Some feel suffocated, like one man who felt his life comparable to that of a dying fish lunging about at the bottom of his rowboat; his possessions and commitments had stifled him—the real him. Others feel that they have become old fogies prematurely; still others feel that life somehow has passed them by. As Herbert puts it: "For a large part of life, we are looking ahead, looking forward to various new experiences, fresh and exciting goals. And then, one day, the individual realizes that he has completed most of his tasks. . .there is nothing really new to look forward to, no particularly exciting goal to attain."

The malaise of middle age is a favorite topic of the literatures of Western society. The critic Frederick Losey identifies the fascination of *Antony and Cleopatra,* a drama of Shakespeare's mature years, with the theme of "the tragedy of middle life":

Idealism and inexperience will ever protect youth from a similar tragedy, and age is exempted by coldness of blood; but middle life, with the dimming of its idealism, its awakening sense of the worthlessness of earthly honour, and its consciousness of abundant physical powers, will always be peculiarly susceptible to mistaking a new and strong sexual appeal for the "nobility of life."

A different aspect of passion is portrayed in Thomas Mann's *Death in Venice:* Gustave Aschenbach, a novelist in late middle age, enmeshes himself in a strange silent infatuation for a handsome boy, and forsakes the dignity and discipline of 30 years to assume the dyes and other tricks for disguising age.

Simone de Beauvoir was barely 60 when she wrote her massive *La Vieillesse* for which she herself hardly qualified as a subject. Besides, since her youth she had had a brilliant, productive life. Still, she writes with melancholy of the "vast miscomprehension" that exists between what people conceive a successful man to be and what he experiences himself to be. And she refers to an earlier judgment of hers in *La Force des Choses*, with which she still concurs: "The promises of my youth have been kept—nevertheless, I have been swindled." In Arthur Miller's play, *Death of a Salesman*, on the other hand, the promises have not been kept, and the sense of time running out on a life unable to identify with its dreams produces a tragedy of middle age unbearably poignant.

In the film, *Sunday Bloody Sunday*, Peter Finch plays the role of a middle-aged physician, an admirable doctor and human being, himself engaged in a dual love affair with a girl and a youth that he is unable to resolve. At the same time, he sees among his patients an executive in his 50s who has developed into a hypochondriac, and who can no longer compete with the youth cult, which has at last penetrated his sphere of business. In fact, the executive explains bitterly to the young personnel officer who is going to try to get him a job: "They gave me the golden handshake." And he adds, "How can I tell my wife?"

These situations are the stuff of excellent drama, but the middle-age malaise for most men and women is closer to the experience of Herman Hesse's character, Harry Haller, in *Steppenwolf* and Louis Bromfield's *Mr. Smith*.

Haller lives on a plateau of mediocre and toneless existence: the lukewarm days of discontented middle life pass, unchallenged, purposeless, unswept by great devotions or emotions, beyond dreams. There is safety in this "normal and sterile" life, and a kind of contentment, but "it is just this contentment that I cannot endure. After a short time it fills me with irrespressible loathing and nausea. Then, in desperation, I have to escape into other regions, if possible on the road to pleasure, or if that cannot be, on the road to pain."

The same was true of Haller's contemporary in North America, in Bromfield's novel, written when Bromfield himself was in middle age. Mr. Smith is a successful middle-aged executive, a charming man who finds that he is drowning in business and social roles, commitments, committees, engagements, obligations to his wife and his wife's friends—he has lost his self. His wife is obsessed with "togetherness," a favorite cliché of the 1950s, and delights in the thought that she and her husband are always together. If Smith goes to the bottom of the garden to read a book by himself, she comes flying down to be with him so that they will be "together." He is a man of peace who has no peace. Among his business circle is an older executive in his early 60s whose special form of the malaise is to indulge in a bacchanal once a year when away from home at a convention—a fact well known to and lovingly accepted by his wife, who actually understands his needs. When, however, he dies in the excess of emotion of one of these escapades, and when Smith's wife refers caustically to "that dirty old man," this is the breaking point for Smith, who deeply respected his associate. Smith seeks escape to one of the war fronts of the Far East, and achieves freedom—and death.

Mr. Smith was a later phenomenon of middle age. At an earlier age, during perhaps the vigorous decade of his 30s, when he built up his array of roles and activities, he undoubtedly assumed that they were himself. In modern North American society as well as other Western cultures where failure in vocational achievement and material ownership is the unforgivable sin, men and women of the middle and later years condition themselves to believe that their personal self can be identified by the labels, titles, functions, and participations that present them to others in various social and business roles.

In fact, there can be so extreme a misidentification of self with a vocational or social role that a man or woman can literally die within a few weeks or months after the severance of a job or of the death of a spouse. However, all this does not mean that there is some kind of pure and idealistic "I" wholly divorceable from the self's many different social roles. We are "a part of all that we have met," and usually we are the richer for it.

Adults in early and later middle age are likely to feel a malaise, which for many will intensify as they move into the late years of the adult drama, but it is important to note that maturity also usually brings its own repertoire of compensating skills and resources. Bernice Neugarten writes about what she calls "the executive processes of personality in middle age: self-awareness, selectivity, manipulation and control of the environment, mastery, competence, the wide array of cognitive strategies." As one British authority of motivation notes, people in middle and late adulthood usually have some conception of how to cope with failure and frustration: after all, they have met these conditions many times. Mostly, adults in the age range 40-60 have learned such simple strategies as when to postpone decisions; how to be patient and wait out a personal dispute; and how to relate things seen and read to the experience of one's life—like the man of 50 who understands *Antony and Cleopatra* with a depth his adolescent children cannot.

Neugarten sought her data from a special group of college graduates and *Who's Who* individuals who also had the alleged advantages of money, prestige, and power. However, anyone who has seen enough of life to have met many older adults of limited means and education, from small towns, farming areas, and working-class areas in great cities can testify that many of them have acquired mature resources with which to confront the frequent stresses of middle and later adulthood: courage, wisdom, and love deepened by time, and strategies of coping and winning.

It is also true that there is a large group of adults in late maturity who feel that they have successfully completed their life's work and are content to rest and relax. Some may have set their own life goals, and felt—or at least declared—that they had met them; some may have accepted goals directed by others, and have acquiesced also in their termination and the approval of this action by others. Amongst these seemingly contented finishers are the people who declaim somewhere in full course that "I have found my niche"—a chilling phrase to the Ulysseans within earshot.

Whether content and passive, discontented but passive, or still seeking (the Ulysseans), all adults in their middle and later years are exposed to some degree of self-discovery—small or large. The motor of our lives is the self-image, and it is the self-image that essentially differentiates the Ulyssean adult from those adults who, at the opposite extreme, are immobilized by disgust and despair.

The wonderful phrase, "Yes, I can," which Sammy Davis Jr., uses as the title of his autobiography, contains a response to life that is not just a jolly-jump-up attempt to meet its often formidable problems with a momentary show of spurious self-confidence. Rather, it grows out of a self-image that unbinds and liberates the self that must do business with the world, and generates creativity. The reverse is summarized in the short and moving memoir of an anonymous British writer describing the deluge of misfortunes he feels he cannot handle: *The Answer to Life Is No*. For some adult people the answer to life may indeed be No. We are not engaged here in making judgments about the morality or validity of the choices people make in their response to life—nor are we capable of doing so—but the role of the self-image in arriving at these Yes, I Can's and No's is clearly a powerful one. Consider the symbolic suicide of a young man who shot himself on top of a garbage dump. The deed described and underlined the self-concept.

Soaked in crimes and stupidity though man undoubtedly is, as Stephen Spender says, he is still the "beautiful creature" with his extraordinary brain, hands, and language systems. These, and the domains of thought and creativity they make possible, give the human species an unmatched magnitude of self-awareness: a Promethean gift that carries its own torments with it.

Popular speech uses the word "self" millions of times daily without defining it, in compounds that are like signs pointing the way but never really going there: "self- centred," "self-inflicted," "self-pitying," and so on. In fact, the "self" has never yielded its ultimate mystery, although enough light has been shed on it by contemporary and earlier seekers to make discussion of one's own self possible. The most striking thing about it is its personal uniqueness. It appears in the individual vocabulary as "I," and as such enjoys a designation that cannot be confused—as terms like "star," "king," or even "you" can be confused.

Yet the self is also the product of human interaction. If a solitary child were born into a dead atomic world from the womb of the last mother and by some miracle survived and grew physically, it would have or be a kind of self, but one so different from the selfhoods we think we know as to be grotesque. The emerging self of the child in a so-called normal world—which is to say a world filled with human transactions both good and evil—achieves much of its identity by innumerable relationships with other human beings—parents, peers, strangers—and from many seemingly less important human interactions and events. He or she "encodes and decodes" thousands of messages about moral systems, social roles, folklores, political and legal habitats, and other influences of organized society and what might be called the "hidden" society (the officially rejected sub-cultures). He or she is also the inheritor of the historical memory of the world.

Thus, it is possible to speak of the self under different titles: the environmental self, the psychological self, the mythological self, the physical self, the mysterious quintessential self, or "core self," and which has connotations with Kant's "pure self." In *Man and His Symbols* Carl Jung wrote about this self as seeking to speak to us and guide us by means of our dreams. Jung's "self" is a "regulating centre that brings about a constant extension and maturing of the personality. . . . It may emerge very slightly, or it may develop relatively completely during one's lifetime. How far it develops depends on whether or not the ego is willing to listen to the messages of the self"—the messages from dreams.

Perhaps the reverse of the solitary child born into a dead world is that of the individual fully equipped by the world and the many contributions of social and psychological interaction who finds himself in the position of having these brutally and systematically stripped from him. The writings of Viktor Frankl and others indicate how men and women under sadistic treatment in concentration camps have had almost every level of existence taken from them short of death and still maintained their selfhood. These cases help illustrate how far or not there is quintessential self and how it is formed or appears. Certainly, nothing removes the strange enchantment for many thoughtful adults of the venerable phrase: "I know that I know."

In very late adulthood there sometimes occurs the terrible phenomenon of open self-hatred—that revulsion against the self which has wasted or destroyed many lives. Chilling reports exist of an old man or woman found standing before a door-length mirror in a nursing home bitterly cursing his or her own image. This is one dramatic and pathetic form of the rejection of the self-as-seen, which can assume psychoneurotic forms as in cases where once-confident elderly adults are intimidated and almost destroyed by their subjugation in a youth-obsessed society. In the case of the elderly self-hater, it is curious and sad that the sense of loss and alienation is so overpowering that the individual wholly rejects or ignores the astonishing number of good choices and actions made and good knowledges and skills acquired: the attempts also to love and be loved which in themselves form part of the art of the self-in-growth.

In advanced years, in hostile environments like bad nursing homes, this same terrifying rejection or alienation of self may, of course, derive from conditions all too close to Viktor Frankl's prison camp experience. Consider what it means for old men and women to find themselves stripped of all possessions, all friends, all contacts, all respect, all authority, all love.

Karen Horney underlined the importance of the self-image as a dynamic force by noting the presence in therapy of two forms of the image: the way each of her patients regarded his (or her) *present* roles, status, and abilities; and the way he regarded his *potentialities*—specifically, his aspirations for himself—the *idealized* self-image, as Horney called it. The idealized self-image provides much of the generating power of human adult life. At its best it supplies what Gordon Allport has called "an insightful cognitive map"; at its worst it can be both so unrealistic and so obsessive that it maims and destroys much of the life action.

Erik Erikson, who is loath to let go the Freudian term "ego" in discussions of the self, ultimately abandons what seems to him to be the seemingly irresolvable debate on the roles and relevance of the "ego" and the "self," a pronouncement that shows the dynamics he clearly conceives to be part of any individual's existence: "The ego, then, as a central organizing agency, is during the course of life faced with a changing self which, in turn, demands to be synthesized with abandoned and anticipated selves." And this leads him to the concepts of self-identity and self-diffusion as powerful generators and inhibitors of wholeness and creative action.

Many of us, in moments of seemingly unbearable stress, at all ages, have felt a temporary slackening or dimming of our ordinarily strong feeling of self-identity. In Franz Werfel's novel, *The Forty Days of*

Musa Dagh, the hero-leader of the besieged city, although he successfully brings his people through their long trial, is occasionally overcome by the experience of what Werfel describes as a "whirling" of the little world about him. This occurs at periods of extreme stress, and may well be the novelist's shorthand for a form of identity crisis.

At times the anxiety of the self to escape from the unbearable challenges to its identity results in a marked dimming of the photographic plate. Or it may lead to an attempt at self-diffusion: to project oneself onto other identities, which in extreme cases may lead to the attempt to assume other roles and backgrounds altogether, for better or for worse. At all events, the anthology in which Erikson's paper appears bears the significant title, *Identity and Anxiety.* And Frieda Fromm-Reichmann, writing in the same anthology, speaks of anxiety as "the most unpleasant and at the same time the most universal experience, except loneliness. We observe both healthy and mentally disturbed people doing everything possible to ward off anxiety or to keep it from awareness." She quotes Poulson, Berdyaev, Riesman, and other social psychologists as finding "the source of man's anxiety in his psychological isolation, *his alienation from his own self* and from his fellow men." (My italics.) And she notes Rollo May's definition of anxiety as "the apprehension set off by a threat to some value which the individual holds essential to his existence as a personality."

All adults are need-bearers, including the hilariously titled "man who has everything" (everything except the consciousness of his enormous need to become a fully actualized human being?) and the often grotesquely misnamed "beautiful people." The supreme need for each individual adult is surely to achieve identification and fulfillment of self, not to be the echo or carbon copy of others, or to merge oneself totally with giant thought systems whether political, economic, or religious, so that one can never be exposed as a divergent being or scrutinized as an agent of change. Yet the paradox is that our selfhood also grows from interaction, from love for others and love for oneself.

In Franz Kafka's terrifying story *Metamorphosis,* the central character is a young salesman who in the course of his routine and empty life has lost any love for himself and any real love for others. His life has become so much a matter of routine and his rejection of the claims of growing self-identity so complete that he awakens one morning to find himself a cockroach. The story is a parable: to be a human being is to develop a unique and growing individuality. To be a cockroach is to exist by living from the refuse of others.

"The essence of neurosis," remarks Rollo May, "[is] the person's unusual potentialities, blocked by hostile conditions in the environment (past or present) and by his own internalized conflicts, turning inward and causing morbidity." And May aptly quotes from William Blake, whose own life demonstrated his constant nourishment of his selfhood and the fertility of his self-concept: "Energy is Eternal Delight: he who desires but acts not, breeds pestilence."

We are the product of the days of our years, of 20,000 days by the time we are age 55. The adult in his later years has lived a very long time with himself, with his *self*. Is it possible over so long a period to avoid in all possible ways confrontations with the inner voices of the self, or to flee from the invitations to more vivid and fertile selfhood, which the small mobile cosmos of our personal life successively opens to us?

It is indeed possible, and very common, just as it is possible to actualize the experiences of the life drama to help bring into being a self open to all the potentialities, at least, of creativity. Those who do so will become the Ulyssean adults. Yet so complex is the life journey, and so varied the network of experiences that occur even in the apparently most commonplace lives, that Ulysseans and non-Ulysseans cannot be finally classified and divided at the gateway of the mid-50s.

If the human adult is subject to a high degree of rigidity and passivity in the course of life experiences, he is also a being who is never wholly programmed. Far more, he is capable of some degree of virtuosity, however small, to the end of his life. Thus, it is wiser not to speak in absolute terms of Ulyssean and non-Ulyssean adults whenever one is speaking of *potentiality*. In this sphere of discussion, it is better to speak of comparative degrees of the Ulyssean life, spirit, and performance.

There is an important piece of good news about the human life drama which, if one could only get it distributed widely enough and listened to carefully enough, might surprise by joy a great number of adults in their later years.

The good news is that the human adult can continue to grow, to learn, and to create up to *and through* the very late years. Traditional folklore, which likes to believe that it can reduce life to certain huge sentimental generalities, likes to conceive of the life drama as a simple curve, the arc of a semi-circle, rising from childhood to the full prime of manhood and womanhood and descending to second childhood. Jaques's familiar description in *As You Like It* of the "seven ages of man," in which the sixth age is that of the "lean and slipper'd pantaloon" and the last age is that of the individual "sans teeth, sans eyes, sans taste, sans everything," is widely quoted as the epitome of folk wisdom, but in fact it is murderously naïve and misleading.

The human life journey cannot be intelligently charted by a single curving line. Such a line is perhaps a fair approximation of an adult's physical progress, since there is a certain decline in the power of the various physical senses. Even here, however, there are instances galore of men and women who survived a sickly childhood and early adulthood, or who emerged vigorously from a period of flabbiness in their 30s and 40s, to enter and maintain glowing health and strength in their later and even very late years. Single-line curves ignore the incredible complexity of the life drama, the varying domains in which adults live out their lives, and the kaleidoscope of individualities, as numerous as the sands of the seas, that have to be taken into account.

Adult individuals do indeed play many parts, but of a complexity far surpassing Shakespeare's wildwood philosopher.

An important denial of the concept of the single declining curve was developed by the University of Chicago sociologist Robert Havighurst in the 1950s, partly as a result of his work with "the Chicago group," which studied the nature of the later-life profiles of aging and aged adults in Kansas City. Havighurst writes about three facets of the life journey that had been virtually neglected in earlier years. One was to examine any life from early to late adulthood in the light of ten-year "cohort" groups—that is, that people whether, say, in the 30s or 60s, would share the notable characteristics of their age group. A second was to describe progress on the life journey for men and women as being made up of a series of "developmental tasks"—a good phrase because its name indicates quite clearly that throughout adult life we are all presented with one task or challenge after another, and if we handle the task reasonably well or meet the challenge, we develop and move on as maturing adults. If we do not, then in that respect and to that extent, we fall back into immaturity. A third was to look at these tasks as emanating from certain "roles" we all play. Thus, any of us in our time plays simultaneously a number of roles: parent, spouse (or single adult by choice), employer or employee, citizen, union or club member, church member perhaps, friend, son or daughter, relative, personal learner or teacher, seeker or creator (and others).[1]

Havighurst's first major statement tied together the multiple tasks we all simultaneously perform (even when much of the time we never think about it) with the special features of the decade we might be passing through at any particular year: these are the typical tasks and responses of the 20s or the 50s, say, to which Havighurst gave descriptive titles 20 years before most other commentators on the life journey began to do likewise. Thus, for him, the 20s were the decade of *Focusing One's Life;* the 30s, those of *Collecting One's Energies,* especially with continuing thrust toward career and personal development and advancement; the 40s, called, not very convincingly, *Exerting and Asserting Oneself:* a kind of peak period as many adults see it, a time of heavily investing energy in the "outer world" of affairs—still in careers or in civic and cultural activity.

The years 50-60 in Havighurst's scenario are a period of *Maintaining Position and Changing Roles.* Many adults reach a plateau in their world of work. For women the "empty nest" phenomenon appears. "Libidinal fires die down, producing a threat to the ego." The self sees the world as complex in ways not perceived before, and doubts its ability to master it. Many adults begin the secret process of "disengagement" (a concept made popular in the 1950s by Elaine Cumming and W. E. Henry); that is, the adult disengages from certain earlier affairs and attachments while, on its part, society begins to withdraw certain responsibilities or opportunities from men and women in this later decade. The parent becomes the grandparent, and a sense of constricted time leads to an urgent feeling (among many) of priorities.

In the decade 60-70, to which Havighurst gives the title *Deciding to Disengage, and How*, disengagement continues as an important process. Most men lose their jobs by retirement, as do many women. Many women also lose their husbands and need to cope with widowhood.

Not surprisingly, the life journey closes with the designation for ages 70-90, *Making the Most of Disengagement*. Havighurst's tone, here as elsewhere, is hopeful and humane, and he wisely quotes Charlotte Buhler on the role of "seeking self-fulfillment" in these late years. This sounds, although Buhler did not mean it as such, as though the self were the least of our possessions, and when life may have stripped us of everything else—power, money, sex gratification, prestige, and most of our friends—we can turn to the fulfillment of self!

Havighurst's scenario of the life journey is valuable for its emphasis on developmental tasks, richness of social roles, and its reminder of the disengagement phenomenon as a factor to be handled (and handled well) in later adult life. However, this schema is dominated by the disengagement concept, and lacks the important qualities of later adulthood in our time portrayed recently by Bernice Neugarten in her identification of thousands of older men and women as "young-old" adults. These are people 55-75 whom Neugarten has recognized in her studies as heralding the arrival of a new type of older adult in our society who lives with marked vitality, grace, and self-growth. (See also page 68.)

The Ulyssean concept, however, goes beyond Neugarten's "young-old" premises, and differs sharply from certain assumptions that may arise from the disengagement theory. For example, the Ulyssean would warmly endorse James E. Birren's definition of a human being as "a biological, psychological, and social constellation moving forward in time" (the word 'constellation" is particularly apt). But the Ulyssean indicates by his or her life performances that the splendid dynamism inherent in Birren's definition need not disappear. Disengagement can be a positive, dynamic, creative process, not a dreary slowing-down, turning-off, opting-out, giving-up retreat from life. In fact, the term "disengagement" is too negative a term for Ulysseans. It carries with it the false assumption that somehow the real business of a human life is to be totally engaged in career and social obligations and expectations. On the contrary, the real business of a human life is to fulfill itself, partly no doubt with the aid of societal dynamics, but *in any event* on its own terms in many, many ways.[2]

The Ulyssean has a revolutionary concept about the middle and later years: that for many they are years of beginnings, not conclusions. He or she would quote C. G. Jung's dictum that it takes a human being about 50 years simply to assemble and truly identify the self; or the challenging assertion of Frank Underhill, the Canadian political scientist, when in his late Ulyssean 70s, that "nobody knows anything until he is 50"; or the statement of Professor (later Sir) Fred Clarke at McGill University that used to send me and my undergraduate classmates into bewildered fury: "Really, no one is fit to begin teaching until he is 50."

Even when we accept the fact that adulthood is a lifelong developmental process, it is often difficult to translate the theory to the particular individual we happen to be contending with in some bleak hour of a routine day. Is it possible to believe that, for example, this self-promoter with the wide cold smile; this jolly nonstop trouble-maker, busy poisoning her wells; this cynical derogator of all great plans and sweet hopes; this arrogant intellectual, lost in his own petrified forest of unrevised views; this square-voiced traveler, proclaiming as loudly as ever the superiorities of his own environment over other cultures; this ferocious junior official, busy demonstrating her equality with the worst of masculine qualities—is it possible to believe that these individual human adults, in so many ways not adult, in too many cases seemingly unloving, unlovable, and unloved, bear any relationship to the good news that adults can grow and increase their creative powers to the very end of the very latest years?

Yes, it is possible. To put the matter succinctly: not merely youth, but the whole of life, is potentiality for all types of adults.

Herbert L. Klemme, head of the Industrial Mental Health Division of the Menninger Foundation of Topeka, Kansas, offered an important insight on this during a lengthy interview in the *New York Times* in July, 1971. What Klemme found absorbing and often tragic was the number of times that people could not successfully negotiate a major period of life transition, and the effect this had on them. He describes how adult people "may spend the rest of their lives making futile attempts to work through" an unsuccessful negotiation, and how others who after early success are suddenly overwhelmed by disenchantment:

> Those who have difficulty making such transitions, regardless of age, often resort to similar behavioral patterns. Such a person may retreat temporarily to struggles of an earlier phase, which by comparison are now more comfortable. . . .A man in his late 30s may resume extramarital dating behavior more characteristic of his earlier 20s, and enjoy the relative comfort of behavior already learned, *perhaps to avoid the pain of advancing to another development level*. (My Italics.)

So great, in Klemme's view, could be the mid-life crisis[3] that failure to make the transition smoothly can begin a long process of personal frustration and failure. A woman whose children have grown to where they no longer seem to need her may become depressed or decide to have another baby. To restore a sense of excitement, a man may resort to risk-taking behavior, indulging in rigorous physical activities or investing in risky stock ventures—a common symptom of middle-aged physicians and dentists. And alcohol often becomes an escape route leading nowhere.

Those who weather the crisis, according to Dr. Klemme, often do it by finding new meaning in their work or by switching to a more satisfying career. On the other hand, persons who have endured the financially unrewarding aspects of such a job through young adulthood may suddenly find meaning in their work and a sense of newfound purpose in life. No wonder that a rich new emphasis in life-planning for the 1980s is on alternative lifestyles and radical career changes. Richard Bolles in *The Three Boxes of Life* foresees a society in the comparatively near future in which adults will study, work, and take extended recreation or renewal periods in "flexible life scheduling." If study, work, and play are good things, Bolles asks, why do we not flexibly interschedule them in our lives from childhood through the very late years, instead of confining ourselves to the "three boxes of life"—the study box up to age 20, the work box from 20 to 60 or 65, and the often unproductive or unfulfilling "play box" after "retirement"?

Two powerful factors are at work that make it probable that for many people Ulyssean options remain, in spite of perhaps a former anti-Ulyssean lifestyle. One of these factors is that most people are not totally classifiable in absolute categories. Few adults, for example, can be described as totally adventureless. With everyone in life the questions have to be put: "At what place and time?" "In what circumstances and conditions?" Surely the mature phrase in all adult assessments and controversies is, "It all depends."

An absorbing study published in 1976 by Florine Livson on midlife transition for women partly reinforces this point. Livson's project studied two groups of women aged 50 who were earlier members of a longitudinal survey of personality which the women had voluntarily entered in adolescence. Livson was able to select women at 50 who clearly seemed to have a high measure of psychological health. One group she termed "traditionals"—women whose past years clearly indicated that they had performed ably the traditional female roles of wife and mother. They seemed to have had few crises during their 40s, and arrived at 50 rich in what Erikson calls Generativity: a fine, nurturing, human capacity. The other group of women Livson called "independents." They had early been "skeptical, unconventional, more in touch with their inner life." During their 40s these women evidenced psychological depression, irritation, unproductive daydreaming. Yet by age 50, these "independents," though not showing the same strength in Generativity, showed to the perhaps rather astonished researchers, strong morale, emotional health, and a high capacity to be open, sympathetic, and trusting. Thus, any confident and despondent forecasts about them during their 40s, in their quite different individual lives, would have been wide of the mark. "You never can tell."

The second powerful factor mitigating seemingly irreversible life processes is the influence of psychological intersections—branches where men and women can choose between life-giving and life-corroding alternatives. In spite of a number of informative reports on the nature of 'adult life stages" appearing during the last half of the 1970s,[4] and which deal with early adult and mid-adult (to about 50) turbulence (what I have long called "white-water passages"), the case is still unproved that easily categorized crises and branchings or intersections can be shown to arrive at sharply definable times. What is clear enough is that all men and women are subject to a multiplex of changes and branches in their life progress, including turbulent intersections, which can harm or heal them depending upon the circumstances and the choices. Consider in this connection the stimulating and liberating conception of the later life journey by the American psychologist, Robert C. Peck, who developed a theory of life investments and alternatives. Peck's career involved him in the psychological analysis of personalities and life processes of several thousand people, mostly men, in business. However, his findings transfer easily to women also. From these studies, he became convinced that to try to sum people up in various time capsules (the 30s, the 40s, the 50s, and so on), was too categorical and fixating. Neither does he describe precisely identified years as major stress times for all adults.

Peck asks the sensible question: Is there not a great variability in adult life in the years of arrival at situations of psychic crisis? For example: young fathers and old fathers—how can their lifestyles possibly match, or how compare the effects upon them, therefore, of children growing up and moving out? We do not grow across adult life as students move from one grade to another; but rather, we progress vertically in different masteries and skills. Therefore, Peck discards much of the chronological and imprisoning classifications. He accepts two giant classifications by age: Middle Age and Old Age—but he is driven to this by the sheer semantics of the whole life-journey controversy. The tacks upon which he hangs his concepts of adult people-in-process are not ages but stages: the female climacteric, for example, regardless of age; or the retirement point for men, which now is beginning to vary enormously.

Furthermore, Peck tackles the needs and potentials of adults age 50-plus as no one except Bernice Neugarten (see pages 68 - 69) has done—almost uncharted territory compared to the recent exploration of the age arenas 20-50.

I was sufficiently fascinated by the potentialities in Peck's schema of "dynamic" alternatives to attempt to illustrate what they might mean in a simple pictorial chart (Chart 1). In designing, and designating it, as "The Major Game Adults Play," I have tried to convey the movement and flow of alternatives that present themselves innumerable times in continuing daily life. The circles representing arenas of behavior I have shown as intersecting, because which of us is ever totally and at all times in one circle or the other? I have drawn the circles equal, but in fact—complex and interesting creatures that we are—each of us has a larger circle in which we participate more than in the smaller. Readers may find it an interesting exercise to consider what their own life graphs would look like if projected on a screen.

"What does it mean to age successfully?"

Peck found that a critical point seems to be reached somewhere between the late 30s and the late 40s. This is a turbulent period for many middle-agers because it confronts them with the waning of certain physical powers, either of strength and sports prowess, in the case of men, or of physical beauty if defined as "young-looking" in the case of women. Many adults have invested themselves heavily in these powers, and the confrontation with loss forces upon them a major traumatic alternative of choice: *valuing wisdom or valuing physical powers*. Peck naturally distinguishes "wisdom" from "intellectual capacity." Wisdom is the ability to make the most effective choices among the alternatives that the wide repertoire of middle-aged adulthood provides in compensation. Some people cling to physical powers as their chief tool for coping with life; as the powers decline, so does the individual's competence to take on successfully life's inevitable frustrations and disappointments. They become more and more depressed, disillusioned, and bitter; and this affects and infects their reactions and relationships. On the other hand, in Peck's words, the successful "agers calmly invert their previous value hierarchy, now putting the use of their 'heads' above the use of their 'hands', both as their standard for self-evaluation and as their chief resource for solving life's problems."

The second of four major alternatives that Peck sees as confronting adults in the middle years is a choice between *socializing* vs. *sexualizing* in human relationships. When I first introduced Peck's concepts into my own seminars on the adult life drama, I found some students very hostile to what they felt to be his moralistic antagonism to sexual activity and play, perhaps because Peck uses terms such as "egocentric sex-drive" and "sex-objects" in describing the negative "sexualizing" alternative. However, Peck is really saying that in negotiating the turbulence of middle-life "climateric" and anxiety, adults must try to view other men and women as companions and friends in increasing

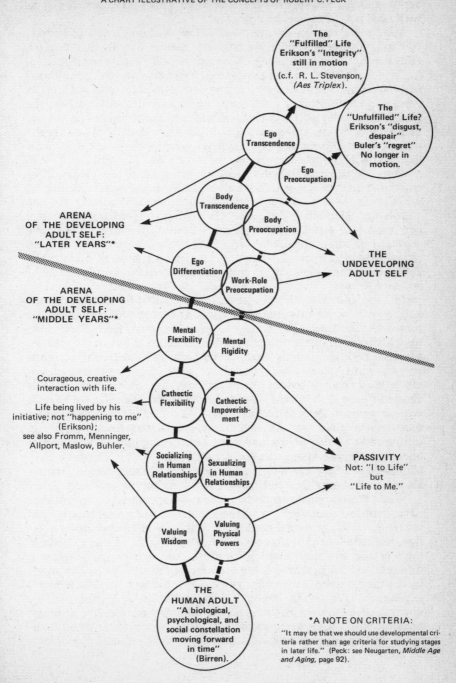

CHART 1
THE MAJOR GAME ADULTS PLAY:
A CHART ILLUSTRATIVE OF THE CONCEPTS OF ROBERT C. PECK

The "Fulfilled" Life Erikson's "Integrity" still in motion (c.f. R. L. Stevenson, *Aes Triplex*).

The "Unfulfilled" Life? Erikson's "disgust, despair" Buler's "regret" No longer in motion.

Ego Transcendence

Ego Preoccupation

Body Transcendence

Body Preoccupation

ARENA OF THE DEVELOPING ADULT SELF: "LATER YEARS"*

Ego Differentiation

Work-Role Preoccupation

THE UNDEVELOPING ADULT SELF

ARENA OF THE DEVELOPING ADULT SELF: "MIDDLE YEARS"*

Mental Flexibility

Mental Rigidity

Courageous, creative interaction with life.

Life being lived by his initiative; not "happening to me" (Erikson); see also Fromm, Menninger, Allport, Maslow, Buhler.

Cathectic Flexibility

Cathectic Impoverishment

Socializing in Human Relationships

Sexualizing in Human Relationships

PASSIVITY
Not: "I to Life"
but
"Life to Me."

Valuing Wisdom

Valuing Physical Powers

THE HUMAN ADULT "A biological, psychological, and social constellation moving forward in time" (Birren).

***A NOTE ON CRITERIA:**

"It may be that we should use developmental criteria rather than age criteria for studying stages in later life." (Peck: see Neugarten, *Middle Age and Aging*, page 92).

depth, and less and less as objects of mere sexual play. Sexual play as such need not, of course, be derogated.

Middle life also brings the periodic loss of the nearness of people, young or old, who were or are beloved. Elderly parents die; children grow up and leave home; long-cherished friends die. At the same time, the bridge position of middle age, stretching between young adulthood and late adulthood, carries with it access to a wide traffic of human types and relationships. Thus a new and major alternative arises: the middle adult who is drawing steadily from whatever capital he has left in the bank (these analogies are all mine, not Peck's) can allow the passing years to become increasingly impoverished; or he can reinvest his emotional sympathies in new relationships. In addition, he can redefine and imaginatively deepen or extend or adapt his "cathexes" or emotional investments within family and friendship circles. (Consider, for example, how successfully or not many parents in middle and late middle age adapt their cathectic relationships to sons and daughters now grown-up and married to persons new to the circle; or to single grown up children, themselves struggling to adapt to the assets and deficits of not being married.) This third major alternative of middle age, Peck calls choosing between *cathectic flexibility and cathectic impoverishment*.

Finally, and crucially, people in the great middle span of the life journey can, again by countless choices at branch alternatives on the route, choose *mental flexibility* vs. *mental rigidity*. Here Peck deals trenchantly with one of the most seductive temptations of the middle-agers: to seek continuous warmth and security in reflecting comfortably upon the value of one's experience after 40 or 50 years of life, or more. Experience is indeed one of the best advertisements for middle age—but only if well used. *It must be reinvested, retested, used to build new perspectives*. Peck is dealing here with a phenomenon supposedly most typical of old age: the rigid mental set, harping upon experience, testing and rejecting liberating ideas by measuring them wholly against one's own unswerving attitudes drawn from "life." However, mid-adulthood may present us with a false security where past experience alone seems to provide ready answers to significant life problems.

When the late years are at hand in a society where too many men have identified their "self" with their career or work role; where it has set their clocks, governed their style of life, produced whatever prestige they have—can they accept the shock of loss when this all-absorbing working self disappears? With most older women the problem is different and has perhaps chiefly occurred at the menopause; however, increasing numbers of women with careers will now know the men's experience. Peck calls the problem presented here that of *ego differentiation* vs. *work-role preoccupation*. Simply and briefly, he is saying this: in the later years we have to learn how to differentiate ourselves among different roles—to find *self-worth* in varying ways of love, service, and creativity. One invests one's self in various fields where the harvests continue on through later and later seasons.

A second life-giving or life-dimming choice opens before us in the very late years where by the clock of life we are indeed old. This is the period when we are often beset by feelings of debility, loss of recuperative powers, bodily aches and pains. We can, Peck suggests, become preoccupied with our physical deficits: become querulously self-centred, full of complaints, a late sad state of egocentricity. Or we have an alternative: we can transcend the physical unease of the body, finding continuing joy in human relationships, in the wonder of the world, in mental activities. We are presented with this choice: *body transcendence* vs. *body preoccupation*.

Inevitably, especially in the very late years, death is a presence that becomes a reality, not a philosophical question. To Peck, this raises the alternative that concludes his schema: *ego transcendence* vs. *ego preoccupation*. The imminence of death may immobilize many late adults as bringing into view the terminating of the "one and only life" (in Erikson's phrase), the night of the ego. Others, however, will transcend their fear of extinction, which is the natural human tendency, by investing their emotions and their energies, however weakened, in people around them. They might also, as Simone de Beauvoir suggests, conclude their life with an attachment to great social or cultural causes that will somehow better the condition of mankind. They may also find a special new strength in the reinforcement of faith or in new trails to the mysterious cosmos: frankly, to ongoing cosmic life. Thus they extend the arena of creative activity beyond egocentric fear and despair so that the self, in investing itself in other people and causes, affirms or reaffirms its own healing self-worth.

Thus, by conscious and life-enriching choices among the seven major alternatives, you may continue to fulfill your "best" self, so that you need not live at any age as though life were simply "happening to you," but that you are happening to life.

So far from moving "over the hill" and steadily down into an arid valley, the proper comparison for the progress of older adults should be that of moving up the sides of a splendid mountain with the perspectives and strategies of the wise and experienced mountaineer. Like him, the older adult should have acquired dynamic wisdom—wisdom that is not simply dormant but used and constantly reinvested. And, like the mountaineer, the man or woman in later adulthood should have become equipped with enough self-knowledge and self-reliance to negotiate the difficult, often dangerous, places on the route not merely with fortitude (which is admirable though passive) but with creative thought and imaginative action—which are active and potential and, in the course of time, Ulyssean.

The verb forms "should be" and "should have," however, are

conditional—they reflect the attitudes and the acts of individual men and women. In them lie both the opportunity and the tragedy of later adulthood. George Laughton, a noted British-born preacher, once built a famous sermon upon the slogan of the Watchtower sect (now Jehovah's Witnesses) which was "Millions Now Living Will Never Die!" Laughton's sermon title was "Millions Now Living Are Already Dead!" He was talking about death-in-life, the conditions wherein men and women never risk looking fully into the eyes of life. A recent book title (1976), *Fully Human, Fully Alive* (by John Powell, S.J.), makes the same point. The alternative is to be half-human, half-alive!

We have rich evidence that in middle and later adulthood we are not simply the hopeless prisoners of psychosexual neuroses dating from infancy and early childhood. Likewise, we have learned that the anxieties and inferiorities generated from psychosocial encounters can also find healing in the comradeships and assuagements of society. Institutional society, which many of us have criticized with burning anger, provides multitudes of supports, guides, healings, and stimuli for psychosocial man. "Do you realize," asks the old alcoholic Church of England priest, in John Masefield's *The Everlasting Mercy*, of the wild naked youth running down the road, half-mad with the world's injustice, "do you realize how much effort it takes just to get the world up and moving every morning?" Much of the apparatus of routine life is itself a valuable safeguard for healthy living, or even for creative activity.

Yet the chief end of man is not to be found in safeguards, survival kits, and guaranteed highways—least of all Ulyssean man, that seeker to the end of life of the full state of what Abraham Maslow, using Kurt Goldstein's term, called "self-actualization." For Maslow there was something saddening about "the ease with which human potentiality can be destroyed or repressed" by what he called the lack of "good preconditions": in the family, in the physical body, in the chemistry of life, in the ecology, the culture, the interactions of people. Why should a "fully-human person," he asked, seem like a miracle—"so improbable a happening as to be awe-inspiring?" Yet Maslow became one of most optimistic of modern observers of the human scene. His optimism, which bears directly upon Ulyssean adulthood, arose from a view of man as need-bearer—Maslow called him "the wanting animal"—and from the plain evidence before all our eyes that remarkable human beings exist who have apparently somehow managed to "actualize" all or nearly all of their potential.

For Maslow, self-actualization was an achievement of middle and later life. He agrees with Jung: that it takes much of a lifetime to assemble and integrate a personal self that is capable, not simply of many-sided self-activity, but of rich self-*actualization*, which is a very different thing. Neither Jung nor Maslow, of course, is saying that the steady addition of years and of "experience" bring self-actualization in and of themselves. Otherwise we would not have the phenomenon that the "fully-human" person seems "like a miracle." You typically look for self-actualized individuals among people well or long past youth, but even in these supposedly maturer phases, too few are embarked upon what Maslow calls "good-growth-toward-self-actualization," a process already found among a certain proportion of the young. (Maslow's term recalls John Dewey's lovely definition: "A good man is someone trying to be better.")

How far, in fact, is it possible for the self, contending with the many influences, incentives, and frustrations produced in the complex life journey, able to continue the process of "becoming"? Is man, when the chips are down, simply a behavioral animal as perceived by a Pavlov or a Skinner? Does he merely react to powerful drives when stimulated so as to remove the feeling of tension, in order that the whole organism can then achieve a sense of homeostasis, or return to the normal state?

For anyone who believes in what I call "the Ulyssean concept" this point of view is untenable. It derives from certain excesses of what critics have recently and unkindly called "rat-oriented psychology"—the conviction that there are overpowering analogies between rats and man. "If only," Maslow once asked innocently, "we could really know what is going on in the rat's mind." The being, Man, soaked in cruelty and ignorance though he is, is much too versatile and elusive a creature to be trapped in the box of the Stimulus-Response mechanism.

Researchers have, of course, learned much about functioning by experimenting with rats, monkeys, and pigeons. Still, human beings are not simply classifiable as animals, and experiments seeking analogies fall ludicrously short of the mark. Maya Pines puts the matter trenchantly when she writes:

> People have allowed themselves to be burned at the stake and have murdered other human beings for purely ideological reasons. We are governed by a whole world of abstractions that never affect other animals. Our large cortex produces a complex interplay of associations, memories, and learned programs. Our forebrain, with its planning areas, allows us to see the possible consequences of our acts. What we will do in any circumstances is never simply the result of an electrical stimulus or a drop of chemical. . .

Maslow turns a flood of light not only upon what motivates human adults but also specifically on what motivates men and women to become Ulyssean or not.

The title—even the order of the words—of Maslow's chief work on the subject is itself significant: *Motivation and Personality.* In it, Maslow introduces his conception of a "hierarchy of basic needs." So far as man is an animal, he is a wanting animal: no one satisfied desire keeps him satisfied for very long. He is not so much governed by drives (although of course they have a role) as pulled by fundamental goals or needs—and these needs arrange themselves in what Maslow calls "a sort of hierarchy of prepotency." Thus the needs at the base of the hierarchy or ladder are *physiological;* and although while he is satisfying them the human being already has the potential for higher needs, these physiological wants must usually be satisfied before the man or woman can get on to less body-centred desires. For example, intense hunger normally monopolizes the whole attention of the "wanting animal," who otherwise with his restless, never-satisfied desire system would be moving on to yet new domains of needs and goals.

Next are the *safety needs* (for example, security, protection, freedom from fear, good order, and so on). Maslow, concerned as he is with adults, notes also how crucial safety needs must be in childhood. Consider the case of the child threatened by parental break-up, by assault, by the name-calling of his fellows, by a hundred seemingly uncontrollable threats. Some of the roots of adult neuroses are here. For Maslow, a neurotic adult is

> . . .a grown-up person who retains his childhood attitudes toward the world. . .it is as if childish attitudes of fear and threat reaction to a dangerous world have gone underground, and untouched by the growing-up and learning processes, were now ready to be called out by any stimulus that could make a child feel endangered and threatened.

Hence arises the "basic anxiety" of many adult people that Karen Horney wrote about in *The Neurotic Personality of Our Time*. Likewise "the whole complicated structure of neurosis," which Andras Angyal described as being "founded on the secret feeling of worthlessness, that is, on the belief that one is inadequate to master the situations that confront him and that he is undeserving of love." Maslow's self-actualized adult, and just as much so the Ulyssean adult, are individuals who have either found healthy surety in the safety needs, so that they can go on to the higher desires and challenges of the hierarchy, or have by various means surmounted the feelings of insatiable craving for safety that otherwise would make them cocoon-dwellers and Milquetoasts.

The third stage in Maslow's hierarchy of human needs includes what he calls *the belongingness and love needs*. Here is a new hunger—the hunger for affection, for inclusion: the longing not to be lonely, ostracized, rejected, friendless, rootless. The phenomenon of sex, with all its facets, is physiological; love, on the other hand, is a generator of deeper and more subtle motivations toward the final two major levels of the hierarchy. Maslow is at pains to stress that the love needs incorporate both the giving and the receiving of love.

Close to the summit of Maslow's hierarchy are *the esteem needs:* the need of the esteem of others, and far more, of self-esteem. At this point Maslow approaches the great sphere of the self-image. He rapidly diverts attention from needs for reputation and prestige, for fame, glory, dominance, and importance to needs for strength, for adequacy, for mastery and competence, for independence, freedom, and "confidence in the face of the world."

To feel that one is useful, to feel that one's life has worth! Offstage one hears again the voice of Andras Angyal, deeply moved:

> Often one wonders why the child accepts the verdict that he is worthless, instead of blaming the parent for being so obviously lacking in understanding, so wrong and selfish. The answer suggests itself that the child needs so much to feel that he has "good parents" that he tenaciously adheres to this belief, and would rather assume himself to be evil or worthless than give up the idea that he has good parents.

Perhaps as a young adult he shoots himself on a garbage dump, or as an old adult obscenely curses his image before a mirror in the antiseptic climate of a nursing home. Perhaps in the long process of "becoming," the child, grown to adulthood, and among good healings and companionships of the world, recovers his self-esteem. Perhaps he is one of the great armies of emotionally healthy people who Maslow insists exist, who carry self-esteem with them to such a degree that it actively promotes feelings of capability and self-confidence.

At all events (according to Maslow), here is another powerful growth need that can pull adult men and women upward in the long process of "becoming." It is one that must be based on deserved respect from self-recognized real accomplishment rather than simply the opinions of others. Thus we approach the summit territory of Maslow's hierarchy: *the need for "self-actualization":* that is the restlessness that develops in someone in whom the other great needs have been wholly or chiefly met, and who is looking for the creativity that he or she must actualize and fulfill.

No one is expected to pass as a human voyager through the various level of needs or goals wholly completing each level once and for all as one goes along. Life is rarely lived that way. On this Maslow himself remarks:

> In actual fact, most members of our society who are normal are partially satisfied in all their basic needs and partially unsatisfied in all their basic needs at the same time. A more realistic description of the hierarchy would be in terms of decreasing percentages of satisfaction as we go up the hierarchy of prepotency.

And Maslow suggests that new needs may appear when the current or "prepotent" need is largely, not wholly, satisfied.

It is important also to point out that Abraham Maslow did not construct his hierarchy simply sitting at a desk, pen in hand, but rather from years of clinical and semi-clinical observations, and from several thousand personal contacts.

All of us have unrealized potentialities that would astonish and sadden us if we knew. For many people there is a kind of general malaise, a soul sickness, that overtakes them when they are frustrated (or frustrate themselves) from developing "the kingdom of the mind." An all too common phenomenon to practising psychiatrists and priests is the man or woman who is blocked from the satisfaction of intellectual curiosity, the constant exercise of perhaps a once supple and lovely mind: to such an extent that the condition is beyond malaise, it is neurotic, even pathological. Maslow writes angrily about the general depression of the body and the steady deterioration of the intellectual life of "intelligent people leading stupid lives in stupid jobs"; and tells of seeing "many women, intelligent, prosperous, and unoccupied, slowly develop these same symptoms of intellectual inanition."

I recall a number of years ago mournfully watching the slow slide into wholly unnecessary senility of an elderly former schoolteacher in a London, Ontario, nursing home—the kind of nursing home where everything was clean, warm, safe, full of official smiles. This resident had, however, no visitors, no money, no books: the thought of books had never penetrated the acquisitive mind of the absentee owners. Here was a bright, normally curious woman only in her mid-70s, bravely trying to draw me or other visitors into conversation, in the room filled with bedridden (sometimes senile) old ladies. Her laughter, in this well-disposed prison, was nervous and uncertain even in the first days. Months later, in the terrible desert of her loneliness and the damming-up of her intelligence, she had become a taunting, increasingly senile shadow, not merely of the woman she might have been, but the woman she had been for years previously.

When Maslow set out to investigate what qualities mark the personality of the self-actualized adult,[5] he and his associates studied the personality traits of hundreds of living and also "historical" persons who seemed to be, by their life activities, fully human, fully alive. What characteristics, then, seemed common among these people? (The following catalogue is my own précis of Maslow's list from *Motivation and Personality*.)

Characteristics of Self-Actualizing People: a Study of Psychological Health

1. More efficient perception of reality and more comfortable relations with it. Unusual ability to detect the fake and the dishonest in personality. In all spheres can see concealed or confused realities more swiftly and more correctly than others. Good perception, much less tinged by wish, desire, prejudice, fear. They are comfortable with the unknown; actually seem to take a certain pleasure from difficult decisions.

2. Acceptance (Self, Others, Nature). Not self-satisfied—but they accept their frailties without undue concern. They see human nature as it is, not as they would prefer it to be. They accept themselves and others at the healthy animal level, at higher levels also; they are the undisgusted. They're without pose and don't like pose in others (but accept it). They don't feel unnecessary guilt and shame. They feel badly about the discrepancies between what is and what may be.

3. *Spontaneity*. Keep up most of the conventions out of consideration for others; but are actually *internally* unconventional, spontaneous, natural. They make their issues over large matters, not the trivia of custom. They often feel like spies in a foreign land. Often they show their inner spontaneity; they're more truly "aware" than the weighted-down "adjusted."

4. *Problem-Centring*. They are problem-centred rather than ego-centred. They like compelling tasks that are not for small or petty and selfish ends. They seem to impart to colleagues a certain sense of larger horizons, *sub specie aeternitatis*, more serene, less fraught with worry.

5. *The Quality of Detachment: the Need for Privacy*. They like solitude and privacy more than the average do. They know the quality of "detachment." They have a certain intrinsic dignity in the midst of misfortune. Their "detachment" is often interpreted by others as "coldness." Actually, even in misfortune they see the problem of the situation beyond or above that of ego or people. They can concentrate to an unusual degree (seemingly absent-minded).

6. *Autonomy, Independence of Culture and Environment*. These people are *growth*-motivated, not deficiency-motivated. Hence they are more independent of environment, more self-contained. Real self-development and real inner growth are more important to them than honors and status. (They must in many cases have had a lot of love and respect in childhood.)

7. *Continued Freshness of Appreciation*. They experience over and over again the same euphoria or ecstasy from beautiful things, people, scenes, relationships.

8. *Mystic Experience; Oceanic Feeling*. They have the frequent experience (including during sexual encounters) of "horizons opening": feelings of awe; feelings of disorientation with time and space—the person then being transformed and strengthened in his daily life.

9. *Gemeinschaftsgefuhl*. They have feelings for mankind of identification, sympathy, affection—desire to help the human race: "they are my brothers." This often brings great frustration and exasperation. Still the self-actualizing person maintains what Adler called "the older-brotherly" attitude.

10. *Interpersonal Relations of the Self-Actualized*. They are less ego-

bound, have deeper interpersonal relations than others. More fusion, more love (but often among themselves!). Kind or patient to almost everyone, they have few close friends—close friendship takes and demands time. They understand pomp and pettiness and meanness; don't condone them, don't like them, but understand them. When hostile, their hostility is situational, not character-based. They attract disciples but try to discourage them.

11. Democratic Character Structure. They are friendly with anyone of suitable character regardless of class, education, political belief, race, or color. These individuals, themselves élite, select élite people for their friends—but an élite of character, capacity, and talent rather than of birth, race, fame, power.

12. Means and Ends. They put their stress on ends; have moral standards. They do right, not wrong, but their "right" may not be conventional.

13. Philosophical, Unhostile Sense of Humor. They are addicted, not to slapstick, hostile humor, superiority humor, authority-rebellion humor but rather to humor that is spontaneous and helps produce perspectives.

14. Creativeness. The creativeness of the self-actualized is different from the "special talent" creativeness of the genius. Rather it is a special way of looking at life all their life: a fresh, even naïve way, similar to that of children. It is a creative attitude not killed by acculturation, and which promotes creativity as a life-style. Thus they often become trailbreakers for all others.

What has this description of the "self-actualized adult" got to do with the Ulyssean man or woman—the adventurer of the later adult years? Both much and not much, depending upon the view from your bridge. "Much" because to be self-actualized, Maslow-style, is also to realize Ulyssean attributes: for example, openness to experience, realistic appraisal and acceptance of others, ability to be solitary without being unsocial, capacity to generate your own growth, and to rely on your own self-evaluation, rather than the imposed values of the world. The more you become self-actualized during the first five decades of your life, the more potentiality you have to become Ulyssean in the later years.

"Not much," perhaps, to the extent that the pure equability of attitude, style, and seeming performance of the Maslovian self-actualized adult presents an idealized state very different from the chaotic, sinsoaked, guilt-ridden, and fear-bedeviled personal arena in which great numbers of adult people live out their lives and still, by personal heroisms, become Ulysseans. Even on a less dramatic scale, the experience of middle and later adulthood is often composed of periods of consecutive or sustained turbulence: especially, in the late twentieth century, the turbulence of change.

For example, in January, 1971, Thomas Holmes, professor of psychiatry at the University of Washington in Seattle, reported a study on the hazards of change to the American Association for the Advancement of Science. Holmes was fascinated by the question: "Up to what load point can adult people efficiently handle the stress of change without breaking down?" Over a period of two years he and his associates carefully observed and recorded the many events causing change in the lives of 80 Seattle adults, and then attempted to correlate their personal-change histories with whatever physical and mental illnesses had occurred. There was a certain level of accumulation of changes and stress in individual lives, Holmes found, beyond which the human adult self could not go without danger to physical or mental health.

Holmes allotted a score of 50 points to the act of getting married, and then established various allotments for 38 other stress-creating life changes. He took advice on his list of scores from people in several countries who rated the change-event against the basic 50-point event of marriage. (See Chart 2.) He cited 300 points as the level at which an adult could not safely take on any further load, "good" or "bad." His theory is a strong reminder of the need for adults to inventory their continuing stress loads (his chart is, in a way, symbolic).

To return to, and close with, Maslow, his valuable portrait of the fully self-actualized adult, nonetheless fails to match the late Ulyssean life in one important sense. Ulysseanism implies, not only that you may indeed have prepared for it through the 50 or more preceding years of your life drama, but that you may have to begin *where you are* in your anxiety-filled, guilt-ridden arena of the self to start the Ulyssean process—*and that such a start is possible.* Maslow has an infuriating habit of separating the population radically into healthy or "intact" people, on the one hand, and "sick, neurotic people" on the other: "sick neurotic people make the wrong choices; they do not know what they want, and even when they do, have not courage enough to choose correctly," and so on. Enormously human and liberating as he is, Maslow does not pay sufficient attention to the unbelievable complexity of people's open and hidden existences; their struggles with Holmes's 39 life-change stresses; confused and mysterious potentialities; and half-aborted neurotic tendencies that make up many of the lives of middle-aged and older adults who *may yet* choose the Ulyssean way.

In fact, what holds back great numbers of later adults from Ulyssean adventures has little to do with neurotic fear. It is rather a fundamental lack of confidence, based on a gigantic misconception: that one's powers must steadily decline and increasingly lose the ability to cope with the challenge of creativity in the later years. To choose between the Good Life and Dark Life—yes, that is different. In North American society where institutional religion is largely passé among the

Chart 2

RATING LIFE CHANGES

Life Event	Value	Life Event	Value
Death of spouse	100	Change in responsibilities at work	29
Divorce	73		
Marital separation	65	Son or daughter leaving home	29
Jail term	63		
Death of close family member	63	Trouble with in-laws	29
		Outstanding personal achievement	28
Personal injury or illness	53		
Marriage	50	Wife beginning or stopping work	26
Fired at work	47	Beginning or ending school	26
Marital reconciliation	45	Revision of personal habits	24
Retirement	45	Trouble with boss	23
Change in health of family member	44	Change in work hours or conditions	20
Pregnancy	40	Change in residence	20
Sex difficulties	39	Change in schools	20
Gain of new family member	39	Change in recreation	19
		Change in social activities	18
Change in financial state	38	Mortgage in loan less than $10,000	17
Death of close friend	37	Change in sleeping habits	16
Change to different line of work	36	Change in number of family get-togethers	15
		Change in eating habits	15
Change in number of arguments with spouse	35	Vacation	13
Mortgage over $10,000	31	Minor violations of the law	11
Foreclosure of mortgage or loan	30		

Time, March 1, 1971

young, those of us in our 40s and older who were schooled in it and (whatever our faith) in the Puritan ethic, still have the feeling in our bones that ethical recoveries and "better lives" late in the day are always possible. We understand the situation of the large, middle-aged, mild-spoken Montreal taxi-driver who said to me in the course of a long ride in the summer twilight: "When I was a child of darkness, before I became a child of light. . ." He astonished and intrigued me with his appearance and style, but I had no problem accepting his premise and his situation—nor would many readers of this book.

But to actualize and continue the *creativity* of the self, to maintain the productivity of mind and hand—this for many is quite a different matter. As the self enters the later stages of its long journey through life, it does not have to lose heart. Although we live at a time and in a society where powerful influences converge to undermine and often sweep away the confidence that is indispensable to people of all ages, adults in their later years must learn to reject the myth of loss of power to learn, to create, and to produce. They need not become bystanders and onlookers in the amphitheatre of active life.

4

THE PERILS AND POTENTIALS
OF THE LATER YEARS

T w o formidable antagonists stand on the great highway that leads to the late creative years, menacing those adults who still seek to be Ulyssean. Their names are Lack of Time and Failure of Powers, and not even the monsters met by John Bunyan's Pilgrim on his heroic journey were as fearful—although they are blood relations of Giant Despair.

Late middle age, for those who are reasonably fortunate, has both a real and a deceptive beauty. The tired analogy that compares the life journey and the seasons was never truer here. For just as in early fall there is a period when nature seems to remain poised between summer and winter, so the later years also have their halcyon period.

Certain excitements, dreams, and pleasures are past. For those who married, the children are grown and away, and at last there is the chance to live for oneself and rediscover oneself. For those who are unmarried, elderly parents and other relatives, lovingly protected while they were here, are gone, and along with the sadness comes the understanding of releases to be more oneself and to reawaken certain subdued aspects of the self. Certain feverish ambitions are past: either older adults have attained much of what they wanted, or else they have become mostly reconciled to whatever their talents, their deficits, and especially the element of sheer luck, have delivered them to.

For those later adults who seem fortunate, there are the satisfactions of a pleasant house or apartment, secure for many years; a circle of friends for encouragement and stimulation; the opportunity to continue and to enrich the reading habit acquired long ago; the chance to travel as never before and sufficient funds to do so; and the possibility of taking up any of dozens of interests that may lead to further self-discovery and creativity. Youngish grandparents welcome adults like themselves as well as younger people for whom such people often represent the good life.

As mentioned in Chapter 3, the gerontologist Bernice Neugarten has written impressively about this sector of older adults which she calls "the young-old." These are men and women between 55 and 75 whom she describes as "vigorous and educated. . .already markedly different from the out-moded stereotypes of old age." She notes that "relatively healthy, relatively well-off. . .they will want a wide range of options and opportunities for self-enhancement and community participation." She differentiates them from the "old-old" of years beyond 75. Their problems in general are different; their still-zestful opportunities are different. (She apologizes later for too drastic time-lines between the two later-age types.)

But even within the parameters of ages 55-75, literally millions of older adults do not meet Neugarten's "young-old" standards of health and prosperity. Millions are pursued into the later 50s and 60s and 70s by all or some of the same conditions that have harassed them during most or all of their adulthood. They are without financial security, without good and secure housing, without good health, saddled with debt, and bedeviled by the anxieties that come from family disruptions and misfortunes—especially by Anxiety itself, the great Fearmaker.

Too often, the accumulation of these negative forces—consecutive sorrows, loneliness, remorse, gnawing insecurity, fear of abandonment if struck down by some crippling illness, and little or no equipment to make use of the kingdom of the mind—may extinguish what is left of the self-actualizing spirit. The fate of the once-buoyant priest in H. M. Robinson's novel, *The Cardinal*, is symbolic of great numbers of older adults. Joyous and confident when he first took on the pastorate of the monstrously debt-laden church, he struggled to bring fresh light and life to it, and at the end his physical and emotional powers were as crushed as though the huge building itself had fallen upon him. The theory of Abraham Maslow's "hierarchy of human needs" finds confirmation enough in the fate of such later adults who are condemned to coping with safety and even subsistance needs at the point when their greatest life concern should be creativeness and self-actualization.

For such older individuals it is possible to stand in a kind of autumn paradise and to have their pleasure senses so eclipsed by fear, worry, and grief that much or all of the paradise is lost. These are the multitudes of people in later life for whom no glib rhetoric or strategies can meet the complex needs of their dilemmas. For them "the loneliness of the long-distance runner" carries a special meaning and poignancy.

For only a proportion, it is true, is there total loss of joy in the halcyon years. For many, in spite of continued misfortune and deprivation,some of the qualities of the enchanted early autumn of the life journey emerge, on their own terms. Life and their own initiatives produce areas which, though radically different from those of the "fortunate" people, nonetheless offer opportunities for continuing growth and creativity. "Nonetheless," because personal growth of the self, which should be a great continuing adventure, may well be aborted among the so-called "fortunate," while, on the other hand, it can be stimulated by defeat and adversity—in some cases, even by despair. Yet many of the physically and environmentally "fortunate" cease to be active seekers. Many of them become as locked into a constricting, spectating, and nonpersonally creative lifestyle as though they were not liberated, as they technically are, to pursue the highest stages of Maslow's hierarchy. Blandness and comfort may be, and often are, the embalmers of the creative spirit. In addition, they also may feel the shadows on the trail ahead of the twin monsters, Lack of Time and Failure of Powers.

But most affected of all later adults by these somber giants are the seekers, the would-be Ulysseans, the truly "beautiful people." For these people are the bearers of dreams. The dream may be very recent, born late in the day, or it may be (and very often is) a dream cherished for years but never actualized because of force of circumstances. Thus Lloyd C. Douglas and Thomas Costain kept their ambitions to be novelists in rein until far along the lifecycle; Grandma Moses did not begin to paint until past 70; Alcide de Gasperi was forced to suspend his plans and hopes for a new Italy until at the age of 64 he was finally released from the obscurity of a librarian's post, where he had waited out the interminable years of World War Two. Likewise, many private "secret dreamers" can be named: the educator who deferred his dream of graduating as a lawyer until he was 69; the elderly woman who waited until her 80s to begin studying a foreign language; the two senior men in Canadian broadcasting, both in the early 60s, their wives recently dead, their children grown, who began at last the studies for the priesthood, which under different life conditions they would have started years before.*

The adult seeker often becomes intensely conscious of Time as the Antagonist through the media's obsession with the ages as well as the exploits of "people in the news." Thus, we get the absurd comedy of the news magazine that brackets the ages of newsworthy adults, regardless of whether age has any relevance to the situation or not. For example: "Unsmiling, balding Wendell Supercrat (48) stumbled out of the 6.30 A.M. flight from Kansas City." The news magazine clearly dislikes Supercrat, but the ultimate idiocy is its obsession with his age.

We are constantly told by one of the few hoary classical tags that still have wide currency in an era too clever for the classics, that life is short and the arts are long—but in fact there is a period when there seems all kinds of time ahead, say, during the 20s and 30s and even into the early 40s. For example, the typical "reading adult" reads widely and carelessly during much of that stretch of the lifespan. Many people realize only at age 50 or 55 that there is only so much time left and so many books to read—books that really matter—that they must establish some kind of rigorous priority system.

---

*A fascinating reverse case is seen in the career of John Tettemer, an American Passionist monk, who in 1924 at age 50 left the order in which he had become the second-highest world officer to assume secular life, marry, have children, and become a film actor in his later years. The separation from his order was without rancor, and in fact with affection on both sides.

As with reading, so with many other countries to be visited, so many talented musicians to be heard; so many new and growth-bearing experiences to be encountered, so many creative efforts, large or small, to be made. And above all, so many enriching relationships to be opened or deepened, so many ways of actualizing one's role as wayfaring companion to the companionless, that it seems that there is world enough, but no time, no time. Where has all the time gone?

Now the temptation is to play a new numbers game—secretly to subtract one's age from the announced average lifespan of men and women in our time, and to balance the difference against the needs and goals of the older adult, opportunities lost and possibilities remaining. Some adults learn to reflect, wisely, that life is, after all, a kind of smorgasbord—we can never have everything we want. To try is certainly to risk the tragedies of Faust or Hamlet. Wisdom is selection: our rational self knows this to be true. But man is also insatiable—that is both his tragedy and his triumph. And for the seeker-adults, there is rarely "world enough and time."

Nor is the longest shadow thrown on the trail ahead in the later adult years that of seeming Lack of Time alone. For many older adults the greater threat is Failure of Powers; many believe it is so, many can feel that it is so, and almost everything in the folklore of the human life journey reinforces their pessimism.

Clearly, the decline of physical powers is one of the rules of the game. Diminution of perfect hearing begins at an early age in adulthood, usually from about 30 on; loss of high tone perception is common among adults over 40, and increases rather markedly for many after 65, for men more so than women. The same is true of sight: visual acuity begins to decline slightly from about the mid-20s to the 50s, and then often shows a rather pronounced deterioration. The bifocal years are a stage in the process, with the late years presenting for some adults the problem of cataracts, fortunately usually solved by modern surgery. Among the aged population of a huge home in New York, 86 percent were described as having from good to adequate vision; in an even bigger institution in California, out of 1,500 late adults, only 3 percent were described as functionally blind. Blindness, although it occurs, is not a serious threat: for those who seek to live as fully as possible, and to create, the fatigue often induced by waning powers of sight may be the greater hazard.

Power to taste is apparently slightly affected for many people by a slight decline in the number of taste buds up to age 70, with a greater decline thereafter. Still, taste is a highly individualized reaction that does not yield easily to research criteria. In any event, for some items of the modern North American diet, loss of the sense of taste would not necessarily be a catastrophe. Consider, for example, the taste of mass-produced bread (loaded, of course, with its rejuvenating vitamins)—

which led the Ulyssean Henry Miller to write indignantly, on returning to America after many years, that "not a bloody mother in the bloody land can bake a bloody loaf of bread."

Investigators of physical decline have tested the power of young and old adults to respond to touch, and of course the power to smell. On the latter, there is little to report, in spite of the occasional complaints of loss of this sense by older adults: for some this may be one form of the pastime, which some relish, of enjoying loss of youth. On the former, the evidence of researchers is that there is no change in sensitivity to touch until about perhaps age 50 to 55. Curiously enough, such loss as occurs in the later years is in the lower body rather than in wrists, hands, and elbows, which retain nearly all of their sensitivity.

What disturbs and saddens many people as they enter and proceed through the later years is their feeling that in addition to generalized infirmities, they are now more exposed to the great organic killer illnesses—strokes, heart diseases, cancer—than before, and this is of course true. Birren's remark, that to live to be elderly is itself a kind of achievement, is some consolation but for the Ulysseans perhaps not much.

The modern writer who has most thoroughly documented what she conceives to be the almost undiluted tragedy of old age is Simone de Beauvoir in *The Coming of Age* (1972.) Old age clearly fills her with revulsion, and few of its attributes reveal anything to her but loss and darkness. Thus she is driven to choose incidents from late life, excerpts from journals, and recorded statements by individuals, that ultimately build an overwhelming portrait of the late years as a time of bitterness, desolation, and defeat. No one escapes. The wonderful Ulyssean, Victor Hugo, at first raises one's heart with the magnificence of love of life and the creativity with which he illuminated his late years, but Beauvoir pursues him into the very late phases, when he lost much of his power after a stroke. Here, as in a hundred other cases, Beauvoir piles everything upon the evils of old age: Hugo, after all, might well have been immobilized by a massive heart attack at 48, or have died at 55! For so fine a writer and thinker, it is extraordinary that she does not see that nearly all lives end in anti-climax. The sad, short finish of Eleanor Roosevelt's life takes nothing away from the splendid Ulysseanism of her last 17 years, after the death of her husband.

Likewise, it is prejudicing the case to quote three or four sentences or brief extracts from the journals that many Europeans have kept, and which reflect their civilized sense of culture and of time. Valéry and Gide are both quoted as hating to look in the mirror when they were very old; yet each handled his late years with admirable style. Gide, especially, quoted by Beauvoir as complaining of "all the little dispositions of great age that make an old man such a wretched being" and that "my mind almost never succeeds in distracting me from my flesh," in fact emerges in the full journal of his last years as a still vital, intensely human being beyond age 80, still attempting to "get up" his Latin, still curious and interested in the human scene. Indeed, 20 years earlier, on his trips to North Africa. Gide had little complaints to make about his physical condition.

Only at long intervals does one get the flash of humor of which Beauvoir is capable, as in her delightful comment on Victor Hugo's eager curiosity to see and to talk to God, "that is to say, another Hugo." But even when Beauvoir seems to be conceding that old age has attributes of joy, she then consolidates her case that all in the late years is vanity and sorrow. Thus, Gide's charming comment, "My heart has remained so young that I have the continual feeling of playing a part, the part of the seventy-year-old that I certainly am" makes her speculate, surely unreasonably, that for Gide it may have been "out of horror of old age that he looked upon his behaviour as a seventy-year-old in the light of an act."

Actually, the long shadow of Failure of Powers appears as early as late middle age (for some people, still earlier) in the two physical areas of beauty and of psychomotor skills.

Beauty, of course, is a "power" since it plays an important role in the building and maintenance of the self-image, which in turn affects both a person's own performance throughout the life drama and his or her day-to-day relationships with other human beings. "Beauty" should mean not merely the "combination of (physical) qualities. . .in human face or form. . .that delights the sight" *(Concise Oxford Dictionary)*, but the whole personableness of the individual that conveys some degree of charm or magnetism. However, to pure physical beauty per se, the aging process is of course considered to be the supreme threat, with the exception of disfiguring illness. Chilling, semi-clinical accounts exist, taken from many novelists and other recorders of life, of the inroads of physical aging upon both male and female beauty. (It is part of the long sickness of Western—and especially North American—society, that it has for so long denied "beauty" to both sexes.)

The eternal footnote, "for his (or her) age," becomes a kind of threnody of comment upon middle-aged and especially later adults which they have to learn to expect. "John jogs daily at the Y; he is in really excellent condition *for his age*"; or, "You remember what a show-stopper Ursula was? Well, she's still a beautiful woman, *for her age*." And so on.

There is, however, a higher maturity that makes different judgments, and sometimes, interestingly, it develops early. For example, a youthful student friend of mine from Finland once made the arresting comment that "No matter how old a woman gets, she never really loses the beauty of femininity." This was the kind of wisdom one might have expected from the Canadian bestseller of the '60s, *In Praise of Older Women*, the account of a succession of love affairs, until it turns out that the "older women" in question were only in their 30s! Nonetheless, the higher maturity wisely notes that for both men and woman what the years take away in the first fresh loveliness of face and form, they restore with a different kind of beauty. In fact, to the highly mature, nothing is more incongruous or disappointing than the constantly "lifted" face, which in the later years shows none of the etching of sorrow, joy, anxiety, compassion, and pain.

Those of us who are moving through the later years of the life cycle had better achieve the higher maturity, because the aging process leaves no one's physical self unscathed. Once in a while, among the men who throng the pools and exercise rooms of health clubs (and who may be of all ages from very young to very old), a man of age 50 or 55 or even older appears who has retained the form of one of the youths 30 years younger who is racing away to the handball court or the weight-lifting room—but he is not the same. In close proximity to him one usually finds him in admirable condition, but he is no longer a youth. Age has put its mark upon his hair, skin, and eyes, and of course upon his suppleness and his psychomotor skills. Likewise, the silly advertisement that attempts to confuse the television audience as to which of the pair of women is mother or daughter is itself as cosmetic an exercise as the product it displays. The mother is not the daughter. The years will continue to make their transformation. Her peril lies in identifying the beauty of her self with the face and form she had as a girl. Her rich potential lies in recognizing the new forms of beauty that arrive along with the undoubted deprivations of the years. And these new forms, which are true of men also, are acquired, not in spite of sorrows and crises and physical losses, but because of them.

As for psychomotor skills, the naked human eye can see the effects of aging in slowing the swift ease of movement that is at least the potential state of most young people. The picture is somewhat clouded because of the appalling deficiencies in carriage, speed, and grace of large numbers of late adolescents and people in their early 20s. The ascending lines of people going up to street level in the subways of the North American cities and often moving at tortoise pace are as likely to be slowed by some slouching and slow-footed teen-agers as by some old man or woman. Older people tend to be slowed down by the thickening and stiffening of their bodies, but many who could walk and even still run with speed and grace actually think themselves into a routine of staidness and slowness. Some rationalize their sloth by claiming that too great haste leads to premature heart attacks. We are not talking, however, about haste, but about the swift grace that adds cachet and zest to the life process.

Birren usefully defines a psychomotor skill as "an acquired pattern of finely coordinated voluntary movements. . . not merely as muscle movements, but rather as complex chains of events in the nervous system, with resulting muscle movement." Thus there is a complex interrelationship between the muscle movement function of the body and the line delivery via brain and nerve cells. For many older adults there is some physiological loss, because of either physical attrition or disuse, and there is the possibility, where mental zest is lost, of increasing slowness or awkwardness in delivery because of a certain slowing of the line communications.

Much of the evidence is concealed because older workers in industrial plants, for example, develop a system of compensations that wipes out or diminishes the losses of performance that aging might bring. Numerous studies indicate little or no change in worker performance through most of the working life of the adult up to the mid-50s. Even beyond this point, the output of many older workers excels that of younger ones. Perhaps, however, a selective process is at work here, only the most proficient of older workers surviving the route to age 65. Temporary losses clearly occur in cases where industry keeps demanding changes in techniques, and they naturally occur where the worker has been injured on the job, although not immobilized.

However, practice also makes perfect: much heartening evidence exists that even into the 70s, a good many individuals continue to show marked proficiency in the psychomotor skills of occupational tasks. There is a minority of remarkable people about whom we need to know much more, if only to gain more and more evidence for the Ulyssean life. Certainly from age 40 on there is as a rule a reduced capacity in strength and in sensory acuity. Reaction times begin to be longer—a factor that surely contributes heavily to the relatively high traffic accident rate of age 65-plus, and very certainly age 70-plus. The twin peaks in North American statistics for traffic accidents are ages 16-21 and age 70-plus. A study by B. W. Marsh in 1961 on "Aging and Driving" cited speed as the major contributing factor for accidents for drivers under age 30, double that of people in the 70s; whereas exactly the reverse was true of right-of-way conflicts, where the older drivers, in spite of usually slower speeds, were also markedly slower in reaction responses.

Athletics provides the most striking illustration of loss of psychomotor power with aging. The problem of adjustment especially affects boys and men, since they are often more involved in sports than are girls and women. From as early a period as age 30 on, the human male has to make adjustments to the increasing limitations that aging places on his athletic skill and prowess. For many men, coming to terms with physical losses is quite as traumatic as a woman's having to adjust to the loss of youthful beauty. The record varies, of course, with the sport; nor do many men realistically expect to become champions. Still, one can hardly name a sport in which champions emerge at age 40 or more.

In some sports the champions are incredibly young. Olympic swimmers, for example, are "old" at 22, and slalom ski champions, gymnasts, and figure-skating champions are often in their teens. In other fields, once considered (almost derisively) the domains of middle-aged men—for example, golf and curling—younger men and women in their 20s and 30s are dominant or are taking over. A magnificent golfer like Sam Snead has represented the older adult who rarely wins a title but is still considered a superb performer "for his age." However, there are not many Sam Sneads.

Practice may make perfect, but it will not put the 45-year-old boxer or tennis player back into the championship circle or even among the near contenders (wonderful exceptions like Archie Moore and Pancho Gonzales only prove the rule). Occasionally an enterprising older adult will create his own arena for conquest, like the remarkable South African of the 1960s who became world record-holder for the running of 60-, 80-, and 100-mile marathons. And some fields of very intense psychomotor activity can certainly be classified as sports—round-the-world competitive yachting, for example—in which remarkable older adults are leading figures.

Yet, says the higher maturity, there is no essential tragedy in the fact that human beings lose long before the middle years the capacity to be championship contenders or even high performers in many sports. "Though much is taken, much abides." There are many exceptions: fishing, hunting, cycling, hill-climbing, billiards (what psychologist of adulthood ever had the imagination to study Willie Hoppe?), and dancing (who has had the wit to do other than superficially interview Fred Astaire?). There are numerous other sports activities that prevent surrender simply to parlor games. In addition, it is probable that with the "new athlete" of recent years we are on the threshold of new breakthroughs in longevity of performance.

The real tragedy is the abdication of too many men and woman from one of the most important domains of the self—the physical. The most disturbing fact about the gymnasiums and arenas where sports are played in North America is the small number of adults in their middle years and older. To participate in no activity that allows the body to delight in its own freedom and movement, and to attempt to replace this loss by constantly watching professional athletes on the TV screen, is a mournful and, in some cases a dangerous, choice of alternatives. Health rationales aside, the tragic loss is psychic. Fortunately, there is a new emphasis in North America on fitness, and people of all ages are running, jogging, joining exercise classes and health clubs, and enjoying sports activities as never before.

To love one's self: this is where all psychic healing begins; to *love,* not to adore, not to condone, not to deceive. And an aspect of self-love almost wholly neglected by the pundits, and by people in general, is the role of love of one's body. To neglect and finally be repelled by one's physical state is a special danger of later adulthood. This destructive self-revulsion, conscious and unconscious, can turn into a sour hatred of youth and beauty and poison the wells of the creative and Ulyssean life. Some psychological historians have traced this state to its most dramatic climax in international and legal affairs. They speculate on the role played by the hatred of old men of power for the youth and beauty of young men in the making of war and the delivery of hideous verdicts in the courts.

No doubt this tendency to transfer self-revulsion to antipathy and hatred for others is at work in thousands of less dramatic arenas every day. But the crucial intersection between Failure of Powers in the physical sense and the capacity to maintain vital and creative growth through the later adult years provides the chance for physical joy *on some terms* for almost everyone. It has little to do with size and shape for those who are on the way to the higher maturity. Throughout nearly all of life, into and through the very late years, it is possible to tap some of the springs of joy in one's body, to keep experiencing some glow of pleasure in the marvelous human system that is one's own, and vicariously in the marvel of other human bodies, including the young.

Regrettably, some older adults seem to get a doleful satisfaction out of the Failure of Powers. One once-noted educator, well known to me, a man who is now as they say, "quite elderly," finds his consolations (or his kicks) in not only noting his own decline and fall but observing that of others, including the middle-aged. For example, he is the originator of the following little hurried dialogues on elevators or on busy streets:

Elderly educator: Oh, hello. Where are you going?
Oneself: Back to the office. I managed to forget my briefcase.
Elderly educator: Yes. Well, that's what happens when we get older.

Or:

Elderly educator: (with anxious pleasure): You're looking rather tired.
Oneself: I didn't sleep awfully well last night.
Elderly educator: Well, that's what we have to expect as we get on in years.
Oneself (drily): There was a four-alarm fire in the apartment house next door.
Elderly educator: Oh. Oh, well, we can't take these things so well as we get older.

Thus in the only game he still plays—the game of Mournfully Enjoying Failure of Powers and in which he must find a partner—he is at least always able to return your shot. But it is a game in which he is also the continual and disastrous loser. Once a handsome and impressive man, with an air of verve and confidence, he has shrunk not only physically (something of this often occurs in the very late years) but in the inner self and in his self-image, which are the generators and creative agents of his life. He is watching what he conceives to be his inevitable decline with fascinated regret, and he is determined to pull others down with him. Anything further from Ulyssean adulthood cannot be imagined.

An enormous need for many older adults, notably the Ulysseans, is energy, physical and psychic—energy to help renew the body, but also to begin new projects and to complete them. "If only I had the energy I had when young" is the frequent cry. And it is surely true that for most adults there is a decline of physical energy in the later years. Still, how real is this state when applied to Ulyssean needs? We talk of the "boundless energy" of youth, without remembering (1) that many young adults suffer from low energy systems and (2) that a great deal of youthful energy, to use another cliché, is "frittered away."

What we should be concerned about in later adulthood is what I earlier called "essential energy," which is the amount of energy essential for the carrying-through of Ulyssean tasks and exercises. This essential energy is usually available to us if we set priorities carefully and conserve personal energy wisely. Thus, the woman who hopes at last to write a novel, learn a new language, or set out on new travels cannot as a rule be simultaneously preparing mountains of refreshments for a succession of church suppers! It is true that for many men and women the days are past when they can pour out energy indiscriminately, go to bed exhausted, and rise exuberantly. But it is equally true that most later adults have pools of essential physical energy quite adequate for Ulyssean projects. And obviously psychic energy need not only *not* decline in the later years, but may reach new levels of power.

In one of the greatest of physical joys, sexual intercourse, there is also, of course, a certain failing of powers across the adult lifespan. Among the adult population a small minority might be described as natural celibates who abstain from all intercourse. A large number of others, in the Puritan idiom of North America, "indulge" in intercourse as part of the pattern of what "normal" people do, and then as the years bring some waning of sexual powers, seem content to relinquish much or all of this area of their lives, in numerous cases almost with relief. A large group of men and women form a third category. They view the decline of sexual virility and fertility as a catastrophic threat to their selfhood, and for them waning sexual strength becomes one of the most disorienting and disfunctionalizing influences in their disappointed later years. This is truer of men than of women. A 1975 poll of a large cross-section of North Americans found that middle-aged and older men rated sex third in their personal priorities, while women rated it eleventh. There is, of course, a fourth category: the Ulysseans—whose style, if they remain interested in sexual intercourse, is simply to go ahead and enjoy it, without worrying that they may not have the full sexual stamina "as in old days," but continue to find a wholesome pleasure in the fact that "much abides."

Does much abide? Certainly it does. Nothing is more absurd than to proclaim that men and women are not capable of rewarding sexual experiences in the later years. According to A. C. Kinsey's study of sexual behavior among North American adults, the frequency of orgasms a week in the male declines in a steadily falling line across the lifespan. Thus, where the "median frequency" of orgasms was more than three a week at ages 16-20, and just under three at ages 21-25, the number lessens to about one a week around ages 51-55, and declines somewhat again in the next few years. These are, of course, median figures, and a considerable number of older adults would exceed the number given for age 51-plus. (Victor Hugo's doctors had to advise him in his late 70s to slow down on his sexual activity!) The frequency of marital intercourse declines on the same steadily falling line—again for the median and with numerous and notable exceptions among individual couples.*

What might be called solo sex, which is to say masturbation, with its accompanying fantasies, likewise declines (if the many respondents were reporting accurately to Kinsey), less so in women than in men (although women in general masturbate less frequently than men). In spite of the often traumatic experience of the menopause, sexuality remains a factor in the lives of many older women. However, it may be sublimated to attempt to conform to what is "expected" and "fitting" in conventionalized society—one aspect of the life of Total Expectedness.

At one time there was an omnipotent pseudo-Christian and Puritan viewpoint that morbidly maintained that all play functions of the body in sex were channels of self-entrapment, venereal disease, and destruction of self. Dr. Alex Comfort in *The Anxiety Makers* has pointed out that the more hysterical promoters of this attitude helped to spawn terrifying books designed to frighten boys and young males out of the "damnable" practice of masturbation. As he suggests, a certain proportion of older men may be sexually crippled by having read books by sadistic physicians and quacks whose nightmare prescriptions to control an innocent practice make an appalling account.

From the same sexually sick society emerged the conception of the "dirty old man" or woman. The same society that so much of the time brutally ignores or neglects its older adults is nonetheless busily attentive to what it considers their "acceptable" behavior. Both Kinsey and

---

*In 1972 an American study of approximately 800 professional men over age 65 revealed that 70 percent of them regularly had sexual intercourse and that clergymen were the most active. For some curious reasons, medical doctors, editors, publishers, and journalists were relatively low performers. The men questioned came from *Who's Who in the United States*, people from business and the arts as well as the professions. Dr. J. A. Silcox of the University of Western Ontario medical school, in commenting on this study, remarked that society wrongly looks on sex for older people as humorous or bizarre.

the now equally important reporters of *Human Sexual Response* (1966), William J. Masters and Virginia Johnson, found a marked reluctance on the part of males over age 60 to give information about their sexual practices or nonpractices. This nervous withdrawal from a mature and valuable area of inquiry is surely one sign of how afraid or shy older adults are to even admit confidentially to frankly sexual fantasies, desires, and thoughts, let alone deeds.

According to Masters and Johnson, "aging males" tend to diminish, and desist from, their earlier sexual activity for reasons having little to do with actual physical competence to continue. For example, these factors contribute greatly to inhibition of sexual play and intercourse: boredom with a repetitious sexual relationship (often, presumably, however well beloved the partner); preoccupation with career activities; mental or physical fatigue; overindulgence in food or drink; various aspects of physical and mental infirmities; fear of failure (which Masters and Johnson consider of enormous importance in hindering and arresting the sexual practice and achievement of the male past, say, age 60-plus).

If an older adult consigns the sexual life to some nostalgic area unattainable to the alleged "failing powers" of the later years, he or she places an undue load upon the success of earlier experience and signs away the possible recompenses and joy of sex in later life.

People persist in looking at "senior citizens" as though they were flat photographs in a sentimental family portrait. Simone de Beauvoir insists that the very young are shocked at evidences of sexual activity in the aging: but in fact it is precisely the "new young" of modern society who are probably most sympathetic.

Surely she is right in stressing the negative and often tragic role that unliberated public opinion still plays in constructing a widely held image of older adults as people for whom it is neither "nice" nor natural to talk about sex, to enjoy it, and to have sexual desires and drives.* They must be, as Beauvoir admirably says, made "ashamed of their own desires." She quotes the thorough research done by the American medical scientist, Dr. J. P. Runciman. Runciman closely studied the sexual practices and the responses of 200 adults aged 40 to 89. He concluded that "psychological barriers" were chiefly responsible for forcing an end to the sexual activity of older adults. In his view, the taboos of the Victorian morality in which they had been brought up were too powerful for their personal needs and desires to prevail.

Western society—by no means only North American society (as witness Beauvoir)—has long sought to make the older adult who continues to "indulge" in sexual interests and activity a figure either of shame or of comedy. Literature across the centuries has always ridiculed men

---

*Fortunately, there seem to be perceptible trends arising in the 1970s and 1980s indicating increased social acceptance of sexual activities among older adults.

whose wives are unfaithful, but none is so absurd as the old cuckold. This assiduous refusal to accept sexuality as a natural and beautiful phenomenon among older adults is seen again in the perennial jokes about May-December marriages. In spite of examples of happy marriages between young women and elderly men, or at least men over 60, in such cases as Pablo Casals, Zoltan Kodaly, Charles Chaplin, and Pablo Picasso, or similar relationships outside marriage, there are people who impute the worst of motives to one partner or the other. When Justice William O. Douglas of the United States Supreme Court at the age of 78 married a girl of 21 as his fourth wife, a group of imbeciles in Congress attempted to get legislation passed to cancel his appointment to the bench. Their real motive was Douglas's long support of liberal causes, but it is significant that they cloaked this in what they conceived to be a widely accepted folk attitude. Significantly, the marriage lasted lovingly until his recent death.

Even more incomprehensible and unacceptable, especially to the species *Americanus vulgaris*, which has its equivalent in all cultures, is the sight of a young man marrying an elderly woman. Yet in spite of the obsessive references to "gigolos and exploiters of women," instances abound of successful and deeply loving relationships between older women and young men, sexual—if not always manifested in actual intercourse—at least in the many loving physical contacts that also are expressions of sexuality. Edith Piaf was a case in point; so was Gracie Fields. An illuminating report on this area is *Older Women and Younger Men*, by Jane Seskin and Bette Ziegler (1979).

No doubt there were numerous cases like *The Roman Spring of Mrs. Stone* or something comparable. In this play by Tennessee Williams a middle-aged woman is driven partly by genuine feelings of love and partly by sexual hunger into a transient affair with a young man of intense physical attractiveness, an affair that fails, and after which in despair she finally opens her hotel suite to the dangerous youthful hustler who has long been watching and waiting in the street below her window. It is also clear that many homosexual adventures in which one partner is an older man or woman often end in bitterness and recrimination and with both partners resuming the eternal hunt. Yet, especially in the arts, there have been many successful relationships, sexual, platonic, and also what can be described as generalized noncopulative affection.

When that wonderful human being, André Gide, was far on in the life journey, he still had a deep fear of contracting venereal disease, and this presumably inhibited him from much sexual intercourse. A homosexual who had married and who loved his wife, but found it—to his later remorse—difficult to maintain a devoted relationship, Gide continued his love of adolescent youths far into his later years. This took curiously moving and innocent forms, which yet were exercises in sexuality. In the summer near the seashore, he would interrupt a game of chess or a conversation with a friend in the garden looking out on the sea, to drag his friend down close to the shore where they could watch adolescents bathing and shouting in the water. Or he would feel a certain pleasure in the accidental touching of a handsome youth in the bus. Once he wrote of his delight in observing the beauty of a young Parisian standing at the side of the pool in a Turkish bath.

Unconventional though these predilections and small adventures in Gide's domain of love would seem to many North Americans, only a very sick mind could describe Gide as a "dirty old man." His "deviation from the sexual norm" (to employ one of the dreary phrases of psychology) was not a block to his creativity nor a disgrace to his old age. He was, of course, often frustrated and unhappy (are we to suppose that these are the attributes only of old age?), but his late sexual life seems to have operated under the code of love: that is, in what he did he tried not to harm others or himself. A certain radiance filled his old age.

When very old people marry each other (often two residents of a nursing or retirement home), the event is frequently treated with amused astonishment or thinly veiled contempt, as if to say, whatever the aged should be doing, they should not at least be engaging in the futility of very late marriage. Since such a marriage is not common, the media play it up, often with a tolerant schmaltziness that is almost as distasteful as hostility. To the press it is all one with the absurdities of old ladies traipsing on a platform as can-can girls, or the hymn-sings that are supposed to be the staple of the institutionalized old. Of course, if the couple are people of private means, the marriage passes in public silence and no doubt in private peace, except perhaps for the exasperated comments of frustrated heirs.

These mixed reactions are not always the case, nor should they be. Pope John's words, "Any day is a good day to be born, and any day is a good day to die," transpose perfectly to marriage at any age, provided it is indeed a marriage of two people who cherish one another. Besides, the sexual encounter is dispensable in a very late married life, although the partners are usually quite capable of it. The Mexican saying that each man has three loves: in his youth, in his prime, and in old age, is a fine example of discrimination between the sexes—women in their very late years have this privilege too.

There are, of course, older adults who bring an atmosphere of nervous comedy to anything in their life that appears to disturb the stereotypes they accept as readily as the rest of a conventional and rigid society. Because they are courageous, or desperate, they take the plunge, but all the time they persist in seeing themselves in the mirrors of "what is expected"; their tense bravado or strained apology partly destroys the calm dignity of actions that are purely their own business. And this includes the decision to marry very late, which often may be a creative decision in the direction of a richer life.

Just as it is beautiful to see adults in their later years deciding to continue their sexual life and interest, making it a natural and continuing function of the life drama, likewise there is another choice among "those that mourn," which is moving and beautiful. For many men and women, when death has taken a beloved companion in the late 50s or the 60s—in our society the one lost is much more often the man than the woman—the rest of the journey is, by choice, a solitary one.

For these people the path taken is well described in the forgotten lines of Fanny Kemble in the poem, "Absence":

> What shall I do with all the days and hours
> That must be counted ere I see thy face?
>
> I'll tell thee; for thy sake I will lay hold
> Of all good aims, and consecrate to thee
> In worthy deeds, each moment that is told
> While you, beloved one, art far from me.
>
> I will this dreary blank of absence make
> A noble task time. . . .
> So may my love and longing hallowed be,
> And thy dear thought an influence divine.

If the consecration so made does not become a kind of mortification and turning away from life, and if especially it lovingly accepts the very different lifestyles of others contending on their own terms with the later adult years—then it is something very beautiful indeed, and one of the loveliest trails to the Ulyssean life.

In the case of long-term marriages, where the partners pass through much of the late-life phase together, an important psychological arena exists in which each must cope with losses of confidence and pride that may result from the waning of sexual power. This requires an empathy and skill in which many men and women are inadequate or, what is more important, unwilling to exert themselves. For the male especially, this can be unfortunate. For example, Masters and Johnson, quoting from their own and other studies of recent years, note that "when the aging male is not stimulated over long periods of time, his responsiveness may be lost." And they qualify an optimistic statement of late-life capacity for sexual stimulation and enjoyment by citing conditions of "*maintained* regularity of sexual expression coupled with adequate physical well-being and healthy mental orientation to the aging process."

Yet the field is full of light for those who will turn to see it:

The incidence of sexual inadequacy in the human male takes a sharp upturn after 50 years of age. . . However , just as the secondarily impotent male over 50 years old can be reconstituted, so can the potent aging male's responsive ability, dormant for physical or social reasons, be restimulated, if the male wishes to return to active sexual practices and has a partner interested in sexual performance. If he is in adequate health, little is needed to support adequacy of sexual performance in a 70- or even 80-year-old male other than some physiologic outlet or psychologic reason for a reactivated sexual interest. . .Even if coital activity has been avoided for long periods of time, men in these age groups can be returned to effective sexual function if adequate stimulation is instituted and interested partners are available.

Nor is the picture any less full of incentive and of potential light for the aging woman:

There is no reason why the milestone of the menopause should be expected to blunt the human female's sexual capacity, performance, or drive. The healthy aging woman normally has sex drives that demand resolution. The depths of her sexual capacity and the effectiveness of her sexual performance, as well as her personal eroticism, are influenced indirectly by all of the psycho and sociophysiologic problems of her aging process. In short, *there is no time limit* drawn by the advancing years to female sexuality. (My italics.)

5

THE UNFAILING MIND

ONE domain of aging takes precedence over every other for those who feel some commitment to keep growing—and notably for the Ulysseans. This is the kingdom of the mind, the "seat of consciousness" *(Concise Oxford Dictionary)* which arises from, but is an entity different from, the human brain, the most remarkable phenomenon in the known universe. In spite of the seemingly fantastic development of computers, the brain vastly outstrips the most sophisticated and elegant of these scientific wonders.

Stanley Burnshaw, who writes brilliantly about the possible role of the brain functions in language, thinking and creativity, describes the human brain as

> . . . probably the most complicated six inches on earth: the supposedly ten billion cells in the cortex, tens of thousands of nerve cells in the spinal cord, with millions of receptor fibres converging upon them—the center of the retina of each human eye, for example with nearly a half-million sensitive cells, each connected with a single nerve fiber.

In the enigma of memory alone, Burnshaw goes on:

> Millions of neurons are involved. Since this is the working effect of a trace, can we wonder that experts regard the profusion of interconnections among the cells as beyond human power of imagining—at least ten billion neurons, each receiving connections from perhaps 100 others and connecting it to still 100 more? The transmission of a "wavefront" may sweep over 100,000 neurons in a single second (it can operate not only on nearby cells but also on distant parts of the cortex); the entire wavefront can advance through as many as 1,000,000 neurons in a second.*

And Burnshaw quotes the striking image of the British physiologist, Sir Charles Sherrington, who compares the human brain to "an enchanted loom where millions of flashing shuttles (the nerve impulses)

*Most current estimates of the number of neurons actually estimate them as 15 billion.

85

weave a dissolving pattern, always a meaningful pattern, though never an abiding one; a shifting harmony of sub-patterns."

It is this wonderful instrument that an older adult is actually worrying about when he or she frets about Failure of Powers. "Brain" and "mind" are very formidable terms and images in human society. And this is manifested in our modern folk culture. Thus, in our time, everything is "stupid": in a hundred cases where what "he" or "she" has done bears no relationship to the mind or brain, they are still "stupid." Thus, you may do something demonstrably selfish or rude or rash—no matter: it is such a *stupid* action. We are living in a Cognitive Age.

Little wonder that when older adults think of Failure of Powers—and they are likely to think of it privately a great deal—the first concern that nags at them is the possible decline of cognitive capability. This concern takes the form of three typical questions: "Will I suffer continuous brain cell loss and disfunctionalizing brain damage?" "Will my mental capacity steadily decline in comparison with younger, more productive and creative adults?" "Will I be able to continue to learn efficiently?"

In short, can older adults create and produce as they once did in the early years and the so-called "prime years—*and even better?*" "*And even better*": these are the daring words that seemingly no one among the gerontologists and sympathetic adult educators will pronounce—yet in many cases they can be true; in many are already true. We will return to this neglected hypothesis later in this chapter in the discussion of "intelligence" and its "testing."

On the subject of physical loss and mental performance, everyone knows that there are severe strokes, either global or selective in their effects, that can temporarily or permanently interfere with the full efficiency of the brain. Likewise, cerebral illnesses of various kinds can also produce senile decay: certain of these can appear at early middle age—although they are rare. Elderly patients who have been institutionalized because of psychoses of the senium are notoriously much inferior in their capacity to perform on so-called intelligence tests than are healthy older adults, who of course form the vast majority.

No one knows how many people in the later years secretly dread the thought of senility. At any rate, the word is used both pejoratively and abusively as an epithet to deride or demean the old—as, of course, "young" is used to deflate youth. The commonest private analysis of politicians who in their late years make various apparent blunders or failures in policy is that they are, after all, senile. If a woman makes her third marriage at age 80 her relatives may well conclude that "she is a senile old fool." These are attributions rather than proven conditions. True senility is all too evident when one sees it: the wonderful instrument of the brain running blank with a few sounds like the TV set after the last show; body and brain ultimately comatose, to match the ever-accommodating folk language: "They say he's just a vegetable." He is *not,* as the late Bishop Austin Pardue was at pains to point out, just a vegetable; he is still a soul. Even if one does not believe *that,* he is still someone to be respected and perhaps cherished.*

No one wants to become senile even if it is the price tag of a very extended life. But the number of the truly senile is comparatively small; even the number of the immobilized aged in institutions is only something like 2 to 4 percent of the whole population past 70. Carl Eisdorfer's recent estimate (1975) is that in the 90s as many as 80 percent of aged adults are still free of senility.†

The concern of many later adults is the effect of the aging of the brain on continuing mental productivity and creativity. The path of anxiety runs somewhat like this: The brain is extremely sensitive to lack of oxygen and quickly atrophies and dies without it; it is the bloodstream that supplies the oxygen and nourishes the brain; interference with the bloodstream reduces the flow of oxygen to the brain; narrowing of the passage in the blood vessels is a common phenomenon of aging. *Therefore,* the process of aging must bring impaired mental efficiency and productivity with it. Anxious older people, and naturally most often those who have learned to prize their mind, are likely to take this simple sequence on its face value without investigating the whole context.

Medical and geriatric scientists, indispensable though they are, suffer from the same occupational hazards as, say, psychoanalysts in that they become preoccupied with pathological or abnormal states. When attention is turned to the great army of healthy or reasonably healthy individuals, some important facts emerge. James Birren in an admirable essay on the psychopathology of aging summarizes the studies done on *healthy* older men at the National Institute of Mental Health in Washington as clearly demonstrating that "reduction in cerebral flow and metabolic rate are not necessary concomitants of growing older. In general, men above the age of sixty-five who were judged to be healthy, or free from significant somatic disease, *had blood flows and cerebral metabolic rates approximately equivalent to those of young men.*" (My italics.)

In 1961 R. W. Kleemeier reported in his presidential address to the American Psychological Association on an intensive study of 13 elderly men (the youngest was 65) tested on four occasions over 12 years, using the Wechsler-Bellevue test of adult intelligence. He found a decline in test scores over the period, but the slope of decline did not seem to be

---

*In Bede's *History of the Church in England,* there is a reference to the extended loving care given to an old abbess until her death from global paralysis by the younger nuns around her.

†G. J. Alexander in a recent paper (Johnston, 1981) speaks of the "alarming frequency" of misapplications of the label of "senility," and from three recent studies estimates that fewer than 5 percent of adults older than 65 manifest true senile dementia (Cohen, 1977; National Institute of Aging, 1978; President's Commission on Mental Health, 1978).

related to age. Kleemeier was struck by the effects of ill health rather than aging upon the performance of his test subjects. Since it may seem at first glance difficult to separate the two, this is how Kleemier put it: "There is no evidence for *age change* in intelligence in the senium, and the changes which are found are better related to the physical state of health of the organism."

In fact, it is an heroic exercise trying to discern the role of cerebral physical functioning in so-called mental performance, if only because of the host of environmental factors involved. This is now becoming dramatically evident in changing attitudes to what the fearsome word "senility" really means. There are reputable scientists who contend that senility, when it occurs, comes usually not from physical/cerebral disease but from psychological sources. Simone de Beauvoir, who usually takes a melancholy pleasure in recording the sad decline into old age and death, finds herself able to report a French geriatric scientist, Bastide, as writing in *Sociologie des maladies mentales:* "It may be asked whether senility is a consequence of aging or whether on the contrary it is not rather an artificial product of a society that rejects the aged."

Further evidence exists in the marked difference in the degree of recovery between adults who are laid low by a massive stroke and in effect abandoned by physicians and family, and those who from the time of the onset are given the constant therapy of communication, encirclement, encouragement, and companionship. Some extraordinary recoveries ensue: for example, this was true of my mother.

In a fine chapter in his book, *Don't Give Up on an Aging Parent* (1975), Lawrence Galton calls senility 'a wastebasket diagnosis. . .too often no diagnosis at all, but, rather, an easy disposal category." Galton lists a small catalogue of physical conditions, including hardening of the arteries, that contribute to seeming senility, which are treatable and controllable, and in many cases curable. Galton remarks:

> Senility involves the whole person. It is not an isolated disease, confined to a single body compartment. Many alterations, often subtle ones, individually or collectively can conspire to create the appearance or actuality of senility . . .when these disturbances are sought for and actively treated, the diagnosis of senility may be abandoned or the hopelessness about it may vanish very quickly.

Galton discusses at length the contributions of "attitude therapy" in returning aged human beings from alleged "senility" to active, meaningful life. He describes the brilliant work of Karl A. Menninger and Howard V. Williams in restoring to health numbers of patients once classified as suffering "senile dementia." He quotes a superb statement by Menninger: "I apologize for this abominable term. It is what we called the state of utter despair and demoralization some of our old people reached as they lost their faculty for readaptation and coping. We know now that the condition is not properly called a "dementia."

An important development in the past decade is the rich use of the arts in later-life environments to help prevent senility among adults 70 and much older and to draw back those perceived to be not truly senile but pseudo-senile. Everyone in the later years will be assailed by certain deficits and threats that are inalienable from the aging process. Mindless euphoria about aging does nothing to improve the situation: it worsens it, and in some cases increases its elements of pathos. Alzheimer's disease, for example, is a reality that affects a substantial number of older (as well as younger) adults, and must be coped with. The brain ages, and Birren reminds us that the brains of some distinguished men whose competence was universally accepted through their active phases until the period just before death, have been shown to contain large amounts of senile plaques, indicators of brain disease. If so, this merely testifies further to the stamina and the mysterious virtuosity of the human brain.

Even in dramatic cases of severe cerebral injury, the marvelous brain is still able on occasion to employ, as it were, reserve circuits and operations that confound the experts. Many readers of this book will have known cases where the physicians have decreed that So-and-So "will not walk again"—but he or she *has* walked again, not merely because of the wonderful courage of the patient, but because of mysterious and unforeseen powers in the organism. The physicians were not usually inexpert; sometimes they were among the finest in the world. There simply exist in the anatomy and physiology of the brain and nervous system of the body hidden forces and channels of recuperation still undeciphered by medical science.*

Where physical and psychological loss occurs among older adults—loss notably of some swiftness of reaction or response—the powerful factor of compensation enters in. Where some damage to brain functioning occurs through aging, the process is usually a lengthy one. There is time to make use of the wide repertory of adjustments and solutions that men and women have usually developed in their work life and personal living. In addition, few of us—none of us?—ever deliver the full potentialities of our body and mind, of our *self*. Most of the time, when we fancy that we are highly integrated and strongly motivated, we deceive ourselves. It takes the stimulus of threat or danger to spur us to reach into the repertory of our skills and strategies to live at a new level of creativity.

Robert de Ropp, enlarging the discussion to include the whole of the inner self, remarks that "within the psyche of man are secret rooms, vast chambers full of treasures with windows looking out on

*A close friend of mine, who had suffered terrible head injuries and undergone massive operations, heard the ultimate verdict: "We are sorry to tell you that you will not be able to walk again, and you will have to expect a considerable amount of pain during your life." He recounted this to me, a year after the verdict, at a party, limping across the broadloom of a large hotel room to give me the details. Some pain intermittently appears.

eternity and infinity. Man does not enter these rooms, or does so only rarely. They are locked. He has lost the key. He lives habitually in the lowest, dreariest, darkest part of his inner habitation."

Yet, although many older adults do not use their talents and experience well, most develop some or all of the life strategies Adlai Stevenson described in discussing what a man knows at 50 that he did not know at 20: "The knowledge he has acquired with age is not a knowledge of formulas, or forms of words, but of people, places, actions—a knowledge gained by touch, sight, sound, victories, failures, sleeplessness, devotion, love—the human experience and emotions of this earth and of one's self and other men." Add to these, neuroses mastered, obsessive anxieties controlled or overcome, terrible sorrows transcended, the nightmare of debt survived, certain expectations and disappointments in love, marriage, and careers encountered, and the silent company of many secret fears endured. In many of these cases, failure has been aborted or transformed, problems unlocked, and resilient strategies acquired.

From all these experiences many older adults have acquired two major strategies that serve them well in encounters between the physically aging brain and the needs of learning and living.

First: they keep the mind active, growing, life-loving, problem-solving: as close a guarantee as one can get—barring the cosmic disasters that can befall any of us *at any age*—that a man or woman can inhabit the kingdom of the mind with rich pleasure and creativity to the end of life. Second: they accept as a rule of life that older adults possess in the human brain, even when it has suffered some deficits, a magnificent instrument that at any phase of their existence could serve them better than they permit. And they accept as generally true the statement by the noted gerontologist Wilma Donahue, "Cerebral function is the most dependable servant that can be called upon over a long span of years."

Many adults would feel that Donahue's statement neglects the supposed significant decline of the memory faculties in later adulthood. However, here again is an area of adult mental capability that swarms with myths.[1] It is true that a few reports of systematic research into memory retention, using structured materials with both young and old, indicate somewhat less efficiency in memory performance by some "old" adults as against some "young" subjects, taking the same tests.

The question, however, that researchers ought to be addressing (and do not) is whether memory powers in the active later adults are sufficient for the many learning, producing, and creative tasks that can fill the later years with rich achievement. If the nature, activities, and performance of the brain are still shrouded in mystery, our knowledge of memory as a function is likewise deeply mysterious.

However, the folklore is always glad to supply the myth. At a recent public lecture, one questioner (she was perhaps 65 or 70) asked: "Why is it that we can't remember names as we get older?" This is what might be called the myth-as-refuge. In this case a personal condition is universalized because the general myth of Decline of Powers indicates that it must be so.

In fact, it is not proven that capacity to remember fails because of age. So complex is the arena in which memory performs, and so complex are the life environments, motivations, and individual differences of the performers, that in both old and young functional memory deficiencies of every kind turn up.

Here in the sphere of memory function, the global tendency of the myth-makers again appears: "the young," "the old." From time to time I ask a room full of older adults, age 50 to 80: "How many have the experience of starting out from one end of an apartment or house to get something, only to find that you've forgotten what you sought for at the other end?" Every hand goes up. And when I ask the same question of classes filled with young graduate students, every hand goes up! It's a small but important symbol of the folly of categorizing "young" versus "old" functions—in this case, memory.

Another of the myths of memory is that, as you enter the late years, you will remember early events in your life, but can't remember events and needs of the current week. So far as the seeker-adults are concerned, this is pure nonsense. Aside from certain brain pathologies that can affect memory, the most likely explanation for this condition among aged men and women where it exists is that they withdraw to that early sector of their lives where they happen to feel needed, respected and loved, and at home. The withdrawal is that of the whole being, not just of the memory.

We are learning more and more of the awesome intricacy and compensatory powers of the brain/mind functions. It cannot be stressed enough that what matters in memory performance is whether the mind has sufficient power, not whether there are decrements in some portions of structured tests. Is there memory power enough in this man or woman, 50-plus and through the late years, to write the novel, take a degree, learn a language (always supposing the person has the aptitude!), invent new organizations or objects, hold a public office, travel in a well-organized way, lead spiritual seekers, and so on? The people I call Ulysseans are part of the rich evidence that it is indeed so.

Older adults who virtually immobilize themselves at the mere thought of Failure of Powers specifically affecting their physical brain have not only lost the key to treasure chambers—they have thrown it away. Most adults are quite able physically or with compensatory skills to take on the tasks of continuing mental growth and learning, but the will to learn may be gone.

And what of those powerful twin motivators of learning: curiosity and the sense of wonder?

The American psychologist William James, who by 1900 had become a giant figure as the founder of the North American school of pragmatism, and who had brilliant and provocative opinions on all too many topics, was at least on home territory when he asserted categorically in his massive *Principles of Psychology* (1893) that:

> Outside of their own business, the ideas gained by men before they are 25 are practically the only ideas they shall have in their lives. They *cannot* get anything new. Disinterested curiosity is past, the mental grooves and channels set, the power of assimilation gone. Whatever individual exceptions might be cited to these are of the sort that prove the rule.

Twelve years later Sir William Osler, in the course of a farewell address at Johns Hopkins University, caused an international uproar by his half-jesting references to the unproductivity of men over 40 and the possible advantages of chloroforming men at 60. (Osler was himself age 55 and heading for yet another creative phase of his career, at Oxford.) Osler did not deny that "occasionally there is a sexagenarian whose mind, as Cicero remarks, stands out of reach of the body's decay." And he went on to recommend that, at the least, all men over 60 as they felt "the silver cord loosening" should do as the Athenian philosopher Hermippus did, "who cut himself clear from all companions of his own age and betook himself to the company of young men, mingling with their games and studies, and so lived to the age of 153." Osler deduced from this that "only those who live with the young can maintain a fresh outlook on the new problems of the world."

An enormous and hostile uproar ensued from editorials, cartoons, letters to the press, and a flood of letters to Osler. There were even some threats! Osler handled the situation with his usual high good humor and intrepidity but the notoriety followed him for years, and he suffered somewhat because of his enormous previous popularity. Mrs. Osler, who had a sense of humor, remarked shortly afterward to a Johns Hopkins friend whom she and Osler met as they walked in Baltimore on Sunday, "I am escorting the shattered idol home from church."

However, for all his fame and authority, Osler was not a specialist in the science of the functions of the mind, as William James was. A single speech, for all its notoriety, has nothing like the effect of a massive text; nor did Osler have his disciples scattered across the United States as professors and practitioners of the relatively new field of psychology, as James did.

The devastating answering cannonade to James and Osler by Edward L. Thorndike and associates of Columbia University, published in 1928 as the now-celebrated book, *Adult Learning*, must have been one of the longest-delayed counterattacks in the history of controversy. In the mid-1920s Thorndike was age 50, and his attention had been caught again and fascinated by William James's statement, which he used as the text for his attack.

Thorndike and his colleagues examined a large number of the many small, obscure studies done on adult learning during the period from 1900 to 1926. One issue that had attracted research attention was the ability of adults to improve in simple sensori-motor abilities. The trials were varied and curious: improved accuracy in tossing shot into a glass; learning not to blink when an empty object was struck; keeping balls going in the air; tapping a telegraph key at maximal speed. All adults participating improved steadily and at rates that were in a number of instances on a swiftly climbing curve. The data, however, were of young adults still in their 20s. Other tests had measured adult ability to improve in forming simple habits, in learning more elaborate systems of habits, in memory (for example, remembering series of nonsense syllables), and in complex abilities. In all cases, practice, if it did not make perfect, at least led to marked improvement. That partly confirms the point Wilma Donahue makes so insistently: we must not simply sit back and relegate adults of any age group to some category of non-learners; we must bring them into the practice field where old skills and habits that have gone rusty can be made to shine again and new ones learned.

The Thorndike group next decided to test adult ability to learn a new hierarchy of habits by getting eight people who had always written with their right hand to try writing with their left.[2] The ages of the volunteers were 22, 28, 28, 33, 34, 41, 42, and 52. Thorndike remarks:

> When one changes the hand in writing, not only do none of his old habits of movement fit the new demand; they are distorted in a complicated way. Nevertheless, the mere general control given by knowledge of the desired appearance and by vision enables the adult learner to counteract tendencies to write in mirror fashion, and to establish rather quickly a new hierarchy of habits.

And he concludes that:

> . . .In general, the gain of these eight adults from less than sixteen hours of practice was greater than the gain proposed by experts as suitable to be accomplished by children using the right hand in two years of growth and schooling, including one hundred or more hours of special practice in handwriting.

Thorndike was struck by the motivation displayed by his eight adults—yet, as he says, the motivation was surely less than that of some adult compelled to learn to write with the other hand because of accident. And is not the economic motive a powerful factor, he asks, in the case of the great numbers of adult men and women who are required by industrial changeovers to learn new skills? He speculates also on the motivation of sheer pleasure, as in learning new games.

The zest with which Thorndike and his associates attacked the question of adult capability to learn is apparent in their search for the right test content for what they cited as "learning a systematic logical subject."[3] Esperanto, the artificial language designed as a means of international communication, seemed to the investigators to have the virtue of presenting to the would-be learner a consistent, logical, intellectual system that could be said to be largely representative of the intellectual efforts required in the learning of various foreign languages, sciences, mathematics, and social sciences.

The test groups are particularly interesting because they were formed of people with almost identical scores on a standard "intelligence" test and were of *three age categories:* a group of 18, aged 20-25; a second of nine, aged 26-34; and a third group of 21, aged 35-plus. The youngest was 20, the oldest 57. All were university students, the older ones presumably senior people from the teaching profession taking graduate degrees.

In global returns, the 20-25-year group gained 31.5. The 26-34-year group gained 26.3. The 35-plus group gained 24.7. However, Thorndike adds that "the superiority of the younger adults is due almost entirely to their greater gain in the oral directions test. In the other three tests, there was little or no difference." (The "other three" were vocabulary, printed directions, and paragraph reading.)

Thorndike raised a highly controversial point in concluding his descriptions of this experiment. In a separate experiment, this time using pupils nine to 18 years of age from "a good private school" who had twice as much class study time as the adult group aged 35-plus, and theoretically with much more home study time, the school group gained scarcely more than half that of the 35-plus adults. Slower still were the children aged nine to 11.

Actually, David Ausubel of the University of Illinois argues in a cogently reasoned paper (1968) that the "widespread cultural belief that children learn languages more readily than adults do. . .is highly vulnerable." Ausubel states that whereas children have unequaled powers as mimics in language learning, "their cognitive immaturity and lack of certain intellectual skills preclude many approaches that are feasible for older age groups."

A fascinating section of the Thorndike studies is devoted not merely to whether adults can continue to learn and learn well but whether they can unlearn. This involved not only familiar skills but attitudes, prejudices, and antipathies. Thorndike tried to probe into such questions as when the fear of snakes, of thunder, or of blood was first aroused, and at what age, if at all, it was overcome; at what age certain prejudices arose regarding race, religion, and political affairs, and when these prejudices were put aside, if at all. His questionnaire, although primitive, would be a marvelous exercise for any reader of this book who, at long last, will school himself to sit down and really analyze how his prejudices and fears were aroused, and how they were solved or healed, if they ever were. This is the learning of unlearning. Not surprisingly, Thorndike and associates were unable to report conclusive *quantitative* results, one way or the other, on attitude change.

Along with this, Thorndike examined a number of more familiar things: how late can people learn to dance, swim, and skate, for example? ("Age is evidently not an insuperable barrier, learning to swim and dance occurring at all ages to 50.") Thorndike's study of attitudes was based on a sample of 99 people, all with a college education or its equivalent. Thirty-nine of these were age 40 or older. The qualitative summation of replies established certain general principles repeated by subsequent investigators in subsequent years. Thus: age inhibits the learning of "things of the mind" less than it influences motor skills; and if adults in their middle and later years find it difficult to learn or even to begin to learn something outside their usual life and routine, it is (to quote Thorndike): "in part due to a sensitiveness to ridicule, adverse comment, and undesired attention, so that if it were customary for mature and old people to learn to swim and ride bicycles and speak German, the difficulty might diminish."

Thorndike was convinced, when his comprehensive review of his own studies and those of others was finished, that James's assertion 35 years previously was grotesquely wrong. "Age in itself," he asserted in his conclusions, "is a minor factor in either success or failure. Capacity, interest, energy, and time are the essentials."

In fact, Thorndike became obsessed with two factors he considered crucial to getting adults to learn, unlearn, relearn: first, the will to learn. In a splendid throwback to the James dictum, Thorndike writes: "By the age of twenty-five most persons have, within certain limitations, learned a great part of what *they wish to learn*." (My italics.) And second, he rates as crucial *the opportunity to learn* under conditions that maximize the potentialities of the individual.

Adult Learning although, of course, a pioneer study, is a kind of Universal Declaration of Adult Rights to Learn. Thorndike calls for a society in which there will be a redistribution of the formal hours of learning experiences—so that these might be spread into and throughout adult life.* He notes how usually inadequate both content and teaching strategies are for adult learners. He cites the need for the availability of counseling for adults—the mature counseling by peers for those who hesitate on the brink of learning, or may drop their learning adventure because of discouragement. He urges a more sensible approach to the "dropout" from adult classes—perhaps the adult happens to know what he needs and does not need, and perhaps there is a message for the instructor and the institution. He notes compas-

---

*In Thorndike's day, libraries, galleries, and classes were often closed just when millions of adults were free to learn in these places! Can we be complacent about our own progress?

sionately the many pressures that converge on adult learners. He stresses that wonder—James's "disinterested curiosity"—is perfectly available throughout adulthood. And Thorndike deplores people who apply to adults tests validated and standardized for child and school use.

In "The Age of the IQ" or 'the Cognitive Age," performance on intelligence tests would seem to be an obvious diagnostic instrument to find out whether adult mental abilities hold up with advancing age.

The intelligence-test approach is so clean and definite. It lends itself beautifully to curves on a graph; and its potential efficiency lends it an unmistakable charm for the North American system. There is, however, a slight problem—what is "intelligence"?

Is it so straightforward a thing as "the ability to solve problems"? So anatomical and baffling a thing as "a function of the cerebral cortex"? Is it a number of things—a plurality of intelligences as developed by Thurstone and Guilford? Is it a product of nature or nurture? And how does it relate to wisdom? Where is the Wisdom Quotient?

In the early days of testing, just after 1900 when Binet devised his tests for atypical children, it was widely accepted that intelligence was a genetic factor, fixed or predetermined at birth (so-called "innate cognitive intelligence"), relatively fixed at age 16, and readily assessable by standardized tests.[4] From this general position, together with careless teaching and learning and slipshod communications, arose what one might call the cash-and-carry concept of the IQ (codified or indexed by dividing the subject's Mental Age, or MA, by his chronological age, or CA, and multiplying by 100).

The so-called "intelligence test" was administered either individually or as a group process. The IQ was determined, and then unfortunately extrapolated from the whole life of the person being tested, usually a child or early adolescent, attached to his records for various future directions in educational choices or for the opinions of teachers and, far too often, of others. In "good" situations it usually formed part of a cluster of judgments. For example, achievement tests, "interests" tests, school performance, or in the case of suspected neurotic students and others, such tests for abnormality as the Rorschach Inkblot tests, and the Minnesota Multiphasic Personality Inventory were variously used. But the IQ retained its aura for better and, too often, for worse. It is interesting to speculate on what effect the knowledge of a supposed "IQ" (often derived in slipshod testing and bandied about in slipshod talking) has had on educational motivations in later adult life.

Compared to the primitive conception of intelligence as a fixed inheritance from the genetic system, some much more attractive definitions of "intelligence" have been advanced within the past 20 years. R. B. Cattell and D. O. Hebb described two kinds of intelligence, not one. In Hebb's concept, Intelligence A is found in the genetic potentiality or basic qualities of the individual's central nervous system; Intelligence B, however, is mainly the result of experience, learning, and the interplay of environment with the self. Cattell's concepts are of "fluid" and "crystallized" intelligence; like Hebb's, they have had wide influence.

The psychologist H. J. Butcher suggests an interesting verification of these views of intelligence in the following comment:

An astonishingly large portion of the cerebral cortex has been surgically removed from some adult patients with very little effect on their scores on standardized intelligence tests, whereas cognitive development in children is severely impaired by similar damage. It thus appears that brain cells needed for the development of intelligence are no longer essential to maintain a high level once it has been developed.

David Wechsler's definition of intelligence is comprehensive and illuminating: "Intelligence is the aggregate or global capacity to act purposefully, to think rationally, and to deal effectively with one's environment." However, the Wechsler definition raises a host of new problems in its adverbs: What is "purposefully"? Who judges "effectively"? and so on.

Jean Piaget has suggested that the nature and functioning of intelligence change quite radically from one age of a person to another. He suggests that it is impossible to place under a single convenient label such different entities or functions as the formal intelligence that adults typically use, the concrete intelligence of mid-childhood, and the sensori-motor intelligence of infants and very young children.

There is a fearful simplicity and arbitrariness in the idea that mental capacity can be plotted on a curve and that ability to learn will follow the curve across the life journey. Folk knowledge, which for centuries, and long before the rise of psychology, thought it could speedily recognize the "dullard" and the "wit," probably rarely pursued the classification into the late years. Dullness became camouflaged by the myriad disguises of old age conventions. Thorndike believed that a dull young man would certainly be a dull old man; and that a bright old man was certainly brighter than an average young man.*

Reports of performance by adult people at various age levels are now normally given, not simply as composite scores on tests, but rather as performances on various sectors of whatever "intelligence" test is used. Thus, typical tests examine verbal competence as seen in strength of vocabulary, skill in handling problems designed to test abstract and practical reasoning, and rote memory. Later adults hold up well in the sections of the tests requiring competence in vocabulary, in informa-

*Even here, dullness could often be the result of lack of opportunity. Generations of men and women, ignorant by necessity, cry out to us.

tion, and in conceptualizing ideas. They typically show declines in sub-tests dealing with rote memory, digit symbol arrangement, and picture arrangement; they naturally show a decline in psychomotor skills. These are, remember, general summations. One of the most essential things to recall in reporting all adult testing is that there are numerous older adults who surpass younger in certain and in all categories; and that there are greater disparities in individual scores among a given age group, say 60-65, than between the ages of 60 and 40.

David Wechsler made a brilliant effort to design a mental abilities test especially for adults, and which would be standardized for each adult age group (instead of against children and youths)—the Wechsler Adult Intelligence Scale. His studies convinced him that there is a progressive decline in intellectual ability as the years pass. In Chapter 9 of his interesting study, *The Measurement and Appraisal of Adult Intelligence*, Wechsler argues that on all subtests of the WAIS the decline is found, and he states categorically in summation:

> . . .whatever it is that the tests measure, the argument advanced does not controvert the fact that the abilities involved alter with the aging process. The least one can say is that for most persons intellectual ability, after reaching a peak in early maturity, declines progressively with age. The correlation between age (after age 5) and scores on tests of intelligence is always negative.

Wechsler is a formidable scholar in the fields of adult testing and learning. He assembles and presents the results of his research with power; nor is it possible to argue that he had an axe to grind. He devised the WAIS, not to prove that adult mental capacity declines in pure curves, but simply to determine what the picture is, and also to provide a far juster measurement of "intelligence" than had previously been possible with child-oriented tests inherited from Binet.

Nonetheless, there are enormous cracks running through Wechsler's rock of finality. The convolutions through which his arguments go in attempting to arrive at a clearly acceptable definition of "adult intelligence" are themselves evidence of this. In fact, he fails. *"Whatever it is that the tests measure"* is a remarkably obscure statement of the enigmatic central domain of "intellectual ability," which, however, by an easy bridge hardly noticed perhaps by either the writer or the reader becomes the centre of a summation statement of dazzling certainty.

Perhaps the most impressive evidence that could be brought forward of the continuing power of operation of the human mind would be its intimately observed ability over considerable lengths of time to find creative solutions to problems or challenges produced from within the domain of its ongoing interests. And this is virtually untestable by the ingenious tests so far devised by psychologists of learning—brief, usually closely timed tests, with, in effect, "canned" exercises which it is hoped will display the varying competences of younger and older adults. The mature mind at its best is not engaged in once-for-all enterprises, even though it is true that conventional or routine living does present its own version of closely timed trial test situations, day by day. For example, how does the driver of a large automobile most rapidly and successfully make his way through the glut of traffic separating him from the city boundary and his downtown committee meeting? But this is a far cry from the solution of abstract problems for which one may have to assemble one's forces time and again, after perhaps successive failures.

James Birren, in *The Psychology of Aging*, notes that tests of intelligence to a great extent measure achievement or stored information, and goes on to define the essential quality in the performance of intelligence that the tests *fail* to measure directly as "inventive concept formation" or "inventive conceptualization." Birren is referring to "the more labile that is, fleeting qualities displayed by individuals who are able to integrate simultaneously available, but previously disparate that is, diverse, or essentially different , facts *into some new synthesis*." (My italics.)

The difficulty of testing and plotting wisdom on a grid has already been mentioned. One indirect approach to this is the struggle to determine whether people have become more or less rigid in their attitudes with the advancing years. Testers seeking to determine this have employed such devices as trying to find out how far different age groups agree with clichés, how far they seem to cling to settled habits as against trying out new approaches, and so on.

Some studies in the past 20 years in Great Britain and the United States claim that rigidity, inflexibility, and dogmatism increase after, say, age 50 or 55. However, the control problems are overwhelming. In probing for rigidity in attitudes and opinions, the line is very thin between middle-aged stability or thoughtful conservatism, for example, and rigidity. The probing exercise may be too brief, too impersonal, and too judgmental without the real data for judgment. The subject's apparent drawing-back and drawing-in may be symptoms of deep anxieties that were as acute at 30 as at 60. Surely the best device for studying the onset and progress of rigidity in attitudes and opinions would be longitudinal case studies—biography supplies some of these, but one would need many hundreds more.

A valuable study at Wayne State University conducted by Paul Cameron had investigators interview three generations: Wayne State University students, their parents, and their grandparents:

First, we discovered that the older generation actually depended on fewer persons for advice, emotional support, and general information than did the middle or younger generations, and that they made fewer demands on the persons they did depend on. In fact, *the grandparent generation seemed to give more interpersonal support than they received from others.* . .

The older generation did express more caution when they faced decision-making situations (and) were less likely to take action under all conditions. However, it was possible to make almost all of the younger subjects as cautious as or more cautious than the elders by adjusting the amount of information and interpersonal approval. *When the young adult grandchildren saw themselves as deprived of factual information, they, too, became cautious.* . .*By taking away information and social approval, we can establish conditions among young adults that resemble those in which many elders must function.*

And Cameron also cites the study of Clarence and Sylvia Sherwood on the supposed political conservatism of elder adults, noting that the older people studied in the survey were actually more liberal than their offspring. In any event, he goes on to point out that "many old persons develop conservative streaks because of what society has taken away from them—status, work, social opportunities, privacy. If fewer things were taken from them, they would feel less threatened, less need to cling to whatever is left." (Reported in *Psychology Today*, December, 1971.)

Within the testing domain itself, a large number of important studies refute Wechsler's position that a downward curve is the normal direction of adult mental abilities. Irving Lorge was struck by the extent to which the intelligence tests were dependent upon the level of education of the adult. (Older adults earlier in this century had had notably less schooling than the young adults they were often pitted against in intelligence testing, and this is in general still true.) Besides, Lorge disliked the rigid and (he thought) unfair controls that closely timed testing imposed upon people in their middle years and older. What was the special virtue of the frozen time limits, other than that the tests were devised in a modern society especially obsessed with technology, so-called efficiency, and the clock?

Lorge had not been Thorndike's disciple for nothing. He took three adult groups, aged 20-25, 27-37, and 40-70, and tried to match the people in them as carefully as possible, person to person. In initial runs he turned up a declining curve on efficiency, working under rigid time limits. He took this and computed a handicap, including corrections for slowness, for time away from school and consequent loss of learning habits, and for lack of motivation. Lorge's conclusion was that if the same individuals could be followed in *longitudinal* studies, there would be no decline in the curves of tested mental capacity.

He maintained this after many years of experiments:

Age as age probably does little to affect an individual's power to learn or think. His performance may be reduced because of changes in his speed, sensory acuity, or self-concept, or shifts in values, motivation, goals, and responsibilities which come with aging. Adults learn much less than they might partly because of the self-underestimations of their power and wisdom, and partly because of their own anxieties that their learning behaviour will bring unfavourable criticism. Failure to keep on learning may affect performance more than power itself.

Lorge might well have also cited the role that arguing with seemingly arbitrary or even puerile test questions plays in the slower responses of intelligent older adults.

Support for Lorge's main thesis came from a study by E. E. Ghiselli and associates in which they worked with a group of 1,400 adults aged 20-65. Ghiselli used only well-educated people, and his testing situations, as in Lorge's case, excluded speed as a parameter. Ghiselli found that his older adults held up as well as the younger. The Fels Institute tested 72 women and 59 men over a period of about 17 years, using the Otis Mental Ability Test as the instrument. During that period the average level of the IQ calculated for the group remained almost unchanged. There were many *individual* changes in the scores: as many up as down.

The great need, of course, was for more such studies that followed the same adults over a period of many years, and in testing them pitted their performance at 20 or 30 against their performance 20 or 30 years later: that is, longitudinal studies. This would remove the educational inequalities and reduce certain control problems of trying to match personalities—an almost insuperable task.

Longitudinal studies are not as impossible as they at first seem. Testing of adults goes all the way back to World War One and in addition, devoted researchers like Nancy Bayley and others reported below set up programs deliberately planned to retest the same adults at periodic intervals. Bayley decided in 1933 to do a longitudinal study of the same 74 subjects from babyhood into and through adulthood; she found after 40 years that the 54 subjects who remained in the project were showing little change from their performances at 18. Bayley's study still falls short of the Ulyssean boundaries, but the returns so far do not support the "declining curve" theories.

The most important report of recent years on adult ability to retain learning powers is that of Jarvik, Eisdorfer, and Blum, *Intellectual Functioning in Adults* (1973). In this anthology of studies, Samuel Granick and Alfred S. Friedman note how research

. . .has, to a large extent, followed the orientation of our culture in focusing on the debilitating aspects of aging. It seems to have inadvertently helped to justify the tendency to view the aged as infirm and in constant need of support and protection. Associated with this are the powerful social, cultural, and economic pressures that lead the aged to disengage from active, dynamic involvement in society, and into a depressed, deprived, and unproductive existence.

And L. F. Jarvik, in making the summation review of dozens of *longitudinal* studies, remarks that, while psychomotor skills "relentlessly decline" beginning even between the ages of 16 and 36, *"the stability of intellectual abilities emerges once more."* (Jarvik's italics.) For example, in R. Schoenfeldt's longitudinal study of Iowa subjects, those "entering the seventh decade at the time of their last testing, had maintained their relative standings on mean total Alpha scores *for 42 years.*" (My italics.) This was true even into the late years: Jarvik notes that "Eisdorfer and Wilkie, and Rhudick and Gordon, whose subjects were followed from the seventh to the eighth decades, were also impressed by their failure to find rapid declines in these later years."

It is true that the same studies found that good health and good education were powerful factors in maintenance of these abilities at the full. Jarvik is able to quote from research at the New York State Psychiatric Institute to the effect that "if illness does not intervene, cognitive ability is the rule and *can be maintained into the ninth decade.*"*

Thus, in the most persuasive of all testing approaches—longitudinal studies—strong evidence exists that adult "mental abilities" performances hold up well, and in the case of some subjects increase, even through the very late years. Who in our time would agree with Freud's incredible statement, "Old people are no longer educable"? Freud's own productive later years gave the standing lie to this fatuity.

On the other hand, every careful observer can see that great numbers of adults in their later years do little or nothing to keep alive the fires of mental alertness and learning capacity. They confront rich potentiality only with passiveness, which is indeed a form of resistance. Or they have organized their lives as a flight from the occasional discomforts and real delights of systematically breaking into new fields. It is a truism of the adult learning world that performance is transformed by an active rather than passive mind-set, and by a life filled with the thrust for learning. Passivity and a turning-away from the challenges to learn are not part of the aging process per se; they are self-induced or peer-induced attitudes about the roles and purposes of older adults.

Yet not wholly. Something else happens to older adults, some of whom find themselves in the corrals of the testers, which has little to do with aging but much to do with time. Many adults get beaten up by life. By the time they are age 50 or 60, not only have they often encountered immense personal sorrows and disappointments, but they have experienced social and psychological shocks simply as participants in a

*Recent studies (1979+) by the Australian gerontologists, E. Harwood and G. F. K. Naylor, add strength to the assertion for over-all sustained powers of later learners.

succession of upheavals in political and economic life, and in the sphere of customs and morals. Only unusually sensitive young adults recognize in older people the heroic achievement it has been for many of them to carry on their lives usefully and lovingly in spite of these stresses and storms.

Select from these men and women a group for testing, to see how they respond to paper-and-pencil or laboratory episodes skillfully conceived to test strength of vocabulary, stored information, conceptualization, and such psychomotor performance areas as object assembly, digit symbol, and block design. What you will obtain is "whatever it is that the tests measure." The result is not unlike a stop-action photograph in black and white of this remarkable creature Man whose life runs on like a full-color film. Remember, too, that each of these lives also is governed by what might be called an expectations threshold. Many older adults no longer expect as much of themselves as they did in their younger years. They are usually no longer as hungrily competitive, as superficial in certain inner values—nor does the folk eye of society expect them to perform as though they were younger.

By contrast, the numerous Ulysseans I have met in my life have continued to expect a great deal of themselves throughout their lives, if not in old fields, then in new. They seem to have their own measure of "adult intelligence," and so far as I can discern it, a Ulyssean would put it in about such terms as these:

"Yes, I feel certain physical losses from my earlier years. *But otherwise* I feel that whatever you call my mind is burning more brightly and beautifully then it ever did before. It isn't just this or that—it's the whole of myself, everything running together, not just adding sums and repeating from rote as in schooldays, but a whole complex, a constellation: perceptions, understandings, judgments, selectivity—the great feeling I have that I'm free but not chasing up and down every meadow, as I did when young. Insights, answers, and compassions keep pouring from all the experiences I've had in my life. Not that I have all the answers! Sometimes I feel that I know nothing—there's so much to explore. When I think of it, it's not just the mind—whatever that is—it's the self, my whole self, that makes me feel young, but a different "young" from my youth, in many ways just as beautiful—in some, more so."

Still, it is impossible really to speak too exactly for the Ulysseans—they come in so many different conditions and personalities. Except that common to all their attitudes are the sense of quest, an active mind and spirit, a loving pursuit of life on whatever terms, and great expectations.

And if this older adult goes on to say that he cannot turn off his mind, that day after day it remains enchanted with the variety and the mystery of life, and that it searches in dozens of ways, no matter how small because of limitations sometimes imposed by circumstances, to obtain more and more sights and views of an horizon that never ceases to expand—then, of course, you have, whether rich or poor, well or wretchedly ill, the Ulyssean Adult.

6

THE CREATIVE PEAK
AND THE THRUST TO LEARN

I
S THERE a peak of creativity? Just as with intelligence, some investigators like to conceive of creativity of the mind as a hill-shaped curve, which one climbs to a presumed peak, then tumbles down the other side. Several of these original searchers have sought confirmation of their ideas by identifying the "peak years" of noted inventors and creators. The theory is intriguing, not least for its simplicity of approach. You look up the career profiles of hundreds of people, living or dead, whose work in science, the arts, politics, athletics, and business has brought them sufficient fame to be listed in the encyclopedias or in the *Who's Who* of their field. You determine at what age each created his or her supposed masterwork, and then you do the necessary statistical runs and correlations and produce a composite figure for the typical "peak" age at which men (in these studies it is almost invariably men) produced their best work as mathematicians, poets, statesmen, chemists, and so on.

This was the approach of the psychologist Harvey C. Lehman of Ohio State University in his study *Age and Achievement*, published in 1953. *Age and Achievement* is important, not only for the massive documentation it attempted, but for its inevitable influence on texts on adult psychology and the life cycle. So able and normally cautious an authority on human aging as James Birren quotes Lehman's book extensively and takes it at its face value in his chapter on productivity in *The Psychology of Aging*. The same cannot be said for Simone de Beauvoir, who refers to it in passing in *The Coming of Age*, accepting Lehman's comments on a handful of chemists, physicists, and inventors and then abrasively dismissing him in the following footnote: "Lehman's statistical method is utterly erroneous when it is applied to art and literature. In science it is easier to evaluate the number and value of the discoveries." Beauvoir's brilliant and penetrating mind, in a single cutting remark, goes at once to one of the central weaknesses of Lehman's whole study.

Lehman inevitably used many available major encyclopedias, dictionaries of biography, and histories of art, science, and literature as resource banks for the lives and accomplishments of famous creators. One approach is illustrative: In trying to determine when the single masterwork of a particular individual was produced, you first determine the pre-eminence of the work by the number of citations it has received in the appropriate resource books. Or you invite the opinions of colleagues at your own (in this case, Ohio State) university. The same "honorable mention" approach helps to identify the most creative period or half-decade, since Lehman divided his graphs into five-year periods.

However, because he was fascinated by the question of the "outstanding" work as indicating the peak, he became impaled time after time on the criteria of the masterpiece. Nonetheless, Lehman does seem to succeed in putting aside personal bias or canceling it out; and he has other merits.

He does not, for example, attempt to deliver some composite score on the age of peak of creativity, made up by sweeping together the top achievement ages of people of almost wholly different fields, but builds his "peak age periods" within each major field. Then, with an ultimately mesmeric effect, he tries to convince us that the summit age for creativity is virtually the same across almost all fields of human activity. Still, he is cautious enough to remind his readers, presumably pounded into acceptance by the deluge of data, that his "averages" are not the whole story—that in every creative category, numerous individual exceptions exist. So, what are his conclusions?

For Lehman, the peak period for the production of outstanding creative work is the half-decade between 30 and 35, closely followed by the half-decade between 35 and 40. Thereafter in all fields except "leadership" (in politics, diplomacy, finance, and the church, where the peak occurs later) there is a decline, usually a sharp one, broken in some fields by lower peaks in the 50s, sometimes, rarely, in the 60s. Lehman often presents additional broken-line graphs to indicate the line of production of works of lesser merit. These lines are often quite different from his main mountain-scopes. Lehman's interest in them is clearly minimal, although it is hard to see why, for example, the production of "510 contemporary orchestral works written by Americans between the years 1912 and 1932" is any less a barometer of age and achievement than "53 very superior orchestral works which have survived the test of time." In the case of the contemporary works, as it happens, the peak of a graph that looks like a profile of almost any range in the Rockies occurs in the 50s, and the next highest twin heights are in the 30s (Lehman's sacred period) and the late 60s.

Nothing escapes Lehman's Zeus-like eye and his ever-ready statistical techniques. At what half-decade did men (women hardly can get their heads in) produce their most important masterworks, not merely in physics, philosophy, and genetics, but in such heterogeneous fields of activity as hymn writing, treatises on education, money-making, movie-acting, eloquent orations, runs batted in in baseball, corn-husking championships, appointment to the American Supreme Court, and the composing of vocal solos? Throughout the whole book one dimly hears the hum of the dynamos set working to furnish this staggering accumulation of data and charts.

Throughout *Age and Achievement*, whatever the domain being analyzed, there on the mountain-chart of "outstanding works" is the almost inevitable peak rearing itself in the 30-to-40 period. However, when the dazed reader puts the book aside for a while and takes a stroll, or does whatever induces his or her creative analysis, some unsatisfied questions begin to rise.

For example, what does Lehman really mean by "creativity"? Incredibly, although he uses the word, and also the adjective "creative," hundreds of times throughout the book, he never defines them. What he really does is to perform an enormous statistical count and charting of years in which certain selected masterworks or master-actions appeared or were performed, and to equate this with the creative apex of the individuals mentioned. While it is true that most people would join Carl Rogers in wanting a product as evidence of creative power, this in no way dispenses with the fact that human beings can continue to be immensely creative thinkers even though they rarely publish—what do you do with the modern philosopher Wittgenstein, as one example? Or if by attentive, almost painful investigation of a large number of musical histories, you discover that Wagner's *Die Meistersinger* is rated 12 times out of 17 books listing "best-loved operas," you are to suppose that this opera was the creative "peak" for Wagner (if you can believe that, you can believe anything); or you find Leonardo's *The Virgin of the Rocks* listed as his one contribution to a naïve list of the 44 "possibly greatest paintings" of the world, painstakingly culled, of course, by checking lists of 1,684 oil paintings in art books and identifying those appearing ten times or more—not only are your criteria wide open to assault, but what were Wagner and Leonardo supposed to be doing with the rest of their "creative" lives? In fact, *Age and Achievement* gives us very few glimpses of the views of the actual creators, and those we have are, to say the least, off-putting.

The very people who should perhaps know more than anyone else about the peaks and valleys, the ebbs and flows of their own creative life—the creators themselves—never get a chance to speak at all. Our judgments of when the writers, scientists, inventors, painters, athletes, musicians, and statesmen achieved the "peak" of creative action are left to paragraph writers in encyclopedias or popular anthologies. Their verdicts are marshaled and counted by anonymous scrutineers in a healthy democratic exercise culminating in the placing of the masterwork in its appropriate half-decade for charting. Since many popular books dealing with the arts and with scientific discovery are highly redundant and simplistic, there is no special safeguard in collecting 17 of them, nor is the creator's "peak" of creativity guaranteed by inviting several university colleagues in separate rooms to identify his single masterwork.

There is probably one excellent approach to the whole question: to examine the life and work of a given number of noted creative people in various fields, including both their own views of their creative lives and those of their most comprehensive and discerning biographers, for example: Leslie Marchand on Byron, G. D. Painter on Proust, Aniela Jaffé on Jung. A review of the whole life is necessary, not just of the composition and production date of a single masterpiece.

In the rare instances in *Age and Achievement* where Lehman and his associates go so far as to mention human creators, one wonders where everybody has gone. For example, in Chapter 14, in a very fair effort to reinforce his point that "although man's creative achievements occur most often during the thirties,. . .any stereotyped conception of later maturity is quite untenable," Lehman provides a list of some 25 "older thinkers and great achievements." (He takes away the fragrance of this reluctantly offered flower, however, by prefacing it with a catalogue of dull things—largely recapitulative—which the elderly are "more likely to do.")

The omissions from Lehman's list of older thinkers and great achievements are grotesque: one can only conclude that someone not otherwise well equipped has been busy again with one of those confounded lists of "Two Hundred People Who Contributed to World Culture." Lehman's people, diligently searching through their pre-packaged lists and popular encyclopedias, had apparently never heard of William Butler Yeats, Robert Frost, Edith Sitwell, Saint-John Perse, André Maurois and Boris Pasternak; of Thomas Mann, Hermann Hesse, Tolstoy, and Kazantzakis; of Titian, Tintoretto, Claude Monet, and Picasso; of Henry Moore, Le Corbusier, Frank Lloyd Wright, and Inigo Jones; of Colette, Costain, Rose Macaulay, Wallace Stevens, and Rabindranath Tagore; of George Santayana, Alfred North Whitehead, Jacques Maritain, and François Mauriac; of Charles de Gaulle, Benedetto Croce, and Thomas Hobbes; of Auguste Piccard, Arthur Eddington, Lise Meitner, and Buffon; of Samuel Morse, Lee DeForest, and Gilbert Lewis; of Hieronymous Bosch, Wanda Landowska, Claudio Monteverdi, and Joseph Haydn; of Wyndham Lewis, Richard Burton, Ivy Compton-Burnett, and Shaw; of Charles Doughty, Henrik Ibsen, Henry James, and James Barrie; of Oliver Wendell Holmes, Thomas Jefferson, William Ewart Gladstone, Winston Churchill, and Kurt Adenauer; of Sophocles, Euripides, Claudel, and Voltaire; of Edith Wharton, Ellen Glasgow, William Hogarth, and Kathe Köllwitz; of Freud, Jung, William James, and Auguste Poulain; of Bruckner, Stravinsky, Schoenberg; of Delacroix, Goya, Donatello, and Max Ernst. This informal list of more than 70 Ulyssean names could be put together in an evening's reflection.

Even Lehman's very fair attempt to include more among his "older thinkers" who are scientists falls flat, since his list omits at least 165 of the noted scientists' names that turned up as Ulyssean in a small sub-study of mine, which is reported in the Appendix. From that study, which I entered on Lehman's terms, half expecting his thesis to have special force, I emerged startled by two undoubted facts: the continu-ing creativity of great numbers of scientists and mathematicians, and their longevity!

Lehman evidently meant to console his readers for the depressing effects of his main thesis, that "man's creative achievements occur most often during the thirties," notably in the sciences and in mathematics—a thesis that everyone seems to accept. In fact, no conso-lation is needed. Lehman works wholly with publications and pro-ducts, but it is naïve to suppose that these alone measure creativity, or that ultimate break-throughs are the only criteria. One cannot say, for example, that a scientist was "uncreative in his later years" simply be-cause his efforts to derive a satisfactory generalized field theory in as-trophysics did not solve the enigma: he may have shown brilliant cre-ative power in the assault without taking the bastion.

Writing about "creative output versus age" in *Physics Today* (July, 1975), Lawrence Cranberg of Austin, Texas, well defines the weakness of commentators who make easy generalizations about age and creativ-ity based on identification of so-called peak achievements. He writes:

> It is plain confusion to identify creative output, which may be readily defined in simple terms, with creativity, which is some-thing quite different, and is at least as hard to define and measure as intelligence, emotional maturity, integrity, and other personal-ity traits. . . .

And Cranberg concludes with the valuable comment:

> The role of reward and recognition systems may also be impor-tant in shaping the output curve. In this connection, it is interest-ing to compare the careers of Newton and Galileo.
>
> Newton, showered with honors, terminated his scientific ca-reer in his early forties. But Galileo, under house arrest to the end of his years for his challenges to the "establishment," continued his remarkable scientific career into his seventies.

It is impossible to conclude this commentary without referring to one other extremely interesting approach to creative powers in the life cycle—that of Wayne Dennis of Brooklyn College. In 1966 Dennis published a paper in the *Journal of Gerontology* entitled "Creative Pro-ductivity between the Ages of 20 and 80 Years." In it he used the Leh-man method of consulting various bibliographies, encyclopedias, and catalogues of scientists, writers, historians, philosophers, mathemati-cians, and musicians (for some unknown reason, he omitted artists). Otherwise his approach differed sharply from Lehman's, because Dennis was concerned with the peak or peaks of *productivity* of 738 persons, all of whom lived to age 79 or more. The governing factor in Dennis's study is described, oddly enough, almost at the end of the paper: "It is our view that no valid statements can be made concerning age and productivity except from longitudinal data involving no drop-outs due to death."

Using these ground rules, Dennis found that "the highest rate of output, in the case of nearly all groups, was reached in the 40s or soon thereafter." Productivity remained strong throughout the 50s in all categories except inventors and opera composers. In the case of these groups, the inventors were on a rising curve to their production peak in their 60s; opera composers were on a drastically dropping curve, which continued to fall through their 70s. Five categories reached their production peak in the 60s: historians, philosophers, botanists, inventors, and mathematicians. Other very strong producers in their 60s were "scholars," geologists, composers of chamber music, and novelists. Poets and biologists maintained something like a 65-70 percent production of their "best" decades, in each case the 40s. Sharply declining categories included architects, dramatists, and librettists. Chemists dropped in the 60s to about half their performance in the 40s, but recovered somewhat in the 70s.

In fact, in Dennis's study the 70s have a special fascination. Six categories continue as powerful producing groups: historians, philosophers, "scholars" (I quote the word because although Dennis is quite clear what he means by this category—English historians, English philosophers, and English scholars of Biblical, classical, and Oriental literature—I am at a loss to know how these persons differ from other scholars), botanists, inventors, and mathematicians. Three categories, all in science, continued through their 70s to produce half as many publications as in their "best" decade. Seven categories, all in the arts, fall off sharply in the 70s—the percentage of their best decade is indicated after the category: composers of chamber music (43), poets (40), novelists (24), composers of operas (16), architects and librettists (12 each), and dramatists (9). Even in these sharply declined groups, the production of poets, novelists, and composers of chamber music in the 70s is surely impressive.

Although Dennis was wholly concerned simply with discernible productivity, and not creative power as such, his data have some significant references to two important sectors of the whole discussion of the relationship between age and continuing achievement. First, productivity, even if defined as undifferentiated by quality, cannot be wholly divorced from quality. For example, if poets (who, unlike historians, cannot be accused of surrounding themselves in their 60s and 70s by cadres of research assistants) are still producing at about the level of 40 percent of their "best" producing decade, the 40s, there is no reason to believe that whatever they produce is second-rate. In fact, we have ample evidence to the contrary. Second, productivity has a great deal to tell us about the energy banks of adults in their later years. Since two factors that have nothing to do with "decline of intelligence" may be powerful inhibitors to creative production in the later and very late years—namely *loss of will* and *loss or diversion of energy*—this surprisingly strong series of production performances may have important messages to convey to all who, like the Ulysseans, wish to set out on new enterprises in their later years.

And what of the thrust to learn? Where are the records of creative action of those remarkable people, the later adults whose names are not found in "celebrated" lists; who in their late 50s, 60s, and 70s, and far older, cannot turn off their minds; who remain entranced by the wonder of the world; and whose later years make a mockery of the claim that the curve of the life journey is a simple hill with a summit at age 50 and a progressive decline thereafter? Who plots the curves of the lives of these creators whose creativity extends to dozens of domains never mentioned in the conventional studies of famous performers in the arts, sciences, politics, and invention?

The answer is that nobody plots them. Nobody does longitudinal studies of these fascinating human beings of all cultures, whose immensely varied creative adventures enrich their own lives and spur on by example the later-life exploits of others.

These Ulysseans have one thing in common: they are all seekers, and this is reflected in the trajectory of their lives. Some are chiefly thinkers and readers, adventurers in ideas, some chiefly doers, many are both. All are in pursuit of new enterprises for the mind, the body, or the spirit. The scale of the enterprises, whether large or small, is incidental; the thrust is outward, ever inquiring, searching, dreaming, *growing*—outward, not downward.[1]

Among these people is one group that so interested the adult educator Cyril Houle, of the University of Chicago, that he devoted a small but unforgettable study to the subject in his Knapp Lectures at the University of Wisconsin-Milwaukee in the spring of 1960. It is the self-compelled adult learners, who maintain their addictive activity throughout their whole lives, who fascinate Houle. Calling his report *The Inquiring Mind*, he asked a neglected question: In a world that "sometimes seeks to stress the pleasures of ignorance," what are the men and women like whose lives seem governed by the desire to learn, so that the act of learning "pervades" their existence? (Houle accepts the fact that all adults are affected at some points and to some degree by the desire to learn, that no one lives a permanently vegetative existence—if only because one "must occasionally learn how to be more like everyone else.")

Houle decided to base his inquiry on the responses of adult learners themselves—22 men and women selected in the first place because they had been identified by friends and colleagues as deeply and continuously engaged in all kinds of learning. His interest was not in older adults as such, although ten of the group were over age 50, and two of these over 65. The distributions of income and education were rather curious: 16 of the group were estimated to be from the lower-income groups, yet only four had less than high school graduation. All lived within a 75-mile radius of a great city (Chicago), and the responses to questions were obtained in the course of relaxed interviews of an average of a little over two hours in a quiet and congenial setting.

Houle found that his voracious learners could be divided into three categories. First were the goal-oriented—people who took courses or began self-directed study with "practical" or fairly clear-cut goals in mind: often a succession of short-term goals. Next, the activity-oriented—people who took part in courses and other group learning experiences for other reasons than the ostensible objectives of the course. And finally, the learning-oriented—people who pursued knowledge "for its own sake." The categories are best thought of as intersecting circles, one of which, however, represents an individual's chief orientation.

The *goal-oriented* are an obvious category: it is not their motivation but their unceasing persistence in pursuing goal after goal that gives them a special interest. An example of how goals can drive learning can be seen in the following case.* A woman, widowed for some time, begins to stir into new life after a passive period of sorrow. She has to make some kind of sense out of her husband's investments, and enrolls in an extension course in investment management for lay people. She finds the area about her home threatened by the cruder type of city developer and joins a group to make a confrontation. In doing so, she discovers the value of public speaking, and for the first time takes part in the public-speaking group of her women's club. Persuaded to accept office in the club, something she had never agreed to before, she finds as one office succeeds another that a knowledge of parliamentary procedure is useful, and studies this.

Inflation undermines her income from insurance and investments, so she decides to return if she can to the only professional field she has had, namely nursing. This involves not one but several "refresher" areas, since much has changed in the 20 years since she left nursing. Often very tired between the demands of the program and of her private life, she is tempted to just sit and watch television night after night for weeks on end—but that is not her lifestyle. She has the inner hunger of "the inquiring mind." Thus she takes up oil painting as a side activity. She keeps an easel always set up, not only because she finds

*This illustration is not Houle's; it is a composite portrait I made up from people in my own seminars; but it illustrates Houle's "goal-oriented" learning arena.

relaxation in painting, but because she loves small oils, cannot afford to buy them, and has found an acceptable talent of her own.

There is a travel plan for nursing employees where she works, and she can go on a charter trip to Spain, a country that has long intrigued her. She could go in a sealed and packaged group without the pains of contact with a foreign language and strange people—but that is not for her. Her goal is to savor the country, to sense something of what it means to be Spanish, to try to get the feel of Spain. So she enrolls in a group at the nearby university who for one winter are studying Spanish life and language. The trip, her studies of the preceding winter, and the contacts made both then and later remind her of how little access anyone in her community and city has to the arts, music, and culture of Spain. There are, for example, no authentic shops. She thinks, "Suppose I could start a very small charming one in a good accessible location. But then I know nothing about how you import things. Where can I find out? Who would know? I must find out—" Thus a new goal appears, clear, practical, one of dozens in her life, and seemingly with no connection whatever with her earlier adventures in public speaking and the refresher courses for nurses.

The *activity-oriented* people, like the goal-oriented, pursue learning activities continually throughout most or all of their adult years, but their motivations are complex and indirect by comparison. Personal loneliness may drive many of them into learning groups. One woman remarked tensely to the interviewer that she wished adult educators would start "selling cordiality or something," that she and others like her would "learn anything," but the world was drab, and what they sought was "the real joy of participation." Or the deeper motive may be the search for a husband or wife; escape from the frictions and unhappiness of a bad marriage, from the claustrophobic atmosphere generated by a demanding elderly parent, or from a monotonous or unpleasant regular job. Or, it may be, for a more unusual reason, because family tradition dictates that one must be seen to be growth-oriented and progressive. Houle supplies the delightful illustration from John P. Marquand's *The Late George Apley* of Apley's collecting Chinese bronzes, not because he liked them, but because he felt compelled in his position to collect something.

Houle does not make the point, but there is some peril that the so-called *"activity-oriented"* will be viewed judgmentally by adult educators and other watchers of the scene as being less serious or "less well motivated" (whatever that means) than the other two categories. But in fact one can make a strong case out of exactly the opposite position: *almost any reason that induces people to begin and to continue learning is a good reason*—so crucial is learning to the process of successful living.

The third major category, the *learning-oriented* people, clearly entrance Houle, as they would anyone interested in human beings as learners. Searching for a terse description of what motivates these remarkable people, Houle adapts Juvenal's famous phrase, *cacoethes scribendi* ("the itch to write") changing it to *cacoethes studendi* ("the itch to learn"). Thus, a 38-year-old skilled laborer in an automobile assembly plant, the son of poorly educated parents who was himself forced by poverty to leave high school, describes how from childhood he was an avid reader. Reading was more important than any of the usual activities of boyhood. No one discouraged him at home. His father, with a grade-three education, had trained himself to be a critical newspaper reader and zealous conversationalist; his mother, much less fond of reading, still indulged the boy, who would "roller-skate twenty blocks to the library, and back." Sleeping in a bedroom just behind the elevated tracks, he would read until he fell asleep. When awakened by the screech of a passing train, "I'd read until I couldn't fight off sleep any more. Then I'd wake up at dawn and reach under the bed and get the book and read again. I always went everywhere with a book, always, my whole life." Yet this book-addicted father of four children was a participant in his union, in many courses, in the YMCA, in *active* listening to FM radio, in personal social life. He thought that he was regarded as a "character"; people seem to think you must study only for a purpose that you can "see, feel, touch," and that "a dollar must come out of it." But he, long ago pursuing his personal adventures in three fields, philosophy, history, and economics, can only describe this governing passion of his life in this way: "All I can say is, negatively, there was no one to discourage me and positively I always enjoyed it. The more I fed my appetite, the greater my appetite became."

The joy of learning: this appears over and over again among the responses of the learning-oriented. It appears in a wonderful interview in the Houle study, that of a 60-year-old woman, the only black respondent in the group. She had been abandoned at birth, had had little schooling and a life full of hardship. Yet listen to this: "When Billy was a baby in his carriage I used to take him out. I used to go up to the University that's built up on a knoll and right in the back of this knoll there is the hall where the lectures are held. Well, I used to sit in there and listen to all those lectures. . . .even when he got to be three or four years old. I still went up there, but I taught him that he must be very quiet. He could take his toys or he could take a book, but he must be very quiet. We were never molested; we were never told not to come there." No wonder that Cyril Houle compares her to Jude the Obscure in Hardy's novel, the untutored handsome working youth who longed to enroll in classes at Christminster (read Oxbridge) a hundred years ago, but whose small and timid efforts to make connections with some don or official never succeeded. This extraordinary woman was endowed with the *joy* of learning, as well as the hunger.

The question of social controls over an individual's efforts to break into new worlds of growth and learning is one of concern to those older adults who want to live their lives as Ulysseans. Many older adult couples and single people find themselves still locked into certain regimens, styles, and protocols by the social group they have come to identify as their "circle"—more locked in, in fact, because the hammer of the years has riveted everyone concerned more immovably to a structure that is accepted as being as indestructible as the pyramids.

In his paper delivered to the Syracuse University Conference in 1962, Raymond Kuhlen describes the case of an intelligent American couple in their later years who have to make what turns out to be the quite unpleasant decision whether to discontinue Saturday bridge-games that have come to be considered the criterion of their friendship in and for the "circle"—a group unbroken for a number of years—or to take on new learning adventures that will entail living out of town some weekends. They choose the new adventures of the mind, but the decision leaves a trail of wounded feelings and alienations.

Similarly, Houle mentions one of his respondents, "a financially successful 50-year-old merchant" who described in detail how he made a similar break with acquaintances of many years: "You take your drinks, you eat your hors d'oeuvres, you have a fine dinner, and just about the time you are enjoying your dessert, somebody says the card games are about to start. Well, you sit down with three people. Any conversation is taboo. If you hear a funny remark or if something occurs to you and you say it, well, you're squabbled at, and so forth. I know some of the leading businessmen and lawyers in this town and all I know about them is that they either bid a strong no trump or a weak no trump. And I have been putting up with that for years. This year I just said to heck with them. I don't go to them anymore. It just isn't my kettle of fish. It's caused a lot of comment."

Lest anyone think this is an American phenomenon, he might do well to spend a year or two in, say, a community hotel of a small Canadian city. Here he will find flourishing and seemingly indestructible the institutional dance—this Saturday the insurance executives, next Saturday the local regiment, following that the Chamber of Commerce, and so on. Most of these, if not all, are attended by the same set of solid citizens; there are inevitably other people according to the purpose of the occasion, but they are incidental. Substantially the same group is there, a large group, engaging in a ritual as mandatory as fire and rain dances, only far more frequent and far less poetic. One young professional man, fond of reading and not fond of dances, told me that once, going up to his room, he met a group of these people and heard the comment, "There he goes, with his book," followed by a trail of guffaws and titters.

Obviously, there is nothing wrong with dancing—it can be one of the dozens of delightful channels to the Ulyssean life, especially for those who have been too shy until later life to try it. There is a great deal wrong, however, when any social group activity acts as a powerful counter-control, ranging pleasure routines against new adventures of mind, body, and spirit.

Cyril Houle devotes a fascinating section of his study of avid adult learners to ways and means by which they can build their own environments of support for learning. They can, he says, form or join what he calls "enclaves." The choice of word is exceedingly apt, since it is defined *(Concise Oxford Dictionary)* as "territory surrounded by foreign dominion." Enclaves can be of many easily recognized types: a whole family devoted to the idea of the individual growth of each as he or she wishes; an extension seminar held regularly throughout much of the year; a study group in a women's club; a university campus. However, Houle cites a type of enclave not easily recognized, one deliberately fashioned by a group of individuals to help sustain mutual learning under normally adverse conditions. For example, a group of young servicemen at a naval base in the South Pacific who had become bored to death with the unvarying routines and shop talk of service life kept meeting informally to discuss questions about life in general ("The other fellows thought we were nuts. I mean, why worry about these things?"). Of absorbing interest in this case is the fact that the young men themselves were curious about why they were like this. They found nothing but diversity in their backgrounds except for this strange hunger to pursue the enigmas of existence in the midst of a highly routinized and socially mandated life. Houle also usefully cites Benjamin Franklin's famous JUNTO or club of mutual improvement, in which every member agreed to contribute topics and essays for discussion on *"any subject he pleased."*

Older adult men and women can enjoy in enclaves, if they only wish to, the best of a Janus-like experience with the mind—looking backward at the best of their heritage to draw strength and compassion from it, but also looking forward to the still marvelous potentials of the species to which they belong. Why are so few adults in their 50s and older to be found in the ranks of the Futurists, the name given in our time to the slim ranks of those people whose chief passion it is to look into the creative possibilities of tomorrow? This is excellent "enclave" territory.

A small circle of adults could, for example, include in their program Douglas Leiterman's film, *The Machine City,* which is a reminder that cities of the future can be so designed as to preserve and advance the human grouping of people and their access to earth, sea, and sun, although the models look like the cities of a science fiction novel. Comparable films for 16-millimetre machines are available at manageable costs to groups of older adults, and nearby schools and colleges may make a film projector available to groups enterprising enough to ask. Likewise, in almost any area architects can be found who are only too glad to describe the work and significance of Futurists like Le

Corbusier, Doxiadis, or Frank Lloyd Wright—but who asks them? And why on earth are there not many TV "enclaves"?*

To live the Ulyssean life is to live the kind of life that believes in the Second Chance, and, for that matter, the Third Chance and the Fourth Chance. Few phrases in the English language are sadder than that which runs through the conversations of many older adults: "I always wanted to be a lawyer or a physician, or a teacher, or an architect, or a farmer, or a nurse, or a journalist. To the tough question: "Well, why didn't you?" there are usually a dozen good answers: no money at the time, no outside incentives, no certainty of one's talent, too early a marriage, older people to care for, no useful guidance, tried but the selection process was too rough, too old to apply, too many family responsibilities and problems, too eccentric an idea unless one is young. (Few seem to think that certain long-held and unfulfilled ambitions could in fact have been built on an illusion.)

Yet extraordinary people among the more than 15 percent of the population in our time who are over 55 have made later adulthood the arena of the Second Chance. There are relatively few of them, but the fact that they exist is proof enough that the Second Chance is possible, and that high potentialities abound among older adults although they require nerve and stamina to exploit them. The meteorologist who becomes a priest, the retired educator who becomes a lawyer, the insurance agent who becomes a teacher, the advertising man who becomes a social worker, the editor who becomes a psychologist—all of these and many other cases testify to two notable qualities among these adventurers. First, they think (correctly so) that they can learn competently and produce richly despite their age; and second, they are prepared to take on the pleasure and possible pains of learning in a group.

A justified euphoria exists among adult educators about self-directed, or what I call "solo" learning—in many respects it does indeed foretell the climate of the future. However, no one, young or old, achieves graduation for a degree, diploma, or certificate without a great deal of participation in lectures, seminars, symposiums, group tutorials, often laboratories or clinical sessions—all involving groups at work. Strong trends exist in certain fields of learning to develop indi-

*When an international conference on ekistics was held in Toronto in April, 1975, the program was well announced as dealing with challenges of the future in the area of the development of great city areas or megalopolises and environments of tomorrow. The assembled cast of expert commentators was impressive: Margaret Mead, Buckminster Fuller, Marshall McLuhan, and other noted scholars were available for a week of discussion. The public were invited to attend all the sessions without charge, and to take part from time to time in the discussion. At the coffee breaks, the delegates mingled easily with those of the public who attended. Few in the age groups 60 and over took advantage of this invitation, although the final afternoon of the seminar, Mead, Fuller, McLuhan (themselves Ulysseans), and others engaged in a wide-ranging summation debate that was so exciting that one left the hall with one's pulses throbbing. Where were the enclaves of older adults who might have attended this seminal experience?

vidual contracts and projects in the midst of group activities to encourage the self-education of students and to replace the sometimes intimidating group tests at the end of the semester or year with small tests more sensitively adjusted to the needs and growth of the individual—even self-testing to an extent. No matter; these excellent innovations in more tailor-made learning are still set in spheres of group or class instruction.

This scene of groups and tests has an important influence on the extent to which older adults, finding time they never had before, and at least the stirrings of hope that they can still seize the Second Chance, will in fact enroll in formal learning activities and will then maintain their studies.

People who take naturally to all kinds of learning, group and solo, may well have difficulty grasping the reluctance of older adults to reenroll after they have been away from formal learning groups for many years. They may be hindered by memories of unsuccessful or unpleasant experiences in classes at school and college. They may make the fine resolution to resume or begin studies in some form, only to find (or to think they find, which in effect is the same thing) a certain indifference and coldness on the part of the institution to older adult students. Dale L. Hiestand, in his excellent *Changing Careers after 35*, found that there was a variety of attitudes among American institutions toward enrolling full-time and part-time adults over the age of 35 and that admissions policies *within* the universities were very uneven. Nor were all instructors attuned to adult learners.

Incredible though it may seem, cases still exist of university departments advertising for "adult learners" while at the same time including in their rosters of instructors people who have little interest and less skill in teaching mature men and women. It is to be hoped that where this occurs the adult students will take swift and courteous action to obtain the teaching they deserve.

One perception of the nervousness of some faculty and officials of universities and colleges about older adult students was put forward at the Syracuse Conference of 1961 by the psychologist Kenneth Benne. He noted that three populations ordinarily inhabit the universities: the largely semi-cultured group of undergraduates, who are viewed as being in the process of being "civilised"; then the graduate students who are much cherished—Benne compares them to the acolytes of priests. Then, says Benne, there are those strange unclassifiable carpetbaggers who come in from the alien world outside the university, and return to work and live therein day after day. These are really disturbing intruders. Their adulthood and its experiences and expertise constitute standing challenges, even if largely silent, to the special world of the dons.

Thus, when men or women in their 50s or older decide to pursue the Second Chance, they may have a mixed reaction from those university officers whose decisions make the adventure possible or not. Some remarkable universities have long been open to older adults, especially in part-time evening and summer credit work; and others are becoming increasingly so, perhaps spurred on more by dropping undergraduate enrollments than by a high-hearted confidence in the creativity of the later years. University extension *non*credit offerings, of which there are thousands in North America, are without prejudice to age.

Many older adults who have little experience in group discussion and reporting, or who feel, as well they may, that at 65 they are marching to a different drummer from the numerous 30-year-old people in the class, may at first have feelings of shyness nad reticence. Then in a great majority of cases, something splendid happens. They find that they are readily accepted simply as people by their class colleagues, and notably by the delightful types of young adults who enroll in these groups. This is the experience reported by the Toronto Ulyssean R. G. (Dick) Frampton, a retired postal worker of very limited education in his youth, who at 67, after the death of his wife, sought and got permission to enroll in a first-year English course at Victoria University, Toronto. He found almost 50 years separating him from the other members of his large class! He continues his studies with zest toward the B.A. degree.

Adults who have decided that one of their Ulyssean adventures will be to resume formal degree or diploma studies might do well to try the temperature of the water first by taking a particularly congenial class or seminar as "special students" on any topic that excites them. Something else may be wise: to make a personal stocktaking of formal assets and deficits in recommencing formal studies. This would include a look at speed of reading comprehension, a check and "tuning-up" of grasp of vocabulary, using some of the stimulating exercises and resources available to expand it; some analyses of strengths and weaknesses in writing; and some of the ways and means to the most productive and efficient study habits. Many adults bring to a resumption of studies rich personal resources in powers of selection, in insights, in capacity for hard work, in stamina, in the repertory of ways to confront discouragement and failure. Nonetheless, in these circumstances a personal inventory is surely at least as helpful as for a lone yachtsman carefully checking his equipment and his physical readiness before he sets out on a transworld odyssey.

In a thorough report (1971) financed by the Canada Council of the number and nature of part-time bachelor degree students in Ontario universities (David A. A. Stager, director) asking "Who are the part-time students?" the late 20s (age 25-plus) and the 30s together contributed almost 59 percent of the total; the 40s, over 13 percent; and the category "50 or more," only 4 percent. Although the breakdown for age 60 and over is not given, it is fair to assume that it was almost nonexistent. This is of *degree* studies. Yet at Carleton University, Ottawa, in 1981-82, no fewer than 15 students aged 80 and over were enrolled in studies for a degree!

Some trailbreaker institutions have made splendid beginnings. As far back as 1965 the University of Kentucky, aided by the Donovan Foundation, began to provide scholarships for full-time study toward a degree by adults 65 and over. They have to be demonstrably capable of taking on university work, and physically healthy. Often married couples come together. Such pioneer ventures in degree credit education for later-age adults have led by the 1980s to the widespread practice of permitting men and women at age 65-plus to enroll without fees or for nominal fees in credit courses of their choice—obviously usually introductory courses first. A fascinating development in terms of its potential for the continuing study of older adults is the Open University in Great Britain, which began operations in January, 1971.[2] Here is a people's university, organized on a home-study basis with a network of various learning channels distributed throughout England, Scotland, and Wales, with outlets in Northern Ireland. There are no admission requirements, the assumption being that adults who are serious enough to come forward to register for studies that will occupy them for a minimum of ten hours a week, and will require in addition attendance at a short annual summer school, are already motivated people with a good deal of life experience behind them. In addition, they are assumed to be readers and in some degree self-directed learners, whatever their field of interest.

An adult enrolling in the Open University for what are called their "foundation courses" is provided with a study guide for each course, a timetable, correspondence study assistance, schedules for the TV and radio broadcast lectures that are another essential component of the scheme, and of course lists of required books. He or she studies much of the time alone, some of the time in groups organized at regional study centres, where the students also meet professors from nearby universities who are assigned to assist them. At the study centres the students can obtain counseling and break the monotony of solo study, which can be one of the frustrations of correspondence and TV-radio broadcast teaching. Library resources are uneven: lists of necessary books are mailed by the Open University to all public libraries, but these themselves may vary in available funds and in the size of their collections. Fees are required, and the Open University expects to be paid, as its stiff language on the subject makes plain. There are no fee exemptions for older adults. At the same time, there are no restrictions because of age, except, curiously enough, for the young!—people under 21 are not usually encouraged to enroll.

Meanwhile, a splendid world of *non*credit education has long been available in thousands of centres in Western society for adult people, including, of course, adults as old as you like. Leaving "skills" courses to one side (public speaking, dancing, cooking, better golf, motor mechanics, and so on), the titles of many of these courses seem inviting to anyone remotely interested in the growth of the mind. For example, "The Universe Around Us" (which was not expected at one university to attract 15 people, yet enrolled 117 adults on its first night, a dozen or more age 70 to 80-plus), "China Known and Unknown," "The Undiscovered Self," "Public Power and Individual Survival," "The Theory and Practice of Creativity," "Best-Selling Novels—A Social Phenomenon," and so on.

Older adults who sign up for and consistently attend the group meetings of a seminar on topics such as these participate in a delightful experience. Whatever tensions may be generated in credit courses by knowing that one must pass and even "do well" in essay-writing and tests, are absent in these noncredit situations where the objective is just to grow and learn in an encounter with a significant topic along with other interesting poeple who are fellow seekers. The encounter is important. There are other delights, of course—reading by oneself, clipping out stimulating material, watching and personally reacting to some of the occasional programs on television or radio that stretch the mind.

But later adults, like all adults, are "need-bearers"; and among their greatest needs are opportunities to express their individual ideas and to exchange insights with other adults who also have become enriched by life experience, and who look for a small, intimate, and fraternal forum. When an elderly woman in a "good" nursing home said desperately to a visitor, "If I can't get some good talk otherwise, I'll go down the corridor and knock on every door until I do," she was seeking something much greater than release from loneliness, and much more than "a chat." Bright and euipped with hundreds of ideas, insights, and compassions, she was searching for an opportunity to interact with other minds and lives. This is one of the precious values of extension education—and of all informal groups meeting regularly as "enclaves."

Short-term residence learning is one delightful route to these group experiences. The "Universities of the Third Age" (which began in Europe in 1965), the recent and valuable Elderhostel Movement in the United States and Canada, the Skills Exchanges, and many summer camps and schools open to or designed for adults in their middle and later years—all offer rich learning experiences at manageable costs. There are also other kinds of learning that the whole self achieves which come from man's eternal need to speak with, to argue with, to investigate, to touch, to encounter, to enjoy, to adventure with his or her fellow human beings. Not many Ulysseans begin and maintain their later-life voyages, small or great, wholly alone.

Still, in the 1980s we are living in a period of human history unsurpassed for adult relearning. Not only is this true of group education but of individual or "solo" or self-directed learning. A phenomenon of our times is the armies of adults age 50-plus who are enrolling in radio or

TV broadcast courses, in do-it-yourself adventures with kits, sets, and recordings, or, of course, in private study, pursuing some personal search or passion. Selective use of television is itself a powerful means of keeping mental powers alive, if the adult watcher plans his or her watching, keeps a looseleaf TV notebook handy, and integrates what the tube gives him with ongoing knowledge. No vidiots here! And, in fact, if Alvin Toffler is right and we are close to a learning society where adults may tune in to hundreds of individual learning TV channels—the horizons widen. It is as Bill Moyers has said of TV at its best: "an endless sea opens to the imagination."

In fact, in most households, rich and poor, there are guitars or other musical instruments, usually discarded, teaching materials on which dust gathers, do-it-yourself kits half used, wholly used, or never used; painting-by-numbers pictures hung up long ago and almost forgotten. These are really not melancholy facts of life. Man is a creature of "temporary systems," a prober, a tryer-out of things, an experimenter, a dabbler. For him to try and then abandon certain exercises is not a tragedy. Because he is fascinated by the changing kaleidoscope of life, he will often try to match himself somehow to the passing scene. The tragedy will come, however, if the end of his continuing voyage of self-discovery, of personal identity and verification, is "disgust and despair."

The extent to which adults quietly but continuously engage in solo or "self-directed" forms of learning particularly interests Allen Tough. In the course of some stimulating study reports on the subject, Tough notes how many thousands of unexpected job situations, community involvements, and unexpected but gripping personal demands and needs all set off what he calls "adult learning projects." Especially intriguing to him are what he calls "high learners," individuals who spend perhaps 2,000 hours a year at learning (not just operating) and who complete 15 or 20 different projects in one year. "In their lives," Tough writes, "learning is a central activity; such individuals are marked by extraordinary growth." In fact, Tough's "high learners" have close analogies with Maslow's "self-actualized" people, and with Cyril Houle's "learning-oriented" adults. The most moving quality about Tough's work so far is, not his theories about "high-learners," but his obvious delight in seeming to establish that in adult life, learning is a natural and continuing function.

This brings us back to a fundamental truth about human beings, well illustrated by an episode involving the great Dr. Samuel Johnson. On Saturday, July 30, 1763, Dr. Johnson and his friend and biographer, James Boswell, set out in a scull down the Thames to Greenwich with a young lad as their sculler. The conversation turned to the advantage, or otherwise, of studying Greek and Latin as part of a good education. (Johnson, of course, thought it essential.)

Boswell: "And yet, people go through the world very well, and carry on the business of life to good advantage, without learning. *Johnson:* "Why, Sir, that may be true in cases where learning cannot possibly be of any use; for instance, this boy rows us as well without learning as if he could sing the song of Orpheus to the Argonauts, who were the first sailors." He then called to the boy, "What would you give, my lad, to know about the Argonauts?" "Sir," (said the boy), "I would give what I have." Johnson was much pleased with his answer, and we gave him a double fare. Dr. Johnson then turning to me, "Sir," (said he), "a desire of knowledge is the natural feeling of mankind; and every human being, whose mind is not debauched, will be willing to give all that he has, to get knowledge."

If this is an overstatement, at least it is a magnificent one. But this still leaves unanswered a great problem: *the apparent abstention in huge numbers of adults in the later years from group-oriented and even self-organized activities that help maintain the growth of the mind and the continuing discovery and actualization of the self.*

One reason for this may be what Richard Bolles has well described as "the three boxes of life." He notes that typically in past decades people have been expected to perform in a "learning box" (ages 6-20), then in a "work box" (ages 20-60 ³), and finally in an adult "play box" (ages 60 or 65 on). If these are good human things—to learn, to work, to play—why, then, does not society provide for them *through life?* (Bolles calls such an arrangement "flexible life scheduling.") Why cannot we organize society so that even in youth, play and work alternate with learning; so also that in the middle years, to "take time out" for personal learning and physical renewal is expected in the system; and so that the late years would also be a mix of work, play, and learning? Instead, we have legions of older adults who enter their late years unequipped for anything but the life of drones—constantly repeating earlier routines and "killing time," that worst of expressions.

Perhaps here is another moment of truth. Repetition of experience, however reassuring or delightful it may be, is not usually learning. Taking up the collection and counting it every Sunday at church is commendable, but it is not learning; lawn bowling or curling for 30 years, although pleasurable, is not learning; playing the same piano pieces for 20 years, no matter how charming, is not learning. Fishing in the same brooks and bays for the same fish (sorry!) is not learning; chairing committees where one's own attitudes and those of one's colleagues are as predictable as the rising of the sun, is not learning; listening to *The Messiah* as one's inevitable musical treat at Easter for 35 years, and eschewing Bach's *The Passion According to St. Matthew* or Leonard Bernstein's *Mass*, is not learning. Participating in the same social, fraternal, organizational, academic, or political rituals for half of the life cycle is not learning; turning to the index of controversial books to confirm your long-held ideas, is not learning. Going only to nice movies that never involve one in thoughts of injustice, violence, anguish, and death is not learning; and neither is attending only films that deal with mayhem and sexual cruelty. Telling the same stories at age 72 as at age 42, no matter how they may continue to entrance the listeners, is not learning. We must be good to ourselves—that is a major obligation for the growth of the self—but learning is never a wholly comfortable business.

The Ulyssean is a man or woman who makes a step in a new direction at an age when the myth-dominated society expects him or her to continue in well-worn paths (and of course to keep steadily slowing down)—even if the Ulyssean step is at first hesitant, tentative, and very small. Alternatively, an older adult can be Ulyssean while remaining in a trajectory of performance established long ago, but which by its nature continually exposes him or her to new adventures and challenges of mind and spirit.

7

ULYSSEANS IN ACTION

ULYSSEANS come in every appearance, role, and characteristic, but their common trait is an irresistible desire to "drink life to the lees," as Tennyson's Ulysses puts it; or, in less dramatic language, to continue to grow, to make life a continuous series of explorations. This common and powerful motivation can be expressed, for example, by Ulysseans otherwise so different as an existential philosopher (Gabriel Marcel), a small-craft circumnavigator of the globe (Ben Carlin), and a blind teacher of the blind (Susan Miller).

Marcel, who died aged 83 in 1973 and was the founder of a French school of Roman Catholic existentialism, was also a literary critic, playwright, composer, and pianist. To him, life should be a matter of "passionate inquiry and of participation in whatever occurs." Man should not seek detachment from the world but "should consider himself an active participant." To Ben Carlin:

> . . .man is not made to go about being safe and comfortable and well fed and amused. Almost any man if you put the thing to him, not in words but in the shape of opportunities, will show that he knows as much. Against his interest, against his happiness, he is constantly being driven to do unreasonable things. Some force not himself impels him and go he must.

If this view gives a too idealistic picture of the state of readiness of all men and women in general, at least it well defines a Ulyssean trait. And in the down-to-earth clichés of everyday speech, Susan Miller, born blind 87 years ago, and an Associate in Music of the Royal Conservatory in Toronto whose devoted avocation in late life is weaving, advised in her 80s: "If you own a rocking chair. . .stay away from it. My plans for the future are to keep on going. The rocking chair doesn't fit in there."

Rocking chairs, which have certain charms of their own, and in which it is quite possible that creative ideas might be born, are nevertheless a very negative symbol among Ulysseans. This is because they usually immobilize the productive activity to which the Ulyssean life is devoted, whatever the scale. In fact, although the Ulyssean life can of course be developing in the deep self without outward signs, most of the time it is the productive or creative act that signals Ulyssean progress.

Of all the arenas in which Ulysseans perform in the modern world, none is more appropriate than that of the original Ulysses—the oceans and the seas. Consider, for example, the striking and (in North America) virtually unknown figure of Alain Gerbault, who died in 1941 at age 43. Gerbault is an exception among the numerous illustrations of Ulysseans in this book, in that he died well before he reached what we have defined as the Ulyssean age: but his lifestyle was so well marked and irreversible that it is possible to include him as a superb example of the Ulyssean type in action.

Gerbault was a man who seemed to bear with him something of the drama and tragedy of the time of the Greek gods. He survived the terrible war of 1914-18, in which many of his friends were lost, and after completing studies as a civil engineer went on to become an internationally recognized football player, bridge tournament star, and tennis champion of France. Society and the press sought him out; he had every attribute that attracts the attention, and often the adoration, of the French and European public, and for a time it looked as though he might become one of the enchanted circle of world tennis stars. Instead, at the height of his prospects, in April, 1924, Gerbault began a 17-year odyssey in a 39-foot English cutter, the *Firecrest*, built wholly of teak and oak, which was his only companion in the circumnavigation of the world, and in many other seaborne journeys.

Gerbault's choice was made not so much out of love for the sea, although that was also a powerful motivation, but because he was repelled by most of what he had already seen of modern urban and corporation life and the seeming inhumanity of men. Although he ranged the whole world, he was especially enchanted by the Polynesians and their islands. In Tahiti he met again the same types of French bureaucrats and would-be tycoons who had partly caused him to set out in quest of a new world in the first place. He was appalled at the vulgarization and defilement of Polynesian life by the arrogant imposition of Western commercial and tourist life, especially in Papeete and the more frequented and exploited islands of a once free and still beautiful people. He cared enough about this to abandon to some extent his personal renunciation of the French worlds of power and politics, and to try to use his considerable personal fame and influence to guarantee the preservation of Polynesian culture.

But these interventions could only be episodes in Gerbault's life—his *life* was his testament. He wrote: "Every man needs to find a peak, a mountain top, or a remote island of his own choosing that he reaches under his own power alone in his own good time." In fact, the Ulysseans never do find the ultimate haven, nor did Alain Gerbault: life is the haven—the quest is the fulfillment. Even physically, Gerbault had many adventures analogous to those of Ulysses. Among the

Pacific islands in a powerful gale his boat was sunk and he was almost literally left naked on the beach. He had to spend six weeks waiting among the hospitable Polynesians until help came, the *Firecrest* was refloated, and Gerbault put out again to sea. He had left Cannes in April, 1924; he returned to Cherbourg in July, 1929, having circled the globe. As usual, he was overwhelmed with praise and publicity. He was named a member of the *Légion d'honneur;* he could have remained a kept hero among the members of café society, but he was indifferent both to acclaim and to the seductions of the so-called smart set.

He continued to rove the world for the next 12 years, during which he wrote two enthralling books, published posthumously, *Flight of the Firecrest* and *In Quest of the Sun.* In the first book he says that he could have settled many times in one of the Polynesian islands, married, and raised a family in a kind of paradise. Like his prototype, Ulysses, who might have remained with Circe and Calypso or at the households of friendly kings, Gerbault was called back to the sea. He writes, "What demon is continually urging me back to the sea?"—and Charles A. Borden, in a brief account of Gerbault, in his fine book *Sea Quest,* says: "Sailing for Gerbault was part of a need for islands, remote anchorages, solitude, simple people; part of a positive need to wander and *a need for streaming in through the sense of new vistas and experiences.*" (Italics mine.) Although he sought solitude as Ulysses never did—one always thinks of Ulysses surrounded by comrades, in spite of periods of enforced loneliness—Gerbault was in no way alienated from mankind. He was alienated from those he conceived to be the dehumanizers of the human condition: the getters and go-getters of modern Styrofoam acquisitive society. For the many simple, deeply human people he met on his 100,000 miles of solitary cruising he had a tender communication and love. This revealed itself also in his passionate crusade on behalf of the preservation of the best of Polynesian culture.

Gerbault's death was appropriate to the nature of his life. Ill from malaria and alone on his boat in a Far Eastern Portuguese harbor, he was found and cared for until his death on December 16, 1941. He was buried on the lovely island of Bora Bora by the French Navy.

There is something especially moving about the sea exploits of those veritable Ulysseans who are supposed to be collecting their "golden age" cards, or at least to be relinquishing any exploits of physical stamina and intrepidity to the young. Consider the remarkable case of Eleanor Wilson, a 59-year-old missionary and pilot in the Marshall Islands who suddenly had to take over as skipper of the schooner *Morning Star VI*, which helped supply the islands and provided all kinds of religious services to the islanders.

When the schooner foundered in the hands of an experienced male captain, she took over the *Morning Star VI*, and remained a familiar figure in the South Seas. Eleanor Wilson had the training and the skill of a pilot, but to be the captain of a schooner with an all-male crew was an altogether different and far more demanding challenge. A woman captain in the islands was unheard of. (How common is it anywhere?) Nonetheless, as Charles Borden writes:

Sailing the rounds of her 500,000-square-mile parish, Skipper Wilson slept on a plank bunk, ate rice and beans with fish and an occasional can of bully beef, and ran a taut ship—one that "the Lord wouldn't be ashamed of" . . . Like most inter-island schooner skippers, she had her share of heavy weather and a few close calls among the coral atolls and the more than eleven hundred reefs and motus of the low, wind-swept Marshall archipelago. Scores of ships have been lost in the tricky currents, unmarked reefs, and sudden squalls of Micronesia. . . .

Everyone knows of the exploits of Sir Francis Chichester and Joshua Slocum. Scarcely anyone knows of the exploits of the extraordinary Tom Drake, whom Borden has rescued from oblivion in *Sea Quest*. Drake was an outgoing man who simply loved sea life better than life on land, and enjoyed people everywhere. Brought up on big ships, he made the personal choice to change his nautical career from that of captain of large brigs to the solitary sailing of his own schooner, the *Sir Francis*, which he lost in a Caribbean storm and replaced with the 35-foot *Pilgrim*. He was 65 and had had a stroke that left him lame in one hip when he sailed *Pilgrim* eastward across the Atlantic from Charleston to London, England, where his attempt to make a temporary docking at one of the more snobbish yacht clubs was rejected.

When at age 66 he lost the *Pilgrim*, this Ulyssean built a new schooner, the 37-foot *Progress*—the fourth schooner Drake had built for himself—and sailed 3,000 miles down the Pacific coast and over to Hawaii. When in a violent Pacific storm he broke one arm, Drake steered a long voyage home with his left hand. He cruised thousands of miles more in the *Progress*, a boat he had come to love: "She'll never fail me. I don't suppose many of you can understand this craving of mine for blue water, but you get mighty close to something big when you're alone at sea. At times I am lonely all right, but probably no more than an albatross or the North Star." At age 73, in November, 1936, this indomitable voyager left California from the Golden Gate to sail for the South Seas, and was never heard from again. Such a conclusion of a Ulyssean life is too poetically true to be tragic.

Sailing was virtually Drake's life. However, other older adults have been able to pursue conventional careers into the late years, and then—to everyone's surprise—become seafaring Ulysseans. For example, a retired army dentist and his wife, Bill and Gretchen Lee, cruised across the world in a 33-foot sloop, and then, with a dental office installed in a new boat, decided to sail to the remote settlements of the Bahamas. In 1966 John Goetzke, at age 72, completed a world circumnavigation during which he was at one time held captive for 39 days by pirates in the South Seas. A former engineer, Frank Casper, occupied his 60s by sailing on a leisurely schedule around the world—a voyage filled with colorful names: Tahiti, Pago Pago, the Cook Islands, Auckland, and Timor.

To launch out across oceans in a little craft, often alone, in one's later years may strike many people as exotic and eccentric—but at least everyone knows that there were ancient mariners and old pilots. On the other hand, the modern motorcycle is wholly identified with youth (often with brawling, delinquent youth), and it is seen as almost a sexual symbol of youthful adventure and power.

Is there any reason, however—aside from society's deeply grooved prejudices about the incapacity of older adults—why the domain of the motorcycle should be reserved for youth? John Pitt, age 62 in 1973, a resident of North Hatley, Quebec, a real estate appraiser by vocation, and a great-great-grandson of the eighteenth-century British Prime Minister William Pitt, thought not—and launched himself upon what was perhaps the most remarkable long-distance motorcycle saga in history.

Thirty years earlier, Pitt had been a daredevil rider of motorcycles at rodeos, so that he was indulging a longstanding passion. In fact, he had kept on riding them from time to time across the years. Yet this takes nothing away from his astounding feat of riding 32,000 miles in nine months to the fabled country of Tierra del Fuego, at the extreme tip of South America. He made the decision to do this one snowbound winter night, after reading a newspaper article about a family living on a sheep farm in Tierra del Fuego. He wrote and told them he would visit them.

John Pitt's itinerary took him down the east coast of the United States to North Carolina, across the South into Texas, down to Mexico, and then to Central America and Panama, where he took a small ship to Colombia. From there he went to Ecuador and Peru, and south on the coastal highway that skirts the lonely and magnificent beaches and dunes of the Pacific. After crossing the pampas of Argentina, and the Magellan Straits, he at last arrived, after three months, in Tierra del Fuego, 16,000 miles from his home in Quebec. Pitt's diary is filled with vivid accounts of the joys, hazards, and exploits of his astonishing journey.

To cross North America on modern transcontinental highways all the way, and without a passport, and to do so in one's early 60s, on a motorcycle, is exploit enough. But in John Pitt's odyssey, he had to negotiate whole networks of often badly maintained national highways, encounter successions of puzzled or surly customs guards or police, make dangerous portages or water crossings, and often sleep out night after night in wholly unfamiliar territory. His journal tells of a collision with a "huge white longhorn steer" looming out of the mist in Nicaragua, a collision that forced him to take an hour to reassemble himself and his machine in pouring rain with trucks going by; of nearly disappearing, motorcycle and all, in an oversized canoe struggling to take him and other passengers across stormy waters to a remote jungle village in Colombia (Pitt's motorcycle helmet saved the day as a bailing instrument); and threading his way, in pitch darkness, along the edges of mountain roads, with precipitous chasms below.

Pitt's odyssey even had its episode of romantic love. In the wake of a landslide across a highway in Argentina, he met a lovely Argentinian woman, a professor of history, half his age, to whom he became engaged and who joined him in North Hatley.

Mayra Scarborough, who in 1972 at the age of 57 began a journey on a Honda 450 motorcycle through all the United States and much of Canada, was, unlike John Pitt, a total amateur in the motorcycle world. Her mission, she told the Canadian columnist Lotta Dempsey, was to mark the two hundredth anniversary of the American Revolution by presenting special flags to the governors of all 50 states. A professional librarian, Mayra Scarborough after age 50 obtained a diploma in librarianship and took a job with a pharmaceutical company. She then learned how to fly.

But why the motorcycle? Mrs. Scarborough makes clear that her choice of this unconventional vehicle for adults grew out of a love-hate relationship. She strongly disapproved of her young daughter's buying one; urged her to to give it up as much too dangerous; then one day could not resist trying the machine out herself. Her only mishap came at that point—she slipped when standing *beside* the bike and broke her collar bone! But after that, Mrs. Scarborough entered a new world hitherto bizarre to her—trans-continental motorcycling. By June, 1974, she had traveled 34,000 miles of her safari, moving along at speeds of up to 80 miles an hour and often camping out.

Dr. Jack Wilmore, a physician at the University of California, who was conducting studies to determine what can be expected as the outer limits of physical fitness for older people, reported in October, 1971, that he had discovered what he termed "a 73-year-old superman—a superman for his age" who had the walk of a teen-ager and "a heart so strong that he can run the mile in 6½ minutes." The subject of Wilmore's study, Noel Johnson, a retired aerospace executive, had developed his own physical formula for a long life: Eat at least 12 times a day and run over 150 miles a week!

Meanwhile, in Great Britain, on May 6, 1973, the *Sunday Express* reported the story of surely one of the most remarkable late-life athletes in the world. Duncan MacLean was a first-class international sprinter in 1904, when he ran 100 yards in 9.9 seconds. In 1973 MacLean was aged 88 and was still regularly timed as running the 100-yard distance in 14 seconds (and the 100 metres in 14.6 seconds). In Toronto, in August 1975, at the age of 90, MacLean ran the 200-metre dash in 49.2 seconds at the World Masters Championships for men over 40. This was 4.5 seconds slower than the gold-medal winner, Fritz Schreiber of

Sweden. "MacLean was not even perspiring or out of breath minutes after the race," wrote reporter Bob Koen. He wanted to take on Schreiber again! Like many Ulysseans, MacLean had returned to an early love after a long career in a totally different medium. Born in Scotland and brought up in South Africa, where he became the country's champion amateur sprinter, he returned to Britain and became a professional music hall artist for nearly 50 years, at one time understudying Sir Harry Lauder. Since MacLean and his fellow competitors had to pay their own way to the Masters Championships (about £150 each) MacLean raised £100 of the amount by appearing on a television show. And his diet, that endless enigma of the students of creative and zestful old age? MacLean remarked: "The secret of keeping fit is in having the right physical and mental outlook. I don't smoke and I eat very sparingly. I have no special diet, except that I never touch fried food. And I don't mind a drop of liquor now and again." He was still active at 95, in 1981, when his life ended.

Another remarkable older Ulyssean athlete is Herman Smith-Johannsen, honored in February, 1975, at age 99 as the Dubonnet "skier of the year." Tributes at the New York gathering in his honor named him as "Viking of the century," and in Lowell Thomas's phrase, "the world's most famous skier"—Thomas, himself a CBS news commentator at 83, was a frequent skiing companion of Smith-Johannsen.

Smith-Johannsen lives in a small bungalow in the Laurentian hills of Quebec at Piedmont, and each morning goes out alone for a five-mile run. In the afternoon he skis four more miles to pick up his mail. He "works up a good sweat," then settles by the fire with a pipe and a glass of beer. His life has had Ulyssean features before: for example, his attempt to enlist in the Canadian Army ski troops at age 64 in 1940 (he was turned down). Among his secrets for maintaining his athletic schedule and his trim physique, he cites "the ability to keep from worrying and *a will to live.*"

The exploits of women in athletics in the later years are rarely disclosed and are presumably far fewer than men's because of traditional lifestyles. There is now, however, a Women's Masters Tournament in track and field, and the exploits of a number of aviatrixes also remind us of the usually unreleased potentials of women. A remarkable example of a Canadian Ulyssean woman is Helen Brunton, who in 1976-77 at age 72 backpacked around the world. Brunton is a cultured and vivacious former university librarian, who, after her husband's death, raised three boys and then found herself faced with what to do next. One of her answers was to go to London, England, where she discovered the Explorers' Club. She signed up for a tour of Europe and found herself in a large group of 30-year-olds who, she reported, "seemed surprised" to be joined by a 72-year-old woman. However, they readily accepted this warm-spirited older comrade. The following year she joined a group backpacking around the world! Returned to Canada, she joined the Ulyssean Society of Toronto, and found herself the centre of media attention, as a result of her exploit. (Brunton's "backpack" which is a feminine rose color, contains, among essentials, a party gown!) She has since backpacked to Alaska and South America, and at 78 in addition to her trips, she is a devoted concert- and play-goer, gourmet cook, and avid searcher of new leads turned up in the course of her wide reading.

For me a most extraordinary example of the woman Ulyssean in physical achievement was the Toronto centenarian Louise Tandy Murch. A professional teacher of voice and piano, Louise Murch considered her last 30 years "the most productive of her life." After shattering her hip at 75, she rejected a doctor's verdict that she would never walk again; after two years of struggle, she not only walked again without crutches but at age 90 took up yoga. She worked out every day in spite of steel pins in both hips, inserted there after a second fall and broken hip at age 94. Her astonished interviewer, Bob Pennington, of the *Toronto Star,* noted that Louise Murch could easily do waist bends and put her palms on the floor, do the routine of bicycling with legs raised, and various yoga exercises.

Louise Murch's whole old age, until her death in 1978, was Ulyssean. Her long-sustained good health, other than the accidents, was a foundation, but her vitality, love of people, eagerness for new experiences, and openness to the future meant that in Robert Peck's terms, she had reinvested herself in life and made great age seem almost incidental. She gave concerts to groups of older people and community college students, accompanying a young singer, Paul Schillaci, whom she coached and who said about her, wonderingly: "You have only to meet Louise to change your entire idea about old age." And he added, significantly: "Many of the older folks we entertain are 20 to 30 years younger than Louise—yet many of them look sad and defeated, reconciled to being old and acting old."

There was no television set in Louise Murch's home. She played the piano for an hour daily, entertained a great deal, did her own baking, welcomed people of all ages who came to see her when they themselves were depressed or lonely. She periodically flew off to Arizona or other places where her three sons live. And as a yoga expert and late-life believer in the joy of the body, she took care to include in her diet a ration of brewer's yeast, cod liver oil, lecithin, and vitamins B and E—and always whole wheat bread.

There continues to be something beautiful and deeply meaningful in the actions and results of the older adult who takes as one form of the Ulyssean adventure the loving care of the body and the faith in it that can vitalize his or her own late years and serve to inspire younger people.

Yet, in spite of the fitness and jogging fads, all too few older adults take advantage of health clubs and spas, although they would be welcome. Some regularly swim; a number (mostly men) fish and hunt; a substantial group of older executives continue to play golf, often for business contacts rather than self-actualization; a few play tennis. Both men and women in their later years continue to curl in Canada, the northern United States, and Scotland; a few continue to do so into the very late years. Both men and women lawn-bowl, a beneficial sport that takes players out into the open air and onto the green grass on a summer evening. Shuffleboard is the game of sea voyagers and of elderly adults—even the name has a geriatric sound.

At all events, we should not just stand around, mouth agape, gazing at the Douglas MacLeans, Noel Johnsons, and Louise Murchs; we should also make physical activity in late human life part of our own Ulyssean experiments, on whatever scale.

Ulysseans of all types share one quality that is an accompaniment of much creative activity in the later years—the quality of deathless childhood: of the child to whom the "incongruous" or the "odd" is intriguing and delightful. If this trait were not present, it is doubtful whether many or perhaps any of the adventures would take place.

Picasso, throughout his immensely long and continuously creative life, seemed to have always retained something of the outlook and nature of the entranced and entrancing child. This accounts for much of the freshness and virtuosity that propelled him on to new styles and experiments in painting and sculpture; but it also appeared in continual glimpses of his personality. When Alexander Liberman visited Picasso for lengthy interviews, the artist was, successively, age 68, 72, and 73. Nonetheless, Liberman's description of their meetings is filled with references to Picasso's childlike qualities or to the way the world of childhood somehow intervened. Thus, when Picasso was expecting some Spanish visitors at his villa on the Mediterranean coast at Vallauris: "He decided to get up and dress—in a polka-dotted blue shirt and wide, baggy shorts. With his extremely large head, this short, stocky man seemed like a young boy dressed in his father's clothes. There was a feeling of youth and at the same time of age. . ."

These might seem to be Liberman's subjective impressions, but then the visitors arrived, and: "The great man walked from one to the other, always with an expression of childish amazement and wonder. He seemed to be surprised at everything—delighted, pleasant, and anxious to put his guests at ease. Time seemed to be of no importance." When the group were ready to go somewhere to eat (no decision had been made),

Skira put on a Tyrolean green hat. It amused Picasso so much that Skira gave it to him. He immediately put it on and looked at himself in the mirror delightedly. He has a need, a sort of childish desire, to take and to get inside other people's possessions. . .He put the hat on and never took it off until we got to the restaurant. This had made his day. The new toy had made possible a new transformation of himself.

And when later Picasso's son Paolo amused him with a variety of antics, Liberman remarks: "Picasso liked clowns."

Passing through a succession of studios, Picasso opened the door to an immense room crowded with sculpture.

A little girl skipping rope was made out of wine baskets. In a corner, a perambulator, made of junk-pile discards, seemed to rock with the weight of a comic-strip baby. This man was playing, trying through play to recapture the innocence of childhood vision, trying through humour to bridge the gulf of years and purge himself of his sophistication. Picasso loves and needs to be near children.

Liberman remarks on the "countless toys" Picasso made for his own children (he was a father at 64 and again when past 70), such experiences "enriching him and transferring to him some of the energy of youth," and he concludes: "His agile, playful mind needs such amusement. The sense of humour, the sense of theatre, the childish delight in play are underlying qualities in many artists. Maybe one dares more under the excuse of play: the creative act becomes less pompous and self-conscious."

This quality of the curious, wondering, and delighted child—furthermore, the child exuberantly showing off, or plunging incautiously into some enchanting project—is typical of many other men and women whose creativity continues to flourish through their later years. In Maurice Goudeket's recollections of his Ulyssean wife, the French novelist Colette, many vignettes of the sensitive and responsive child appear—the creative child whom no number of contacts with the sophisticated and synthetic world of adult protocols nor the sorrows and pain of old age could destroy. Colette's intense and moving empathy with animals was one evidence of this.

Her spontaneous employment of the senses was that of the child to whom the world is new and filled with wonders. Thus, after her third and at last deeply happy marriage, to Maurice Goudeket, in April, 1935, when she was already 62 (and he 44) they lunched at a country inn, and "on our way home, between two sunny intervals, snow began to fall, snow with large flakes of dazzling whiteness. Colette asked me to stop the car and got down to receive this impalpable manna rapturously on her face." Goudeket adds that Colette could never recall the date of her wedding, being usually forgetful of anniversaries, but "she always remembered that springtime snow, to the point of speaking of it eleven years later in *L'Etoile Vesper*."

Colette's reactions to the worlds encountered by her senses were unimprisoned by the usual accumulation of adult postures and defences.

Compare the behavior of this enchanted child, as described by Gou-deket, with the restrained and well-bred demeanor with which we ordinarily walk about and formally observe and comment when visiting gardens:

> Her way of making contact with things was through all her senses. It was not enough for her to look at them, she had to sniff and taste them. When she went into a garden she did not know, I would say to her: "I suppose you are going to eat it, as usual." And it was extraordinary to see her setting to work, full of haste and eagerness. . . She separated the sepals of flowers, examined them, smelled them for a long time, crumpled the leaves, chewed them, licked the poisonous berries and the deadly mushrooms, pondering intensely over everything she had smelt and tasted. Insects received almost the same treatment, they were felt and listened to and questioned. She attracted bees and wasps, letting them alight on her hands, and scratching their backs. "They like that," she would exclaim.

Yet, Colette's fresh childlike empathy with nature in no manner lowered her empathy for human nature. She remains among the small circle of the most penetrating and compassionate observers of human beings to appear in the past century.

There is another aspect in which the child appears in the later creative years of Ulyssean adults—in the plunging of one's self into enterprises that delight the mind and warm the heart, without sensibly and cautiously measuring the costs in advance. "A mature person," we say, "would never have got involved like that": but then the "mature person" would never have acted at all. Ulyssean people and exploits can be born, and beautifully so, from among slide rules and balance sheets, but this is not their natural milieu. It would have been more mature for the *chanteuse* Josephine Baker to have adopted only three or four foster children when she was about 50, instead of filling a large villa near Paris with a dozen or so of these lively young human beings from several racial cultures as an eloquent symbol to the world of the need for all men to love one another. Because of her impetuous humanity, Baker was for years in difficulty with landlords and creditors and a variety of authorities—still, her action was a great action. Its intrepidity contributed to its splendor, and the element of the child that contributed to it may well also have been one of the sources of the singer's astonishing success in continuing as a fine performer up to her death at 69 in 1975.

Elements of what Eric Berne called the "OK-Child" also account for the remarkable ability of Ulyssean adults to abandon old rubrics, to take on new roles, to engage in new ventures, large or small, to try to acquire new skills, to branch off from established paths. Consider

Hella Hesse, a remarkable mother of five sons, a 71-year-old Canadian widow and hospital administrator.

Exiled from childhood on by war and revolution, first from Russia and then from Germany, Hella Hesse finally found herself an exile in Canada in 1959. Her husband had been a political prisoner of the Soviets, and had died in Europe before he was able to help his family in Canada. She and her young sons took every kind of job to stay alive. Mrs. Hesse worked as a hospital kitchen maid and dishwasher, a floor housekeeper in a Bermuda luxury hotel, and, after taking correspondence courses was accepted as the executive housekeeper of a hospital in British Columbia. She was by then 61, and her sons had become young men with responsible posts. Hella Hesse might well have finished her days in comparative calm and security in the British Columbia hospital job.

Instead, "to the amazement of my sons," she told Bob Pennington of the *Toronto Star*, she applied to a number of international agencies for service abroad. The first to reply was CUSO (Canadian University Service Overseas), and the work offered was health administration in Nigeria.* "My sons were startled to see the old lady giving up her job and setting out for another continent, but I'd always wanted to volunteer for an international agency." She thereupon found herself administering one 40-bed district hospital, a rural health centre, and ten dispensaries—work so extensive that during her 1973 furlough in Canada four different people replaced her. She did not view herself as a heaven-sent messenger bringing light to a less developed country, although of course she could see the value of her technical skill. On the contrary, for Hella Hesse the Western world had much to learn from the African people: "The cultural wealth and social attitudes of the African people are healthier and more mature than our own. There is much to learn from Nigeria in its refusal to segregate old people and its absolute acceptance and integration of all generations."

Another striking illustration of a Ulyssean at work on the international scene is Welthy Honsinger Fisher, an extraordinary American woman. I met her briefly at a symposium in Toronto in October, 1969, when she was on a furlough as president of the World Literacy Movement, centred in India. She was then 89 years of age, and already celebrated in special circles: for example, in adult education, for having established Literacy Village near Lucknow, from which thousands of

*The neglected list of older women serving overseas may well be a very long one. Many, of course, join their husbands in CUSO or American Peace Corps projects, making up first-rate teams. However, there is a special quality to the stories of solitary women who, like Hesse and Welthy Fisher, and like Dorothy Schick, the *Ulyssean Newsletter* editor, take on lonely odysseys abroad. Schick, at 64, in 1972 went for four years to Ghana to teach English as a second language. A former university official, she was the only Western woman in an area of 400 square miles. She returned to take up renewed university studies and to help cofound the Ulyssean Society.

teachers have gone out to provide chances for lifelong learning among enormous numbers of illiterate people. I was one of a group of academic men and women who waited for her to appear at a little afternoon reception and tea; almost no one had met her, and we expected to see a bright but fragile old lady leaning on someone's arm. Instead, a remarkable figure entered the room, alone, erect, and poised, handsome and imposing but without pretension, a woman one would turn to look at again. She was dressed gracefully in a sari, and in everything she said her mind was clearly full of India, and of the Third World; yet to speak with her was to feel her intimate interest in people simply as people.

Seven years before, she had published a personal memoir, *To Light a Candle*, which had gone into eight printings and which described at least four lives of Welthy Honsinger Fisher: the girl and young woman who might have been a first-rate concert singer and perhaps an opera singer; the missionary teacher in China with a host of colorful experiences; the wife and companion across 400,000 miles, of an American Methodist bishop, Frederick Bohn Fisher, with whom she worked and traveled throughout India; and then the Ulyssean life, which began about age 60, after the bishop's death.

Because of her love for her husband and her intense companionship with him, Welthy Fisher was extremely lonely. Since she had married late, at age 44, her family consisted of her adopted Chinese daughter and her husband and a little Chinese grandchild, and these comforted her. She was made a lay preacher of the Methodist Church and a deaconess; she tried to take up the conventional parish work of these roles, but they neither eased her loneliness nor met the demands of what she calls her "undiminished energy." The fact was that something Ulyssean was waiting for her. She felt this instinctively, enough to decide to go around the world, "with no basic reason than to find nothing but myself." When she reached India she fulfilled a vow and scattered her husband's ashes at sunrise on the great slopes of the Himalayas. That day she made an entry in her journal, one of the refuges from her loneliness: "Oh God, help me to keep my sanity and not to live in the past, for I am sure Bohn is still living in the future, as he always did here." The entry epitomized the openness of spirit of this 60-year-old widow to new experiences and to the Ulyssean way.

The subsequent years did not yield their special treasure easily. Welthy Fisher found a young American woman as a companion in new enterprises, one of them the renting of a houseboat in Kashmir where she hoped to settle down and write (this proved impossible), and on shopping and travel excursions meant to be joyful. The effort to be carefree was in a way Ulyssean, but it was not enough for Welthy Fisher. For a number of years she continued her "seminars," as she called them, studying educational systems in Mexico, South America, and the whole Middle East—almost parenthetically she recounts how at age 70 she broke her knee and was on crutches for the whole of her journey through Greece, Lebanon, Syria, Iran, Iraq, Jordan, and Israel. She also learned to speak and read Hindustani, something she had long put off in the busy and exciting years before her husband's death.

The signal for the ultimate Ulyssean adventure was provided in 1948 in a personal interview with Gandhi six weeks before his death: "As we parted he took my hands and said, 'When you come back to live in India, go to the villages and help them. India is the village.' It was several years before the message was fully decoded by the steady accumulation of events in Welthy Fisher's life. In 1952 an invitation came from Allahabad to help train teachers in villages to instruct illiterates. This, as it turned out, was the special Ulyssean treasure. Within a few years she planned and built a ten-acre village, the now celebrated Literacy Village, which opened with the support of American funds, wholly deeded over to Indian ownership at Welthy Fisher's insistence. A new and powerful force had been launched in the world as a result of the energy and zest for tomorrow of this remarkable widow already far into her 70s. Remarkable—still, intensely human, as when she stood shaking at the news that there were cobras in her garden, and when in search of a famous English architect now living in the foothills, she found herself compelled to cross a raging river on a temporary footbridge with a slippery rope railing ("clinging to the improvised railing, I set one foot ahead of the other and prayed").

Openness to experience: As a wise European-born Ulyssean friend of mine remarks, one of the most important phrases in life is, "You never can tell." Life from time to time delivers unexpected reverses and disasters, but it also delivers unanticipated achievements and adventures—sometimes, as in the case of the Ulysseans, whole new sectors of life. Thus Welthy Fisher, mourning and lonely for her husband at age 60, in no way anticipated Literacy Village, which did not begin to materialize until she was 72.

Similarly, Pablo Casals in his mid-50s could have had no inkling that he would spend the last 37 years of his life in exile from Spain; nor that in addition he would become almost a sublime figure of political and human freedom; that he would found the Prades Festival, the school and festival in Puerto Rico; that he would become the deeply beloved and admired maestro every summer of the Marlboro Festival in Vermont; and that at an advanced age he would marry a lovely young woman whose companionship illuminated his last years.

Among the Ulysseans openness to experience means openness to new experiments. This includes the creative life, even where that life has been long productive and successful. Thus two modern performers in the arts who died recently at advanced ages—Jacques Lipchitz, the sculptor, at age 81, and Edward Steichen, the photographer, at 94—were both described in their lengthy *New York Times* obituaries as being twice-born—but in each case these were Ulyssean adults who continued to create works that showed the perpetual odyssey of their spirits. They were twice-born in the sense that at least once in their careers they made epoch-making conversions of their artistic lives or their styles. Lipchitz, from being a brilliant early *avant-garde* sculptor, a cubist who never lost what one critic has called "the syntax of cubism," turned his greatest energies to what the same critic has called "the mythological, monumental works. . .that would be capable of sustaining the grandeur and eloquence that haunted him."

Steichen, a painter, became a photographer of such imagination and perception that he transformed photography into a fine art. In his old age he remained as productive and creative as ever, although he could have stroked himself with the innumerable tributes paid to him as the founder of a modern art form. He could have joined the circle of very old men flattered and consoled by endless honorific citations and testimonials. Instead, when a party was given for him at the Plaza Hotel in New York on his ninetieth birthday in 1969, Steichen took the floor to say:

> When I first became interested in photography, I thought it was the whole cheese. My idea was to have it recognized as one of the fine arts. Today I don't give a hoot in hell about that. The mission of photography is to explain man to man and each man to himself. And that is no mean function. Man is the most complicated thing on earth, and also as naive as a tender plant.

Perhaps practitioners of the arts, professional or amateur, in their later years are wise (or fortunate) because they have provided the self with an arena of unusual potentiality for maintaining zest of life and creativity. One example among many has been the American dancer and choreographer Martha Graham. Her life and work, especially in her latest major dances, performed in New York in May, 1973, are powerful examples of how the arts make fruitful the self in the late years, and the self the arts. What is exciting about Graham is not just that she continued to dance commandingly and beautifully with her young company until her retirement at 75. Now it is Graham the choreographer in old age who is exciting. She seeks to find and to express the divine synthesis of the creative self and the deep inner self, and to ally them with what she calls "the surge of life." Her response to the criticism that by emphasizing pelvic movement in her dancers she created a sexual emphasis to many of her ballets (she has composed nearly 150 of them) has been to say: "You have to take life as it surges through you, and sex is part of it."

No wonder it was possible for Graham to tell the newspapers, "I've just entered a new cycle of energy. I'm going through a rebirth—with anything artistic, one must die to be reborn." One of the dances dealt, suitably enough, with the figure of Ulysses; the other, *Mendicants of Evening*, interpreted Saint-John Perse's magnificent poem, "Chronicle." Some conception of the searching, radiant creativity of its chore-ographer at 79 can be seen in her program notes for the four *pas de deux:*

> In the first *pas de deux*, a couple has an erotic encounter ("Divine turbulence be ours. . .") in which the flesh meets but the spirits clash. In the second, the spirits are in harmony, the flesh cool; in the third, the couple oscillates between tenderness and violence. Everything is resolved by the last duet ("We are herdsmen of the future"), as spirit and flesh are integrated, the movements marked by soaring lifts, like birds freed.

A Ulyssean achievement—yet when Martha Graham felt she had to take the decision to retire from dancing, the crisis was almost more than she could bear. Ulyssean decisions are often difficult. What restored her and maintained the surge of life was her almost equally deep love for the art of choreography.

Thus, what the lively arts do for those who participate in them as professionals or amateurs in their later years is clearly to permit the reinvestment of the self in new adventures—where the process of self-discovery is continuous. For an example of an amateur artist and Ulyssean in action, I turn to my own personal journal, and an entry for November 15, 1973. (The entry is necessarily abbreviated.)

> In a pelting rainstorm at about the hour of 4:15, I arrive at the home of the noted Canadian Germanic studies scholar and writer on Goethe, Barker Fairley. . . .
> I look with pleased curiosity at this "later adult" (to put it mildly)—he tells me he is 86—and hear with astonishment the accents of Arthur Lismer's Yorkshire. Fairley is marvelously youthful—not only in his alertness (he also hears well, but seemingly has to strain occasionally), but in his whole appearance and walk. He swims every day, he tells me, at the Hart House pool.
> Noting my wet state, Fairley invites me to the kitchen to make a choice among the drinks. We return to the living room, where small oils hang everywhere, sip our brandy, and consider together the important question: from what sources and by what means has Barker Fairley kept himself across eight and one-half decades a productive and creative human being?
> Fairley's chief claim to Ulysseanism lies with his painting, which he first took up, he tells me, at 45. He remarks drily, "I was supposed to be able to do nothing in art from the age of 7 on, and so they told me—and I believed them" (we had a short burning digression on the damage done by these pedagogical fiats of God).
> At 45 he began to paint because his University of Toronto colleague, Robert Finch, the poet and English scholar, insisted that

he should: "Why can't you?" Finch asked, and the next Sunday morning brought paints and easel and put them into my hands. I gave breakfast to Finch and his friends, and hoped it would rain." It did not rain, and Fairley at 45 began the career in painting which was to bring him a separate distinction from his main career. . . .

In his 60s, Fairley added portraiture to his landscape painting. Again a "happy accident" had delivered to him in London, England, the English portrait painter, Barbara Niven. To Fairley's protests that he could never hope to do portraits, she responded matter-of-factly, "Try a head," and shoved both the opportunity and the materials at him. "I've painted heads ever since.". . .

By now a younger artist friend of Fairley had come in for tea. As we talked, I tried out on him my anecdote about the Toronto publisher brooding over his "daily" loss of neurons. Fairley frowned slightly, and said emphatically, "I never think of it. I live as much outside myself as possible, obeying the outside impulses."

It was now 6 p.m., a good time to end the first visit of what might become a friendship. Still, I managed one more question. Fairley obviously was still a reader; new books dotted the living-room, and there was evidence that he had been into them. But what of music? "There's a stereo around the corner," evidently with quite a few records at hand. It turned out that Fairley's passion is Handel.

My host shook my hand warmly at the door and urged me to return any time I wished. . . .

It is still raining as I go out into the street, but now the rain seems warm and hospitable. I am enchanted.

This remarkable Ulyssean man, by opting for life, not only fills his own path with light but the paths of younger adults to whom his great age is not a barrier but a bridge. In Fairley's case, the painting that is the central motif of his late years is also the force that provides him with a special circle of younger friends who, along with older companions help him to externalize his thoughts and maintain his creative engagement with life.*

Another interesting example of a man who made painting a late second career is Lachlan MacLean Morrison, a former Ontario civil servant. At 70 he exhibited a collection of 22 oils in a Toronto gallery, all of the paintings done during the previous two years in bars and taverns where Morrison finds the people who fill his canvases. Morrison, who for health reasons cannot drink himself, and who has a severe hearing impairment that shuts out most of the noise of the bar, makes his

*At 94 he still appears weekly in the dining circle of the Faculty Club of the University of Toronto, and exhibits new canvases regularly.

sketches there and then paints his subjects on masonite or board back at his tiny studio. Kay Kritzwiser in the *Globe and Mail* brings out strikingly the way in which routine can be allied with Ulyssean adventures. She writes of Morrison and his wife Helen:

> The pattern of the Morrisons' days is predictable. "We watch television until perhaps 10 o'clock," his wife said. "Then Lauchie gets into a pair of old paint-stained pajamas and comes into this corner of the kitchenette." He sets up an ordinary stepladder with a small table nearby. The current painting hangs on hooks on the stepladder. He mixes his oils in old egg cartons, tries out his colours on an age-worn palette, then gets to work. At daylight, he goes to bed. "And I can't wait to come out into the kitchen to see what he's accomplished in the night," his wife said.

The late emergence of an artistic talent can occur in settings and arenas unbelievably different from the scholarly backgrounds and the glowing tea hours of retired professors. Clementine Hunter is a black painter, age 96, living in her birthplace, Natchitoches, Louisiana. Hers is the saga of a Ulyssean adult who did not put brush to canvas until she was over age 60, yet within a few years had the pleasure of seeing Edward Steichen choose one of her paintings "to illustrate an essay he wrote on the meaning of a picture—the inner vision—which sets it apart as a work of art." (The quotation is from a perceptive interview by Mary Gibson, in *Family Circle* Magazine, August, 1973.) Clementine Hunter had no formal education; she was a farmhand, picking cotton, then a worker at the Melrose Plantation in the Cane River county of Louisiana. One evening, according to the writer and critic François Mignon, who was then a guest at the plantation, Clementine Hunter simply appeared at his door with several tubes of used oil paints which she had discovered, and announced that she, too, could "mark a picture." Mignon said, "When I told her to keep the paints, I never dreamed of the talent that was about to be released. At dawn the very next day, she returned with her first picture, a vivid primitive scene. Her talent was unmistakable and exciting."

Yet Hunter's talent had been unactualized for 60 years! She has now achieved a certain modest fame, and she is still—35 years after that summer evening—vigorously producing still lifes, primitives, glowing flower studies, and murals. Mary Gibson's report describes her "standing straight-limbed and proud in a pert blue-flowered dress with big beaded blue earrings, very much a model for her own paintings." She lives in her small house close to the Melrose grounds, chopping her own wood, planting her own garden. Perhaps the earthy simplicity of her life contributes to the vivid humanity that is found all through her painting.

Whether they produce the Ulyssean adult or not, the arts have of course provided a therapy for older adults in times of critical strain or crisis. Thus, Eric McLean, music critic of the *Montreal Star*, tells how the aunt of one of his friends, "a lady in her sixties who was going through a period of deep depression, was persuaded to take up the recorder." McLean goes on to narrate how growing interest in the instrument led to the restoration of the woman's health and morale. Renewal through individual use of the recorder led also to a reawakening of social involvements: "Now blooming in her early seventies, she is an enthusiastic joiner-in with groups of amateur musicians." In fact, she had achieved a Ulyssean victory.

McLean writes with a sympathy rare among professionals in the musical world on the subject of frustrated would-be learners of instruments who cannot seem to find anything tailor-made for them except music appreciation courses at the conservatories: "We know that the eager but embarrassed forty-year-old is looking for a place to address himself for guidance where he will not find himself, like a doltish Li'l Abner, sitting in the midst of a passle of twelve-year-olds." He cites with enthusiasm the English industrialist W. W. Cobbett as an example of finding oneself in one of the arts (in this case music) in late adulthood. Cobbett was born in 1847 in Blackheath, England, and made a fortune as the founder and chairman of the Scandinavia Belting Company. After retiring at age 60, he devoted the next 30 years of his life to chamber music, offering prizes for competitions, and scholarships for talented musicians. Cobbett had long been an amateur musician, but dedicating his whole life to it from the ages of 60 to 90 was Ulyssean. Besides, in his 70s he began the considerable adventure of attempting to compile an encyclopedia of chamber music, which in fact he published in two volumes as the *Cyclopedic Survey of Chamber Music* when he was 82. Cobbett found that taking part in chamber music recitals renewed him, and he put forward an unusual argument for the advantages of playing a musical instrument as against painting or writing:

> The movements of brush and pen are imperceptible, but to play a violin means constant vibration in every nerve and fibre of the body, and it is this vibration which gives to chamber music practice the therapeutic value of which, I may add, my medical friends are all convinced. . . .I am not exceptionally robust, but the considerable strain involved in three hours' strenuous playing of quartets and sonatas not only leaves me unfatigued, but with a greater sense of buoyancy when the last note is heard than when the first note was sounded.

Whatever else was true of the writer of this statement, *writing in his 80s,* he had achieved something far beyond successful personal therapy from the arts. He had achieved a major Ulyssean adventure in his life at age 60, and enlarged it in his 70s so that by age 90, when Cobbett reached "the Happy Isles," he could look back on a long odyssey that was in effect almost another life.

So varied are the approaches to the Ulyssean life, and so diverse are the personalities of those adults who qualify as Ulyssean, that it is difficult to compose a catalogue of their characteristics as, for example, Abraham Maslow did for his "self-actualized adults." Perhaps this is the way it should be: Maslow locked himself into too specified a description of the self-actualized person. For example, could a person not be highly *self*-actualized at 60 although his life violated half of Maslow's 14 desired traits reflecting self-actualization, provided that special creative powers and dynamics of the personality flooded him with energy and the capacity to grow?

Frank Barron recognized this problem when, as a research psychologist he became fascinated with the question of what made, in his words, "delightful normal people" tick. Barron studied a substantial sample and emerged with a catalogue of characteristics. He also noted that at a conference of psychotherapists and psychologists dealing with the "goals of psychotherapy," there was a considerable consensus on what were the characteristics of a "psychologically healthy human being."

The most commonly mentioned traits were: (1) accuracy of perception of reality; (2) stable body functioning and freedom from psychosomatic disorders; (3) absence of hostility and anxiety; (4) capacity for friendly and cooperative relations; (5) spontaneity and warmth; and (6) social responsibility. Barron listened, he tells us, "in comfort and mild edification" until there drifted across his mind the images of a dozen great creators who not only lacked a number of these qualities or skills, but had some quite opposite characteristics—yet was it possible simply to dismiss them or classify them as psychologically unhealthy? His own list of traits discovered in the delightful young people in his own study seemed too pat to him. Nor did his own studies seem to confirm L. S. Kubie's thesis that neurosis only inhibits, never promotes, creativity.

If Ulyssean people from many different arenas could come together to observe one another and to exchange experiences, the whole scene might confirm how difficult it is to devise some formula for the Ulyssean life and personality. Some would seem "self-actualized," in Maslow's terms; others would seem to have deficiencies of personality; some would be flooded with success; others confronted with huge reverses of fortune; some would be in radiant health, others almost immobilized.

Not surprisingly, there are Ulysseans who seem light-years apart in their approaches to self-growth—a fundamental criterion. Thus, Bernard Berenson, the most noted art critic of the twentieth century, was at the very end of his life still engaged in a search for the deeper meanings of the self—this might be called an inland, or inward, odyssey.

The journals he kept from age 88 to 93 are enthralling, and show Berenson in full possession of his powers. He records many impressions of visitors to his villa in Italy, as well as external events; but it is the adventure of his ideas and insights that lends excitement to these late-life entries. Likewise, Carl Jung, at age 80, and aided by Aniela Jaffé as transcriber, composed one of the most unusual autobiographies, *Memories, Dreams and Reflections*, ever recorded, devoted chiefly to Jung's extraordinary experiences in the revelatory world of dreams. Jung compares himself to a mountaineer moving among the awesome ranges and abysses of the inner mysterious self. His course was a psychodynamic odyssey with its own excitements, dangers, encounters, and rewards.

Seemingly poles apart from these probers of the *inner* self are the Ulyssean adults who attach themselves to social and political causes heavily involving the *persona*, the *public* self, which can be seen to respond and to change in various ways.

Bertrand Russell is perhaps the most notable modern example of such an externalized Ulyssean. Russell fulfilled Simone de Beauvoir's exhortation to the very old that they should attach themselves to passionate and burning causes. In his massive autobiography, which he completed only a few years before his death at age 97 in 1970, Russell defined the inner flames that had burned undimmed through his life: "Three passions, simple but overwhelmingly strong, have governed my life: the longing for love, the search for knowledge, and unbearable pity for the suffering of mankind." And how did he feel he had fared, as he reviewed his enormously long life? He felt, he said, that only one yearning—the yearning for love—had been fully satisfied, and this only when he was 80 and married to his fourth wife, Edith Finch, a 52-year-old American. He felt that he had achieved "a little" of knowledge, "not much"; while as for assuagement of his "unbearable pity" for mankind's suffering, he wrote:

Echoes of cries of pain reverberate in my heart. Children in famine, victims tortured by oppressors, helpless old people (a hated burden for their sons), and a whole world of loneliness, poverty, and pain make a mockery of what human life should be. I long to alleviate this evil but I cannot, and I too suffer.

He suffered, but he also knew joy throughout his life. He had remained open to experience (young people always thronged around him); he had grown continuously; he had been creative as both a thinker and a writer, and as a leader of causes, often intensely unpopular (he organized the highly biased International Peace Court at Stockholm in 1967, and was, of course, accused by his critics of being "senile"). He had lived, not one life, but seven or eight—as mathematician, philosopher, leader of social and political causes, prolific writer, exponent of sexual freedom, educator, conversationalist, a friend of an extraordinary circle of people extending from Alfred Tennyson to Graham Green and Jean-Paul Sartre.

Russell's life splendidly presented the qualities of creative performance and of growth-of-self as shown in *both* the contemplative and the intensely socially active Ulyssean adult. Vivid examples exist, however, of a type of later-life performer much further removed from the introspective worlds of Berenson, Jung, and Gide, and closer to what Beauvoir meant when she suggested that older adults can be galvanized by passionate causes. A remarkable example was provided by the Canadian public health physician, Gordon Anderson Bates, described with understandable excitement by the columnist Sidney Katz of the *Toronto Star* in March, 1971, when Bates was 85.

Bates had been a crusader all his life, and had gained early attention as a young physician in heading a movement for legislation to control venereal disease. He was still Director of the Health League of Canada when he finally died at age 94! Almost 60 years later, with the VD problem again resurgent in the country, Bates added it to the list of situations that must be reviewed with the objective of developing new strategies and defences.

The passion of his attachment to his various causes was precisely what Beauvoir was talking about. Thus, when Bates noted that few among the perhaps more than 150,000 victims of Parkinson's Disease in Canada could obtain L-dopa, a new and potent drug to help control the disease, he felt hot indignation and he was not interested in preserving medical niceties and protocols. Katz reported that Bates's blue eyes "blazed with indignation" as he said, "The specialists, like neurologists, are narrow-minded. They think they're the only ones skilled enough to administer L-dopa. And the general practitioners are apparently uninformed, ill-informed, or apathetic." Constant badgering of physicians, hospitals, and government health agencies had led, Bates reported, to one important gain: the University of Toronto medical students were now taught how to use L-dopa in future practice.

Bates had explosive views about the silly custom in present-day society that retirement should occur by at least age 65. His response to a question by Katz about his own retirement was heated: "Retire? Never! A person can keep going as long as he wants to. I'll never quit. I'm working 15 hours a day. Look at the things I have to do! And indeed he was not short of personal projects and professional causes. At 75 Bates flew to Paris, lived with a Parisian family, attended a Sorbonne course, and learned French. He returned to Canada to form the Alliance Canadien and to join half-a-dozen French-language clubs in Toronto. He drove around in a bright yellow Packard touring car, custom-built for the Prince of Wales when the future Edward VIII visited his Alberta ranch in the 1920s.

Needless to say, this veteran of many past health crusades—to fluoridate water, to pasteurize milk, to compel immunization for diphtheria, and in general to support the forces of preventive medicine—was intensely interested in the extension not only of the working life but of life itself. He studied reports from Russia on the large numbers of enormously long-lived people near the Caspian Sea, and checked further with Paul Dudley White, the noted American heart specialist who visited some of the Georgian communities, and decided that the secret of longevity lay in a simple, abstemious life, nonpolluted air, no retirement, and maintenance of an even temper and an optimistic disposition. Bates told Sidney Katz that he himself neither smoked or drank, ate lightly with the emphasis on nonfat protein foods, walked a mile a day, and usually went to bed by 11 P.M. Bates was then able to work out an analogy with the famous Thomas Parr, a 156-year-old wonder still living at the time of Charles I, who (if one can believe it) is alleged to have subsisted throughout his life on cottage cheese, dry bread, and water. Parr, according to Dr. Bates's account, was taken as an exhibit to the King's court in London where he was plentifully supplied with meat, pastries, and wine. "Parr didn't last long after that," Bates told Sidney Katz, presumably with relish.

The sustained, passionate devotion to a cause galvanizes late adults in many political and social arenas, some of them in positions of great power. For example, the astonishing Chou En-lai fascinated Mark Gayn, the Canadian journalist, when he interviewed Chou, then 72, in 1971. Gayn, an able and tough observer of the modern People's Republic of China, was the last person to be taken in by postures and façades. He was enchanted with the premier: "He still looked indestructible—lean, erect, physically fit, intellectually dazzling. The interview ran for more than three hours, but he showed no signs of fatigue." Gayn was struck by the probing curiosity and agility of Chou's mind.

This also was the impression of the Australian-born Harvard professor, Ross Terrill, who met Chou in 1972. Terrill was very much aware that he was meeting one of three or four major architects of a titanic revolution in which, by the nature of revolutions, millions of people had died in order to achieve the desired rebirth. Terrill did not overlook the tough expression, the steely eyes: "from a side angle, a rather flat nose takes away all his fierceness. The mouth is low in the face and set forward tautly, giving a grim grandeur to the whole appearance." Terrill was clearly impressed by the formidable power of Chou's presence—yet his chief impression was one of the premier's youthful resilience in manner and speech: "Recalling his amazing career over half a century, I marvelled at his freshness."

Chou, incidentally, had for years broken the pious convention that the proper time for older adults to go to sleep is about 11 P.M. He himself worked until 4 or 5 A.M. and then slept until midmorning. Any sleeping arrangement in the later years is good if it accords with the individual body chemistry and the cultural lifestyle of the person. For example, older adults who live in or near great cities and who love classical music can hear hours of splendid recordings hitherto unknown to them played from midnight on through the channels of certain FM stations. An unpleasant illustration of a violation of individual needs is the nursing home regulation demanding "lights out" at 11 P.M. or earlier, as though the inhabitants were children and as though they had no individual preferences. (One home considered it an outrage that a vigorous old man wanted to shower at 11 P.M.) These are, of course, the institutions that provide no books, no wine, no facilities for growth. They are matched by the spouse who insists on identical sleeping schedules for his or her partner in marriage. With the obvious exception of physical emergencies, and with the provision that 11 P.M. sleepers also have rights, later-life adults in general need, not "lights out," but *lights on*, with more music, more conversation, more loving company, more zestful talk about the uncreated things in the great world, many more small personal odysseys. And more working schedules for those who, like Chou En-lai, cherish the hours after midnight.

Passionate causes have a way of being associated with "great" leaders and "great" issues, as though the world of human values and achievements were all slide rules and weighing scales. In fact, a cause involving human rights and the preservation of beauty and civilization is just as splendid when played out in a tiny arena. What might perhaps be called "confrontative democracy" in our time is producing more and more men and women in their later years who lead or take part in movements or demonstrations designed to confront dehumanized bureaucrats or so-called "developers" where there is a need to protect and advance human needs and rights. None of these groups excludes older adults; sometimes the older adults exclude themselves. These groups are usually weak and need support, and adults in late maturity who are open to experience are valuable because their commitment is not confused with having to fight Father at the same time, as is the case with some of the revolutionary young.

A late photograph taken of the crusading American novelist, Upton Sinclair, when he was nearly 90, shows a face marked by age, but so radiant with a youthful smile that one cannot look at it without a lift of the spirit. Here is seen the ever-renewed self of a man who not only helped right certain terrible national evils with his early novels (which he had to publish himself), but in the years from age 50 also attached himself to running for public office as candidate for governor and senator of the state, and on one occasion at least missed by a hair's-breadth.

Sinclair's exploits are well matched in the 1980s by the remarkable Ulyssean woman Maggie Kuhn, who at age 73 founded the movement that became the Grey Panthers of America. Kuhn, a retired teacher, was appalled at society's indifference and injustice to many aged people. Like Sinclair, she did something about it. Starting with a small group, she now travels continent-wide as the rousing voice of an international movement to assert the rights of older adults.

Nor does attachment to passionate causes usually demand money—just time, a great deal of commitment, and a sense of humor for the rough spots. Therefore it is all the more astonishing that older adults of all classes and conditions have done so little to head up and take part in movements to improve the general lot of older people in our society. Surely this, for older adults, is the cause of causes! The reasons why so few participate seem clear enough: if one is poor, there is an ever-present fear of reprisals—largely illusory: one cannot be deprived of his pension. If one is rich, it's the sort of thing that isn't done. The central problem usually is the conventionality of the life-style. We have lived too long with the mask, adjusting our faces to the faces that we meet.

Yet there are many causes worth the passionate attention of older and very old adults that do not even demand the added investment of stress and worry about one's image. Of all people, the old have usually the least to lose in expressing their opinions and taking up positions; and some of them show this by a liveliness and forthrightness of attitude and expression rare in their earlier years.

A case in illustration was a Ulyssean adult living in Vancouver, age 86, when reported on by the press. Yin Lo, a Chinese Canadian, was no less remarkable in his way than Chou En-lai, whose revolution placed Yin Lo where he is. A graduate in naval engineering from Cornell, a former supporter of Sun Yat-sen, a former "guerrilla banker" in South China during World War Two where he had to dodge the Japanese to pay out $1.5 million daily in remittances from overseas relatives of the Chinese, and then a merchant in Hong Kong, Yin Lo created a whole cluster of enterprises designed to bring new activity and pleasure into the lives of neglected old people, especially of his Chinese group.

Lo obtained a $16,000 New Horizons grant from the federal government to expand the work of his organization, Chinese Elder Citizens (*Kei Hing Wooi*), which he had founded earlier. He built the group up to about 200, with a program of varied activities. Lo himself lived in a retirement home with 40 other old men—the Immaculate Conception Oriental Home—where he volunteered to provide extra care for those among his fellow residents who needed it. He did this because "I feel I'm such a fortunate old man. I led a very good life before, and *now it is my time to contribute. Wherever society needs my services I go*." (My italics.)

In the retirement home, Lo made it his concern to see that no one felt abandoned. At the same time he found the company of children immensely refreshing and renewing, and he offered his services as a teacher's aide at an elementary school, filling in from time to time for English and Chinese lessons, and for other subjects as well. "I love children. They're very attracted to me, but I don't know why. Every

time I see them I feel ten years younger." Lo noted the difference between the older adults necessarily confined at the home where he lived,
and the group for whom he was providing a repertoire of new activities:
"Once you get them out, a change becomes apparent . . . . They're
spirited. They feel young and they act young."

A highly externalized Ulyssean, Yin Lo is light years removed from
the inner Ulyssean voyages into the self of Berenson, Jung, and Gide.
Activity is the story of his life. In fact, for many contemplative older
adults, Lo would probably be just too much. Yet he is incontestably a
first-rate example of one type of Ulyssean adult: "I'm more or less ad-
venturesome in spirit, and I always liked thrills. I hate to remain in old
things."

8

NAKED ON THE SHORE

AND WHAT if the powers above do wreck me out on the wine-dark sea? I have a heart that is inured to suffering and I shall steel it to endure that too. For in my day I have had many bitter and shattering experiences in war and on the stormy seas. So let this new disaster come. It only makes one more.

The speaker is Ulysses; the place, the island of the nymph-goddess Calypso, who has held Ulysses captive for seven years during his trouble-filled voyage home; the time, the morning when Calypso, on the orders of Zeus, father of the gods, has told Ulysses that he may go, but that much misery still awaits him before he will see his wife, Penelope.

Helped by the goddess's gifts of working tools and the provision of woodlands, Ulysses within four days builds a splendid boat. Well provisioned with water, wine and appetizing meats and aided by a warm, gentle breeze springing up at Calypso's command, he sets out on what he hopes will be the last leg of his long homeward journey. For 17 days, in fact, Ulysses sails on fair seas under a calm sky, steering by the stars. But on the eighteenth day his implacable enemy, the god Poseidon, raises terrible storms and giant waves—seas so mountainous that, "great heart" though he is, "Ulysses' knees shook and his spirit quailed."

The unrelenting storms destroy his craft. Ulysses finally has to strip and thrust himself into the monstrous foaming seas, where he swims for two days and nights until finally, partly by his strength and courage, partly by his shrewdness and common sense, he is able to reach the land which, just before Poseidon's raising of the tempest, he had seen looking "like a shield on the misty sea."

Splendid physical specimen though he yet is, Ulysses seems for a while more dead than alive: "all his flesh was swollen and streams of brine gushed from his mouth and nostrils. Winded and speechless, he lay there too weak to stir, overwhelmed by his terrible fatigue." He is a king, yet at that moment he owns nothing but his life; he is friendless in a strange country. Naked on the shore, he faces the hard decision whether to sleep overnight beside the wet river bed, chancing chills and illness; or climb the hill, lie down in dense undergrowth, and risk

151

being attacked by beasts of prey. No wonder "he grimly faced his plight."

After reflection, the hungry and naked king decides to travel into a shelter on the wooded hill, where he falls asleep. In the morning his fortunes turn. The lovely princess Nausicaa and her maidens come to the river to wash, and their shouts of joy waken Ulysses who, after some understandable hesitation, "crept out from under the bushes, after breaking off with his great hand a leafy bough from the thicket to conceal his naked manhood." At the sight of this salt-encrusted warrior, whom the poet compares to a "mountain lion. . .with fire in his eyes," the maidens scuttle off in every direction, except the princess, in whom Ulysses soon finds a courageous and warm admirer. Nausicaa provides him with olive oil, a cloak, and a tunic and takes him to her father Alcinous, ruler of the country. This is the turning point in Ulysses's fortunes: he is able to reach Ithaca without further peril.

Of all his qualities, the one that makes Ulysses unforgettable is not so much his capacity for success as his intense humanity and his intrepidity in the face of failure—and Failure was his frequent companion, no less terrifying because so often sent by forces he could not control: the capricious and hostile gods from Olympus. Yet even in the midst of groans, and burning tears for comrades lost to the Cyclops, or to Circe's magic, or to Poseidon's storms, Ulysses's fine mind was still at work on how to overcome these disasters, and his strong will, checked for a little while like a naked and battered swimmer resting exhausted on the shore, resumed its journey.

The Ulyssean life is bound many times to encounter failure. Its practitioners do not, of course, court failure—courting failure is the domain of the death-wishers, not the life-wishers—but neither do they pretend that it is nonexistent. The Ulyssean life is possible in spite of failure, *in the midst of failure*. Furthermore, the Ulysseans have often known enough failure in their earlier lives to recognize it for what it is: sometimes the result of their own human misjudgments and missteps, but sometimes—many times—the result of circumstances, the result of Fate.

This truth of the human condition is an important corrective to the universal "I'm not OK" guilt feeling of Western man: the terrible (and false) conviction that whenever and however failure occurs, somehow it is all one's own fault. In fact, this is exactly the neurosis to be expected in a culture that adores success, and in which credit for whatever the "success" may be is typically and publicly attributed to the individual himself.

Rudyard Kipling, who had certain Ulyssean traits himself, touched unerringly on this point in his famous poem, "If," which, whatever its merits as pure poetry, resonantly strikes the chord of the hazards and inherent heroism in certain Ulyssean adventures in later life:

> If you can make one heap of all your winnings,
> And risk it on one turn of pitch-and-toss,
> And lose, and start again at your beginnings,
> And never breathe a word about your loss. . .

Kipling is certainly talking about adults of at least middle age, because he speaks of stooping and building one's life and work again "with worn-out tools."

The Ulyssean answer to great and inexplicable misfortune was furnished by Ulysses himself: to say in effect, "Why has this happened to me? How have I deserved this? Is there no end to such catastrophes?" thus proving that one is a human being. Then after this first flood of sorrow and despair, which coincides with one's being naked on the shore, in a strange and lonely country, bruised and wounded by storms and mysterious forces, to seek new imaginative strategies to recommence the journey.

One Ulyssean exercise is to look upon misfortune as a *learning experience*. Friends of mine have taught me much about the utility of this approach—Helen Ansley of Seattle, Washington, a devoted leader in later-life therapy programs, telling me that the rough business of recovering at 75 from a broken hip and having to have a steel pin inserted was "a learning experience"; and Professor Virgil Logan at 68 remarking how intently and with what interest he observed the doctors' arrangements to help him recover from a cerebral hemorrhage. And then there was Percy Wyndham Lewis's wonderful demonstration of this attitude, in his blindness, at 71, writing his *third-last* novel "in silence, hour after hour, dropping each page as it was completed into a deep wooden tray on the floor at his side."*

Modern times have furnished some striking examples of Ulyssean people who have been cast naked on the shore, and whose creative imagination as much as their undoubted courage made it possible for them to resume interrupted adventures or launch new ones, or both.

An interesting case in politics was Harry S. Truman, who began life as the son and grandson of pioneer farmers in Missouri. In spite of poor eyesight he managed to get into World War One, and emerged with a captaincy and the warm friendship of hundreds of men attached to his battery. It was chiefly the support of this veterans' group that launched him into politics after the failure of his men's clothing firm, due to the Depression. (He spent years trying to pay off the creditors.) Truman had the support of the powerful Pendergast organization in Missouri, but the evidence is clear enough that, far from being its tool, he was sand in the machine. As a result, he waited for years for the preferments to higher offices that went to more pliable associates.

When Roosevelt chose him to be his running mate as Vice-Presidential candidate in 1944, it was not because Truman was a nonentity—

*Hugh Kenner's Introduction to *Self-Condemned*, by Wyndham Lewis.

although the Vice-Presidency was designed for nonentities—but because he had become a respected member of the Senate. He had completed two years of law school by evening study back in Kansas City and had been a county court judge for ten years; he had kept up his omnivorous reading and homework for Senate committees. Although he was a dedicated Democrat, he was very much his own man. On one occasion he sent Roosevelt's press secretary a cryptic message just after supporting a difficult Roosevelt measure: "Tell the President to stop treating me like an office boy."

When Roosevelt died in April, 1945, Truman was catapulted into the Presidency. After a fumbling start, at which point *Time* Magazine with flip omniscience forecast that as he was "a man of distinct limitations. . .there are likely to be few innovations and little experimentation," Truman's first administration became marked by a series of extraordinary events: The controversial Hiroshima nuclear bombing, the creation of an Atomic Energy Commission, the magnificent Marshall Plan to assist in the rebuilding of war-ravaged Europe (it might as appropriately have been called the Truman Plan), new Fair Employment Practices legislation, new unemployment insurance legislation, recognition of the state of Israel (with limitations, however, displeasing to some Jewish groups).

Still, powerful blocs of the Democratic Party were sulking by the time the nomination months reappeared in the spring and early summer of 1948. For those who chose not to adjust their blinkers, Truman seemed to lack the dimensions of a world leader, a "great President": he was, it seemed, too earthy, too gauche, too stubborn, too party-ridden.

A glamorous candidate appeared from the Republican side: Thomas E. Dewey, the governor of New York State, who had once been the gang-busting district attorney of New York City. The media, who had never grasped Truman's dimensions, possibly because of his self-destructive tendency to assign heavy credit for new ideas to legislative and administrative colleagues, had consistently downplayed his record, and now thought they beheld certain disaster for the Democratic Party in the 1948 elections. (There were, of course, enlightened exceptions.) Conservative Congressmen, both Republican and Democrat, viewed the "interim" President very much as conservative members of the Curia must have viewed John XXIII when they discovered they had an aging tiger on their hands.

Truman was by now 64 years old, no longer a young or even a younger-middle-aged man. In a way, nothing had prepared him for anything else, and yet everything had prepared him for everything else—notably how to handle failure and the threat of failure sent by whatever is the modern version of Poseidon.

In the suffocating July heat of the Democratic convention hall in Philadelphia, Truman was indeed renominated, but he rose to accept the nomination in an atmosphere of oppressive gloom. Certain sections of the delegates were unhappy or hostile; the new and prestigious opinion polls week after week rated Truman as being hopelessly behind his younger, seemingly more exciting, and so far unmarked Republican opponent.

In her biography of her father, Margaret Truman would have one believe that from the beginning of this desperate situation in 1948 her father alone exuded quiet confidence. This may indeed have been the outer expression—it is just too much to believe that there were no inward groans. Yet at exactly this moment of nakedness on a very barren shore, the bright, shrewd mind was at work: not just the courageous nature of the man—courage was not enough, courage alone would take you down like the valiant but misguided captain drowning with his ship—but the Ulyssean mind, which at 64 was still young with hope and large plans.

What Truman needed in his acceptance address was not just fighting words, although from his opening sentences, long after midnight on the national radio networks, it was evident that his cocky promise to defeat the Republicans took the delegates by surprise and galvanized them: "Senator Barkley and I will win this election and make those Republicans like it—don't you forget that." It was an electrifying performance—but it was not enough. He had saved the best, the imaginative, wholly unexpected idea, for the very end of his address:

> On the 26th day of July, which out in Missouri we call Turnip Day, I am going to call Congress back and ask them to pass laws to halt rising prices, to meet the housing crisis—which they are saying they are for, in their platform.
>
> At the same time, I shall ask them to act upon other vitally needed measures. . . .
>
> Now my friends, if there is any reality behind that Republican platform, we ought to get some action from a short session of the Eightieth Congress. They can do this job in fifteen days, if they want to do it. They will still have time to go out and run for office.

The effect of the statement was not just the pandemonium that broke loose in the convention hall itself. Across the continent millions of radio listeners (including great numbers of Canadians, like myself) felt the euphoria of hearing a wholly unexpected stratagem outlined in the crisp Missouri voice of the beleaguered President. It was the stratagem of attack, of a supreme and cool disregard for the odds. In fact, when the dismayed and angry Congressmen assembled for their unheard-of brief pre-election session later in the summer, little happened. But the initiative was never lost.

Truman had one other major creative plan, much larger and equally aggressive, in his fight to retain the kingdom that foes and sometime friends were trying to take away from him: the whistle-stop campaign. While Governor Dewey was flying back and forth across the United States to mass rallies and uttering sonorities that would not rock the boat, Truman made hundreds of stops by train to greet crowds that steadily swelled as the campaign progressed—warm, friendly crowds that responded to Truman's intimate speaking style and his relentless attacks on congressional apathy and the smug self-satisfaction with which he claimed the big interests were backing his opponent. He was able to make millions of people feel that somehow his cause was their cause, as to a substantial degree it undoubtedly was.

Even so, Drew Pearson had drawn up in readiness his forecast of the members of the Dewey cabinet; four days before the election *Life* Magazine published a photograph of the "next President," that is, Thomas E. Dewey, traveling by ferry boat across San Francisco Bay. On election night, the new Univac machine began forecasting a Truman victory; engineers and announcers anxiously conferred, and apologized for the machine's malfunction! Even when at midnight Truman was far more than a million votes ahead, one of the three or four best-known national commentators kept insisting that he was sure to lose. A Chicago paper carried the headline of Dewey's victory in the early-morning hours even as the man who couldn't lose was losing past recall. In fact, Truman got a greater proportion of the total vote than Roosevelt had got in 1944: he had over 300 of the votes in the Electoral College, and he had carried a Democratic majority into Congress with him.

Truman was 68 when he left the Presidency—still vigorous, still intensely interested in human affairs. He survived his Presidency by 20 years. He returned to his old home in Independence where one further Ulyssean act climaxed the last phase of his life. He obtained the funds to build a library in the centre of the town, to contain millions of public papers from the White House, thousands of private papers, books on history and politics, especially on the Truman era, and colorful murals. And he continued far into his 80s to rise at dawn and to take the 6 A.M. walks that during his Presidency had astonished and exasperated the reporters.

Ulyssean women, too, in public careers, especially in the arts or in the humane professions or in hereditary sovereignties, have innumerable times been left naked on the shore. There is something intensely moving in the sight of older women who begin the process of resuming their personal odyssey through the courage of simply holding on in the face of failure. The great achievement, however, is to begin new creative enterprises that are highly personal and idiosyncratic, no matter how small and timid at first. Among the many women who illustrate the Ulyssean ideal is the Danish novelist, Isak Dinesen, in private life the Baroness Karen Blixen.

Karen Dinesen, as she was known before her marriage, was born in 1885, into a family of wealthy Danish merchants with highly placed political connections. Her father, who committed suicide when Karen was ten, was a brilliant and versatile man with a marked literary gift, which, however, he was reluctant to develop. Because Karen and her father had had a special rapport, his death affected her more than it did the three older children. She showed early talents for writing poetry, small plays, and stories, and a distinct ability to draw portraits in charcoal. She studied briefly in Paris, and upon return to Denmark began to be published in literary magazines. Thus far her life was bounded by a warm family circle and by the pleasant artistic activities of well-to-do Danish people in the early 1900s.

In 1913 Karen married a Danish aristocrat, Baron Bror von Blixen-Finecke, a year younger than herself. The marriage produced two immense and potentially catastrophic changes in her life. One was her husband's decision to emigrate to Africa where he wanted to buy land for a coffee plantation. The couple left for Mombasa in German East Africa in December, 1913, built a house, hunted lions, and in time bought a farm of 800 acres, chiefly to raise coffee. The other event was that Karen contracted a venereal disease from her husband that forced her return to Denmark for treatment before she had completed even a year in Africa. By that time the war was on; the progress of the ship was slow; and even when Karen reached Denmark she lost still further precious time by trying to make arrangements for treatment while concealing the situation from her mother, a kind woman but a typical Victorian. There were no miracle drugs in those days. The best that Karen could do was to halt the advance of the disease; for the rest of her life complications remained to harass her physically. What the episode did to her emotional system can be imagined. She was a glowing, warmhearted girl, none of whose many photographs taken at the time give any inkling of the inner agony she must have known.

She returned to Africa, where in 1921 she and Bror Blixen separated, and for ten years she managed the farm alone as owner of the Karen Coffee Company, helped from time to time by her younger brother, Thomas, who had always been particularly close to her. Still, his visits could only be for a few weeks at a time. Management of this large African plantation was a lonely, burdensome job, relieved by Karen's remarkably sensitive and warm understanding of the African people who worked on the farm, and of the neighboring Masai and the Kikuyu, whose respect for her was shown in the title they gave her: "The Lioness."

Friends and relatives occasionally came out from Denmark to try to ease her loneliness. She needed all the loyalty and company she could command: the coffee market was falling apart in the postwar years; as her markets closed, her debts rose. By the late 1920s it seemed impossible that she could save the farm, or indeed any personal assets. In the midst of constant gloom and worry, three facets of her world filled her life with a certain beauty. One was her relationship with her native

Kenyans and her undoubted simple joy in much of African daily life. Another was that she had begun to fill the long, lonely evenings on the plantation by writing stories again and she had high hopes of being published again in the Danish magazines. The third was a kind of personal miracle: she met an Englishman, a leader of safaris, whom she rapidly learned to cherish as a close intellectual friend and someone dear to her as a person. Denys Finch-Hatton was the son of the Earl of Winchelsea and Nottingham, a radiant, handsome man then in his late 30s who had had a classical education at Eton and Oxford, loved music, and was a first-class athlete and pilot.

In him, Karen Blixen found the companion to whom she could read her stories and test out her ideas. Life must have taken on fresh hope for her in the late 1920s. Perhaps the coffee market would right itself, after all; perhaps her manuscripts, now in the mail to Denmark, would give her a new sphere of creative life; perhaps in time her relationship with Denys would develop into something even deeper and more lasting than dear friendship.

But Poseidon, or some other vindictive god, was to end Karen Blixen's brief journey on fair seas. The Danish journals returned her manuscripts: Denmark was not interested in what she had to write at this stage. The coffee markets collapsed: by late spring, 1931, Karen was certain that she had lost everything—even the sale of the house and plantation could not pacify her creditors. And on May 8, 1931, Denys Finch-Hatton flew his Gipsy Moth from the farm, saying that he would be back the following Thursday. Karen was waiting for him, but the plane never arrived. It had crashed on the flight from Mombasa to Voi, and Denys was killed.

Karen Blixen was now 46. She was sensitive to the needs and, far more, the rights of the native people, and had seriously considered heading a movement to guarantee greater fairness and justice to the native Africans; she would have done so had not financial disaster overtaken her. She could have recouped much of her loss by selling her farm to developers who would carve it up and dispossess the native people who trusted her, but she refused to do so. (In the end this was the fate of her native friends and retainers, anyway.)

Now everything seemed lost. She had lost her plantation, and was in fact destitute. She had failed to regain entry to the literary world of the Danes, and thus to a second career. She had lost Denys Finch-Hatton, opening a wound so deep that 30 years later she was still in symbolic ways in her life remembering him, treasuring him. She was, in truth, naked on the shore.

She could at least go home—that is, to her mother's home—and she had in addition the support and affection of her brother Thomas. When Karen's ship reached Marseilles on August 19, 1931, he was at the wharf to greet her. Her first act was to look ahead, not back—except for essential books and manuscripts, she unpacked nothing from her African trunks and boxes for 13 years. She then made an early and heroic decision: she asked Thomas (who had had his own family for more than five years) to support her for two years while she stayed at her mother's house and wrote in English, for an English market, the stories that throbbed in her mind. She did this, even though there was no publisher standing by.

The book she wrote, *Seven Gothic Tales*, was finished within the two-year period. Karen went herself to London to urge the claims of the *Tales*, without success, and she returned, surely close to despair. Then her good angel, her brother, as certain of his sister's creative genius as Vincent Van Gogh's brother was of his, was able to make a contact through the American novelist, Dorothy Canfield, with the American market. The result was publication in the United States. (Its publisher could not resist it, but predicted that it would not sell.) Early in 1934, *Seven Gothic Tales* was chosen as a Book-of-the-Month Club selection, and the author, under the name of Isak Dinesen, was famous in England and America. The following year, when the Danish translation was published, celebrations were held in her honor in Copenhagen. Two years later, with the publication of her account of her life in Africa, *Out of Africa*, Isak Dinesen's fame was secure.

Karen Blixen died in September, 1962, at 77. To the end of her long life she continued to produce stories, articles, and taped interviews. In spite of fragile health she traveled much, steadily developed her admirable gifts as a gardener, entertained friends from among the African people who visited her, and encouraged young writers and artists. Her photographs in the later years are filled with warm smiles.

In his foreword to Clara Svendsen's biography of Dinesen, Frans Lasson gives a poignant glimpse of the author's inner life. He remarks that Svendsen, who was Karen Blixen's secretary, had for years watched her, each night before going to bed, open the door to the yard, pause, then go to "Ewald's Room," so called because it had once been occupied two centuries earlier by the great Danish poet of that name. Finally, Clara Svendsen asked Karen Blixen what this invariable ritual meant. She explained that the door looked toward Africa, and that she went into Ewald's Room to look at the map of her African plantation. Frans Lasson adds that Blixen did not say that in the same room, always standing on the windowsill by her desk, and never mentioned by her, was the portrait of Denys Finch-Hatton. And Lasson suggests that all this expressed Blixen's longing for wings, her faithfulness to things living now only in the realm of her mind, and the unhealed wounds that enabled her to enrich her writing through her suffering.

Just as forces of circumstance or whatever passes for fate in our time can deal out crushing blows against Ulyssean people, often when their hopes are high and prospects bright and fair, so also powers and events wholly outside their control can rescue them when the situation looks

lost beyond recall. The intervention of these beneficent strokes of fortune really takes nothing away from the Ulyssean recovery: the intervention simply creates a new potential, which it is up to the individual
to exploit or not.

Examples of this benign interference by outer forces abound, but
two illustrations from the eighteenth and nineteenth centuries can
make the point vividly. One was the case of George Frideric Handel;
the other, a much less well-known episode from the life of Cardinal
Newman. In both cases, forces beyond their personal control had halt-
ed, and in fact almost immobilized, these creators, both in their later
maturity—Handel was in his mid-50s, Newman well past 60. In both
cases good fortune intervened to provide a possibility of recovery,
which both men seized.

Handel was living in London in the early 1700s, where he had
achieved an enormous success as a composer of Italian-style operas.
Crowds packed the opera theatres to hear his music; he was a great favorite at court; and his creative powers seemed inexhaustible. Handel
needed all his genius, because his appearance and manners were unpre-
possessing. He was grossly stout, awkward, often uncouth, imperious,
and difficult to deal with. This unattractive outer personality, however,
partly concealed a noble inner spirit. He had many enemies in the envi-
ous musical world of London in the 1730s, one of them the formidable
Prince of Wales; these he could handle, but not the tidal wave of financial failure and debt that swept down upon him when the London audiences abandoned their interest in Italian opera and deserted his theatres. He wrote with his usual abundant creativity—what was said of
Saint-Saëns many years later could have been said with equal truth of
Handel: that he was throughout his life like a great flowering and ever-
fruitful tree—but the market was gone. Simultaneously his health
failed—the worst blow was a paralyzing stroke from which he slowly
recovered after a rest cure in France.

A fine and rarely seen film about Handel's life, produced in Great
Britain in 1947, shows in an especially moving way Handel's bachelor
life in those lonely and bankrupt days, shadowed by the menace of the
debtors' prison. Except for isolated walks at times when the streets
were empty, the composer remained in the house, which somehow he
had been able to retain, brooding over the dark turn of events—naked
on the shore. Then an extraordinary event occurred that was outside
his control. Late one summer morning a delegation of three men arrived from the Duke of Devonshire to ask Handel to prepare a work
for a charitable performance. Almost indifferently the composer asked
if they had a theme in mind. Rather nervously the leader of the delegation suggested that something involving the New Testament had been
discussed. The effect upon the hitherto indifferent, almost somnolent
composer was remarkable: "Do you mean," he asked, "the life of our
Lord?"

This was what they did mean, and Handel, accepting the commission, shut himself into his workroom, saw no one but the women who placed his food at the door, and wrote the oratorio, *The Messiah*, in 25 days. He was in the grip of a magnificent creative obsession; many times tears flooded his eyes. To his servant he made the famous statement about what was to be the immortal Hallelujah Chorus, "I did think I did see Heaven before me, and the great God himself." He was then age 57, and from the long crisis of terrible financial loss and physical and social desolation, which had lasted many months, he had derived a new masterpiece—to be followed by still others in his late years.

John Henry Newman's experience is a fascinating parallel of seemingly utter failure, intervention by a wholly unexpected event, and creative exploitation of the new circumstance by a Ulyssean adult. Before he was 50, Newman was famous as one of the leaders of the new Anglo-Catholic movement in the Church of England. The idea of restoring much of the ancient, beautiful ritual that had been lost in Puritan days in the Church of England, and of restoring some of its Catholic beliefs and practices, had created so great an upheaval that its leading spokesman became celebrated, hated, and adored. He was the author of a famous hymn; an awesome controversialist and sought-after speaker; a popular and brilliant priest and don.

Then Newman, for reasons that would be irrelevant to enter into here, became a Roman Catholic. At once the whole tenor of his life changed. The huge audience he had once commanded in the dominant Anglican world now left him; at the same time he found a cold welcome among Roman Catholics, notably and specifically at Rome itself, where he had expected to receive at least generous respect from Pius IX and the cardinals. All that he gained instead was the headship of a group of Oratorian Fathers in the provincial city of Birmingham.

Then came a succession of prospects from outside forces and imaginative ideas of his own which he hoped would advance the cause of Roman Catholicism in Great Britain and restore much of his shattered influence in the prestigious circles of thought: the offer of a bishopric, mysteriously withdrawn after he had accepted it and had bought the robes; the appointment to the rectorship of a so-called Catholic University of Ireland, which involved him in a period of intense travel and organization in Ireland, only to find a chimera; the prospect of a Catholic hall at Oxford, of which he would be the rector: this was Newman's own plan and dream, a plan defeated by his enemy within the Church, Cardinal Manning, also an Anglican convert.

In whatever direction Newman looked he was blocked. With all his great gifts, and in spite of his former fame, he had come, so it seemed, to a complete dead end. It was about this time that Newman wrote in his journal that he could hardly bear to get up in the morning; the day stretched before him already dreary and defeated. He was, in fact, naked on the shore.

Then occurred the mysterious interposition of the gods. Newman, who had been neglected for so long, was suddenly and angrily attacked by Charles Kingsley, one of the most noted Protestant writers of the day, for his desertion to the Roman Catholics, for his insincerity, for his opportunism, for his jesuitry. Kingsley's attack also extended to the church Newman had espoused. What was Newman to do with these searing and highly personal onslaughts? Turn the other cheek and let them pass? But this would be both masochistic and provocative to further attacks. Write two or three letters to *The Times* and responding letters to the magazine that had published Kingsley's initial paper? But responses in article form to original polemics never carry the weight of the original; and they die with the temporary nature of nearly all journalism.

No. What was needed was a book that would give real substance to Newman's defence of himself and his conduct, and which would be read long after he, Kingsley, and the other polemicists were dead. It took Newman seven weeks of intensive work to write a reply to Kingsley that was to become one of the most famous statements in the world of theological debate, yet a book well within the range of the average intelligent person: the *Apologia pro Vita Sua*. Like Handel, Newman often wept as, standing at the wooden lectern on which he wrote most of the *Apologia*, he carried forward his brilliant and eloquent defence of himself and of the Roman Catholic Church. He must have wondered whether his will power and creative generativity were sufficient for the work. He was, after all, 65 years old—"retirement age," in twentieth-century terms.

In fact, Kingsley had been the unwitting rescuer of Newman from utter defeat. The *Apologia*, with its fire and zest and artistry, was a triumph, read and acclaimed everywhere. Without Kingsley, it would never have been written—but then, without Newman, it would only have been another humdrum treatise ultimately gathering dust on the shelves of pious Victorian homes. Nor did Newman, to the end of his very long life at age 89, lose his ability to think originally and write creatively. (His career was unexpectedly crowned by the Cardinal's cap when he was 78.) The bright, quick mind, with its sensitive humor, mature irony, simplicity of enthusiasm over human projects, and its tender faith, can be said to have remained Ulyssean until the day of Newman's death in 1890.

"But then," says the inevitable cynic of those Ulysseans, "what options had they?" If they had no choice, it was because of their essentially life-loving and striving natures, always open to the presence and possibility of creativity. To contradict the cynic, they indeed had other options, important options chosen by innumerable older adults just as much today as formerly.

One choice is self-pity—"Who has known such woes as I have known?": one can make a career out of this, and many have. Everyone knows of someone who by personal mistakes or, much oftener, the injury and blockage of external fate, has not written the novel, conducted the orchestra, created the business, bought the long-dreamed-of house, visited Scandinavia, painted the portraits as he or she had hoped to do, and whose reaction has been immobilizing self-pity. (Who, on the other hand, had more excuse for self-pity than the remarkable modern Ulyssean Pierre Teilhard de Chardin, whose brilliant books were forbidden publication by his Church up to his death and in the years preceding John XXIII—but who wrote them anyway?)

Another option is to live more cautiously; play it safe; move back into the comforting conventions of routine life. There is a basis of good sense and reason here, and of human practice. Even the Ulysseans in terrible misfortune are first saved by routine. If you are Thomas Carlyle, and you discover that a housemaid has unwittingly burned the just-completed manuscript of your *History of the French Revolution,* in the writing of which 20 cartloads of books have been employed, you undoubedly feel crushed. For the time being it may be the routine that saves you—the cup of tea, the usual walk, the familiar companionship of a dear friend. But because you are Carlyle, and a Ulyssean, you rewrite the history. If you are the painter, Eugène Delacroix, keeping also a journal fine enough to be published years later and read by thousands of people since, and if you leave one complete year of the journal in a Paris cab one night, and never recover it, you can never rewrite the entries. One piece of creative work done over a whole year is permanently missing. The world of small routines will save you, as it saves years of life of lonely and desolate women in their late years—but because you are Delacroix and a Ulyssean, you recommence the journal.

The routines of conventional living can heal and save. However, they can and do engulf and enslave. Worse, there are also the demonic conventions that wait for all who have suffered terrible reverses and sorrows: alcoholism, drug addiction, cruelty to other people and oneself, sustained bitterness.

Sometimes the type of creativity evoked by the depths of disaster is not what Maslow called "special talent creativity," but "self-actualizing creativeness"—how the Ulyssean person responds in his or her personal life to the blows of Fate. A provocative example of this is the life of the Grand Duchess Olga Alexandrovna, who at her death on November 24, 1960, was the last surviving sister of the Tsar Nicholas II, murdered with his entire family at Ekaterinbourg in 1917, ending the 300-year Romanoff dynasty. After the revolution the Grand Duchess Olga and some other members of the royal family escaped to Paris and other western capitals.

The fleeing nobility and former ministers had certain critical choices to make. If they had enough money (few had), they could try to maintain the illusion of temporary exile in some villa or resort in Italy or France. If they had not, they could seek some kind of dignified work, or as in many cases, any kind of work. Ideologically, the exiles could continue to live in the vanished world of Imperial Russia. Or they could, while preserving loving contacts and memories, look toward a world from which Imperial Highnesses had vanished.

What was remarkable about the Grand Duchess Olga and her husband, Colonel Nikolai Koulikovsky, was that they made a Ulyssean decision when she was 66 and he was 67 to go to Canada to farm a property of 200 acres with the aid of their two sons and a couple of elderly servants. The decision was unmistakable in its symbolism. They had chosen for themselves and their sons not the world of yesterday, including intrigues and jealousies of certain royal and ex-royal circles in Europe, but the world of tomorrow in a wholly new country.

At first the venture seemed successful, but as the years passed, Colonel Koulikovsky found it impossible to hire the extra help he needed for his farm; his sons chose new careers; and as his health failed, he and the Grand Duchess moved to a modest house in Cooksville, a small community near Toronto. There was a garden, and Olga made the house charming with many mementos of their former life.

The old servants died, and Colonel Koulikovsky's health steadily deteriorated until he, too, died in 1957. The Grand Duchess Olga was left alone in the Cooksville house. What was she to do? Although her health was good, she was 74 years of age. She decided not to move, and by living very simply she was able to carry on. She became a familiar figure in the town, shopping and gardening. There was no Russian Orthodox church in Cooksville, and on frequent Sundays Olga made the trip into Toronto to the Cathedral of Christ the Saviour, where after the service elderly members of the congregation and their families and grandchildren would swarm around her to pay their respects to almost the last living member of the Russian Imperial royal family. "Almost," because there was still one other living grand duchess, her sister in London, England, who as it turned out was to die shortly before Olga's own death in November, 1960.

In his biography, *The Last Grand Duchess*, the Greek journalist Ian Vorres tells that he drove out to Cooksville from Toronto to see if he could interview her for an article. One early autumn day, he found a small, spare woman working in her garden—this was the Grand Duchess Olga. From the beginning Vorres was struck by her ease and graciousness of manner, and by her warm, friendly spirit. He found out that Olga had often been invited to write or permit the writing of her life story, but she had always refused. But the young newspaperman and the elderly grand duchess, then 75, became fast friends; and Vorres was able to persuade her to let him write her life story—fortunately completed before her death.

It was not only Olga's vitality and courage that drew Vorres's admiration, but her sense of humor and her wise humanity. She had seen much and lost much—in the material sense, almost everything. She was, of course, lonely; she could not blot out the past, and history continued to pursue her. She still received letters and occasional visits from former Russian subjects who cherished her as a symbol, and also tiresome intrusions from imposters. Yet there was a modernity in her manner and her way of thought that reflected the new country and new style of life she and her husband had chosen so late in their lives.

In midsummer, 1960, she became ill, and had to enter hospital in Toronto, where the routines tired her and made her unhappy and restless. The medical staff, who became fond of her, were willing to send her home, but there was no one to nurse her in the silent house at Cooksville. Then an elderly Imperial Russian Army officer and his wife, Captain and Mrs. Martemianov, invited her to go with them for "convalescence." They had a small flat above a hairdresser's shop on Gerrard Street East in Toronto. It was there that Olga died on November 24, 1960.

Thirteen years later, also in November, I made a short nostalgic journey across downtown Toronto to visit the site where Olga had last lived and made the following entry in my journal:

From Gerrard Street East, the sky could be seen slate-blue on the late autumn day above the quiet Sunday traffic, the air frosty and damp. The building housing the apartments, one storey above the shops was as photographed in Ian Vorres's life of Olga.

It was only in the last four or five months of her life that the Grand Duchess lived here. Released from hospital, which she hated, she apparently found a certain joy in being at home with an elderly Cossack officer and his wife, who loved her, and in seeing the walls around her bed covered with the beloved icons of her faith.

One can, I think, imagine fairly well the final stage on which Olga played out her days. Her small room, filled with some charming things rescued from the past, but with the simplicity of her poverty; the warmth of being in and being home; the smell of good soup; lamplight; the presence of two or three loving people, and some cards and messages from others; and the visits of the young journalist, a close friend across a difference of forty years of time, who revered and loved her.

Here then, passed from this world that lovely-spirited lady, Olga Alexandrovna, the last grand duchess of the Romanoff dynasty, on a commercial street in Toronto, Canada, among little boys whose bikes turn over and whose jugs of milk are upset, among young couples who dash laughing up the stairs, among schoolgirls carrying books across the parks, among pizza takeouts and cut-rate pharmacies, among amiable truck-drivers and elderly ladies carrying shopping bags, among neon signs and parking lots, among church rummage sales and "ethnic" movie houses and restaurants, among thousands of family groups.

It is not all so incongruous as at first it seems. In a deep human sense, it is not incongruous at all. It has something to do with "citoyenne du monde"—something to do with "noblesse oblige." And there is something very Ulyssean about it.

Among the disasters that can overtake Ulyssean achievers are crippling illnesses that severely impair or immobilize the body's action. Sometimes the disease or disintegrative process attacks exactly the physical instrument provided by the body to carry through the creative performance. A notable example was Auguste Renoir, one of the masters of French impressionism, who was overtaken by severe arthritis in his early 50s. His hands became more and more twisted until, by the time he had reached his late years, the deformation was so complete that he had to have the paints squeezed onto the palette for him, and he moved the brush not by his fingers but by his arm, through an apparatus attached to his rigid fingers and wrist. Nevertheless, he continued to paint great works until his death. Nothing exhausted his great talent—in fact it was inexhaustible, even though the disease forced him into a wheelchair at so early an age as 60, and he later became bedridden.

For a long time Renoir was in great pain until at last the arthritic fires burned themselves out. When he was 71, the Renoirs actually found a doctor in Paris who was certain that he could make the painter walk again—something that would have been like a gift from heaven. In fact, he did walk again: a few steps around his easel and then back to his wheelchair. But it required so great an effort that Renoir remarked to the physician that he would use up all his energies, and he needed, he said, all his willpower for his painting. Having to make the choice between walking and painting, he chose painting. In fact, he asked for paintbox and brushes on the morning of his death, and completed a lovely painting of some anemones the maid had brought him. According to his son, Jean, as he completed this painting and had his brush taken away, he said something like, "I think I am beginning to understand something about it."

Still, Renoir's condition in late life, cruel though it was, was by no means wholly tragic. He had, after all, a great talent that he realized; he was famous; and he accomplished much that he was born to do.

But what if you are wholly immobilized at a late age, unknown to the world, and with the feeling that you have never been able to realize whatever gifts you had? In so dire a situation, one form of the ultimate test of the human spirit can be seen. Is there even creativity in the survival of self over senility? Is it possible that this "I," so encircled by "disgust and despair" that its terrible urge is to take flight into somnolence and extinction, nonetheless creatively maintains its own existence and identity?

An example of this most calamitous form of being "naked on the shore" is that of Isabelle Buchanan, an aunt of mine, born in the lovely old town of Parkhill, near London, Ontario, in 1870, who died in London in 1963, age 93. Her case seems to be as clear an example of a tragic waste of human talent as the records could disclose. Nor does the achievement of a very long life do much to make up for it.

Belle Buchanan was born into a Highland Scots-Canadian pioneer family, the oldest members of which had helped build the farms and towns in Middlesex County, Ontario. The family had a heritage of great health and vitality. Belle, a beautiful, high-spirited girl, going to the dances, skating parties, sleigh rides, plays, and church functions of a small Ontario community, had a magnificent obsession: to be a nurse. Nursing was then on its way to becoming a profession, and in those days Detroit was where you went for training in nursing.

But then Fate intervened. One of Belle's grandmothers in a district ten miles away had a massive stroke. There was no one to nurse her—could Belle do it? It would mean a short postponement of her imminent arrangements to begin her training in a hospital in Detroit. But the condition of the imperious old lady did not improve. Three years went by; Belle was told that if she nursed her grandmother through the illness, she would be well remembered in the division of property at death, which was the way payment was often made within pioneer families.

The grandmother died; in fact, no provision was made for Belle, who was by now a young woman. The chance of studying nursing was lost—Belle Buchanan began the life of a spinster in the age of the unliberated woman. Because of her beauty and vivacity, she had a number of offers of marriage, all of which she turned down. In the family, it was said that she was always looking for a Prince Charming who never arrived. She may also simply have been what a later age would call "a career woman." After the death of her elderly parents Belle and a younger sister were left in the old house, and the two women carried on with the slender funds available from renting land, the sister's skills at dressmaking, and interest from modest investments left by their parents. In spite of this, they entertained many visitors and became special figures in the life of the little town.

In 1940, when the vivacious girl whose dream had been to be a nurse, was 70, Belle Buchanan had lost something of her radiant health—she had been drenched too often at her work out in the orchards and the grazing land and she began to develop arthritis. She was still beautiful: you could see the lovely girl that she had been. Then one snowy winter night in 1941, without warning, her sister died. There was no telephone in the old home. Belle, in the wild panic and sorrow of the crisis, threw on some clothes and went to the house of some neighbours to call for help.

After this, events followed swiftly. The home was sold and its contents auctioned off. Belle's health was irremediably shaken by these personal catastrophes, and the arthritis advanced. At first she found a certain happiness and excitement in staying with relatives in London for a few months; then as a boarded guest in the home of a married nurse whose teen-age daughter filled Belle's days with interest and joy; then, briefly, in a Roman Catholic hospital where the nuns were kind; then finally in a nursing home for old ill people in London. She entered the nursing home at age 77; here she remained until her death—16 years during which she finally arrived naked on the shore.

As nursing homes go, it was a good one, clean and warm. Belle was by now wholly immobilized; her weight had gone down to about 70 pounds. Still, frail as she was, she refused to let anyone feed her. She was in a room with seven or eight other elderly women, the majority of whom slept most of the time or were senile. The staff were good, but there were no stimuli for the mind. Belle was so crippled that it was difficult for her to read. Sunday visits from a few family members of the inmates helped to break the monotony. I came from a busy existence 400 miles away, three or four times a year, to stay a day or two; and a cousin, Mary Fisher, came in often to talk with her.

As time went on, Belle had long periods of unbearable loneliness. One calm summer evening, her eyes filling with tears, she hummed for me and half-sang in her still-melodious voice the words and tune of "My Ain Folk," the poignant Highland song of exile: "Though I'm far across the sea, It's in Scotland I would be. At Home, in dear old Scotland, with my ain folk." Yet she was always glad to talk about the old family days and was never morbid or talked resentfully, and she had no self-pity. Only very rarely did she seem confused. Usually her mood was a quiet brightness. I dreaded the day when I might arrive to find her sinking into senility as so many other old women had done in those rooms.

A few years before her death, Belle was moved to a front room with two beds. At first she was pleased, assuming that this was the "best room in the house," which in a way was true. But the location increased her isolation and her loneliness. In the other bed was a timid, very fragile, senile (of course) old lady—this was her companionship. Sometimes when this person was especially silly in comments or actions, Belle would draw my attention to her with an ironic smile. Somehow I dimly resented this as mocking a defenceless old woman and a sister in misfortune. I should have known that it was from this ironic humor, still vividly awake, that part of Belle Buchanan's own mysterious defences against senility came.

The last evening, a Saturday, as usual I had supper with her, eating from a tray as she did, giving her the pleasure of feeling that I was her guest, as I was. That October evening all was at peace; we fell into a contented silence, and I drowsed. Suddenly to my astonishment, she said with great clearness—I am sure that she thought I was asleep—"I should have gone to Detroit."

My aunt was 93. Still, so tenacious was the grip of her girlhood dream that after 76 years she could mourn the great chance lost, the divide in the road not taken.

The following Wednesday I had word from my cousin in London that Belle Buchanan had died in the early morning—gone in the moment between sleeping and waking.

In what possible sense was such a woman a Ulyssean? Because of her terrible immobilization, she could not have done what Major A. F. Graves of the United Nations Society of Ottawa did at the end of his life when, desperately ill with cancer, he went out in his self-propelled chair into the corridors of the hospital, for weeks comforting other people. Was her creativity, then, self-actualization?

It seems to me now that her defeat of the steady menace of senility in an arena where many others had succumbed was in itself a Ulyssean adventure. She had a whole repertoire of defences and counterattacks against being engulfed. She had learned how to handle loneliness. She was sorrowful and angry at times, and at rare intervals clearly felt that somehow she had been betrayed—but she was then angry and outspoken, not silent and bitter. Incredibly, although she read little and saw few people, she remained open to the rich world of fantasy and dreaming which, in a certain sense, was also one of the deficits of her life. And if at the end she was left veritably naked upon the shore, she eluded self-pity. She retained an unconquerable hope into the late, late years; and when that finally dimmed and perhaps died, she never lost the sense of being the protagonist in a significant drama. Thus I came to attach to her the strong and tender accolade: Ulyssean.*

Sometimes the ingenuity and gallantry of the Ulyssean performance outwits death itself. Romain Gary, the French novelist, tells in his memoir, *Promise at Dawn,* of an astonishing adventure that his mother embarked upon during the last two years of her life—during which she expected death.

Refugees after World War One, Gary and his mother had wandered across Europe while she tried to keep them both alive. She felt that her boy should emerge at the top in whatever occupation he chose—from tennis to politics to the army. Her wonderful gutsy sense of life, her panache, filled her young son's life with verve and laughter, and robbed his occasional moments of embarrassment of their sting. Naturally, after 20 or more years of such companionship, with poverty and hard-

*Another remarkable Ulyssean of this category is an immobilized male in his late years in a Toronto nursing home who has trained himself to travel in his mind as though traveling with his body to distant places and to have rewarding encounters with imaginary people.

ship from time to time, mother and son were close in mind and spirit, yet Gary had his own full identity.

In 1940 when Hitler invaded France, Romain Gary joined the Free French air crews flying out of England on sorties over the continent; his mother remained behind with good friends, in what must have been to her a sorrowful separation. Her solution, of course, was to try to bridge the gap by writing her son wonderful weekly letters designed to keep up his morale. When peace came, he rushed home—only to find that his mother had died two years previously.

When she learned that she would probably die before her son's return, she devised a Ulyssean stratagem. She prepared enough letters for a period of more than two years and arranged that the devoted friends with whom she stayed would send them to her pilot son.

The prospect of imminent death may seem too overwhelming for even a Ulyssean to cope with. This all depends upon how powerfully the individuals have learned to internalize their sense of permanent uniqueness or value of life. And, it depends, too, upon their having developed or swiftly grasped toward the end of their lives the undoubted truth that fate is just as capricious one way as the other—that the cause seemingly lost may in time be the cause well won.

The life of the Sicilian prince and author Giuseppe di Lampedusa, who died in 1959, illustrates this strange working of fate. Lampedusa at age 60 was a tall, rather heavy, princely-looking man (this is more than can be said for many princes) who had capably fulfilled the demands of his heritage. He was the master of two palaces in Sicily, one of which was obliterated by American bombers toward the end of World War Two. He was also something of an oddity in his aristocratic circle because he was devoted to study and reading; and had for many years talked about writing a novel, which no sensible person expected him to write.

He was capable of attempting it. He had already written from time to time; and in his later years, he actually won a a prize. But who expects a prince to write a novel that might be published by a commercial publisher and read by all sorts of people? Even in these days when princes have come down in the world, they are embalmed in social protocols, especially if, like Lampedusa, they are administrators of large estates. Administration is the mortal trap of serious activity outside its own sphere.

For many years Lampedusa's duties as an administrator took precedence over his urge to write. He had the Ulyssean's open and sensitive reaction to life, and when the war brought the destruction of a great part of his heritage, he was at first obsessed by the loss. To divert his mind, his wife urged him to write. He did so, and we have Alexander Colquhoun's little cameo of the result:

From now on, his routine—the café tables he used, the waiters who served him, even the cakes he ate—followed an invariable pattern: breakfast at the Pasticceria del Massimo in Via Masqueda; a call at Flaccorio, the imaginative bookseller and publisher whose shop is a kind of literary club, and who was the first to encourage him to publish; by mid-day he would be settled in his personal version of an ivory tower, the back room of the Café Mazzara under the only skyscraper in town.

The brief case opens. It contains, as well as maybe a few cakes from the last café, books, the addiction which made him as great an object of suspicion to his fellow grandees as his great-grandfather had been with his telescopes and comet-finders. . .This concentrated reading throughout the day at the Café table (mysterious scribbling) was in a way creative.

What Lampedusa was soon engaged upon was the actual writing of the novel, *The Leopard,* which had been in his thoughts for 25 years.

He began it in his mid-60s, and finished it in about three years. Meanwhile he wrote other pieces. He had the novel typed and sent off, encouraged by both his wife and by the bookseller Flaccorio. Now, however, another disaster struck. He was found to have cancer, which, as it turned out, ended his life. The publisher, as publishers often will, held the manuscript for weeks. Finally, and just before his death, the letter came—a rejection. Lampedusa received the news with noble composure; still, his inward disappointment must have been intense. A day or two later, while quietly talking with his physician, the prince suddenly died. Within a matter of weeks *The Leopard* was submitted to another publisher, and accepted. It became an international best seller and a notable film. It is accepted as one of the distinguished novels of our time.

The performance was splendidly Ulyssean, but who outwitted whom—Death or Lampedusa? Death is a formidable adversary, and platitudes and histrionics do little to assuage his effects. Yet, in this case, Lampedusa had finished his novel, and its effects far outreached his death. Furthermore, the writing of the novel was, *in itself,* a personal fulfillment, a justification and actualization of the self.

This last point is crucial in considering the adventures and attempts of the Ulyssean life. Ulysses's last voyage was a failure, and it was uncompleted—still, this takes nothing away from the splendor and individual creativity of the act. Chichester's last effort to win a trans-ocean race, which he had to abandon because of the pain and immobilizing effect of his last illness, was no less splendid than any of the other Ulyssean adventures of his later years. Surely we do not have to listen more than once to Schubert's *Unfinished Symphony* (which was not only unpublished at his death, but lost for years in a cellar) to understand that creative fragments are beautiful things in themselves.

One creative person who thought a lot about this last point was Rob-

ert Louis Stevenson, and with reason. Stevenson, who fought a long
losing battle with tuberculosis in the late nineteenth century, when the
medical profession was unable to cure it, dealt superbly with the subject of death and creative achievement in a now almost forgotten essay,
Aes Triplex. In that essay, Stevenson notes how well many old people
deal with possible disablement and death. He takes, as one example
among many, someone he had admired, Dr. Samuel Johnson, of whom
he writes:

> No one surely could have recoiled with more heartache and terror
> from the thought of death than our respected lexicographer; and
> yet we know how little it affected his conduct, how wisely and
> boldly he walked, and in what a fresh and lively vein he spoke of
> life. Already an old man, he ventured on his Highland tour; and
> his heart, bound with triple brass [*aes triplex*], did not recoil be-
> fore twenty-seven individual cups of tea. . . .Think of the hero-
> ism of Johnson, think of that superb indifference to mortal limi-
> tation that set him upon his dictionary, and carried him through
> triumphantly until the end!

Then Stevenson moves to the great question of whether it is worthwhile to begin creative acts that, after all, may turn out to be fragments:

> Who, if he were wisely considerate of things at large, would ever
> embark upon any work much more considerable than a half-
> penny post-card? Who would project a serious novel, after
> Thackeray and Dickens had each fallen in mid-course? Who
> would find heart enough to begin to live, if he dallied with the
> consideration of death?

This is a Ulyssean speaking, even though Stevenson's own life was
to end at 44:

> By all means begin your folio; even if the doctor does not give
> you a year, even if he hesitates about a month, make one brave
> push and see what can be accomplished in a week. It is not only
> in finished undertakings that we ought to honour useful labour.
> A spirit goes out of the man who means execution, which outlives
> the most untimely ending. All who have meant good work with
> their whole hearts have done good work, although they may die
> before they have the time to sign it.
>   And even if death catch people, like an open pitfall, and in
> mid-career, laying out vast projects, and planning monstrous
> foundations, flushed with hope, and their mouths full of boastful
> language, they should be at once tripped up and silenced: is there
> not something brave and spirited in such a termination? and does

not life go down with a better grace, foaming in full body over a precipice, than miserably straggling to an end in sandy deltas?

"By all means begin your folio. . ."

The folio, a natural symbol for a writer, is Stevenson's shorthand for any creative opportunity that exists almost simultaneously with the threat of serious illness. The human tendency, which no one has the right to criticize or patronize, is to abandon everything that seems to interfere with the awesome threat to one's life. But is this always or even usually the only or the wise action? There remains the possibility of the Ulyssean action, which is what Stevenson is writing about. Two incidents from my own experience may illustrate the point.

About 20 years ago I heard the story of a married couple in their mid-60s. They had planned for years to wander through Europe but had been kept from doing so by family responsibilities and business difficulties. At last they were free to do so. The husband had just been able to retire, and retire comfortably; they were, after many years of marriage, much in love; they had spent some happy months in the early summer just before his retirement planning their itinerary, gathering tourist and guide books, and assembling luggage and clothing. They had their tickets for the passage. Then each decided to have a medical examination as an extra precaution. Her returns were clear; her husband's were dismaying—the odds were against the husband's living as long as a year. Shaken and sorrowful, the couple cancelled their tickets; the husband began treatment and in fact lost his fight with his rare illness in about a year.

I learned of this episode from a close friend of the couple. My friend described the wife's poignant double sorrow: not only the loss of someone dearly loved, but that of the long-planned-for, dreamed-about trip to Europe. When she finished, there was a few moments' silence between us. Then she said, "What would you have done?" I said, "I would have gone to Europe." My friend smiled: "I too. But it's easy for us to say. He was faced, after all, with what turned out to be a fatal illness." "That's true," I said, "but there are great physicians in Europe." "They are beautiful people," she said, using the present tense lovingly, as though the husband were still alive. "I wish that they had strolled in the sunshine on St. Mark's Square, and sat in a café in Paris. He wanted so much to see Athens. . . .They could have had a little odyssey."

In 1967, when traveling by bus between Montreal and Ottawa, I met an extraordinary person. He was a 78-year-old Australian, spare and heavily tanned, with rather gnarled working hands, plainly dressed; it was midsummer, and the day and the bus were intensely hot. It was easy to move into conversation with this keen-eyed traveler with the quick, warm smile. Where was he going? To my surprise, I learned that he was bound for Calgary, to see the Stampede. He and his wife had arrived in Los Angeles to cross North America and then Europe by bus, and to find a passage home from the Near East. They were visiting their daughter and her family in Montreal—meanwhile the Calgary trip was his personal side expedition to fulfill a long-held dream. He and his wife would resume their odyssey when he returned. They liked big buses—you could often stop, stroll, have the feeling of being close to the land and the people. Sometimes they stopped over; often they traveled through the night, and in "America" there were usually splendid middle-of-the-night restaurants and rest stops. They had had so much fun seeing things together.

I asked about fatigue: no, this was not a great problem. If they felt themselves getting too tired, they "stopped over." I did not mention, of course, the inevitable thought held in the back of my mind, placed there by the conventions of our society: Suppose one or the other became ill—after all, both were about 78; suppose. . .But it was impossible, talking to this vital, obviously life-loving man to whom I said a warm farewell in Ottawa, to keep dwelling on thoughts like these. I knew that I had met another of the Ulysseans.

"By all means begin your folio. . ."

9

PATHS TO THE ULYSSEAN LIFE

THE ULYSSEAN life is possible, and the Ulyssean way is accessible and free, because in many ways the conditions required for the creative life are *more available* in the later years of adulthood than earlier in life.

It is essential to make this statement with force in order to banish the myth that creativity resides chiefly with the young and the "highly geared." Being in "high gear" is no guarantee that one will be creative—productive, perhaps. Assuming that a constant factor in all creative enterprises is the existence of certain personal gifts, talents, qualities, or self-actualized attributes, there then seem to be conditions or situations that set the stage, or help provide the soil and air for the creative enterprise. And all of them are conspicuously available in the later years.

One is a release of time, not only to think and plan, but to produce. Incredibly, if you allot ten hours a day as released time across any 15 years after age 60, you have approximately 55,000 hours available to invent, to build, to serve, to paint, to sculpt, to write, to learn. Tolstoy could perhaps have written the monumental *War and Peace* three times in that period of time! For most of us our problem will not be unavailable time, but rather how to manage the abundant time we have. And how to manage our self—our will to learn and create.

Another is the rich store of experiences accumulated throughout life, which are recorded in the apparatus of the mind. In older adulthood not only is the brain operating with abundant power, but the great reservoir of the unconscious is surely more potentially fertile than it was earlier. Many possibilities arise from this—one of them Wordsworth's concept of emotion recollected in tranquility. Older adults have the extended experience, usually together with a greater accessibility to tranquil thought—not confusing "tranquil" with "passive" or "bovine." An example of this fusion of experience, perceptive recollection, and tranquility in a creative enterprise is, of course, keeping a daily journal filled with reflections and ideas.

Still another advantage exists among older adults. Surely many are freer than they have ever been to explore and adopt fresh and unorthodox points of view—to release themselves to new quests and adven-

175

tures. At last they can "give themselves permission." For too many years, in too many ways, we listen to the Board of Directors in our mind, locking ourselves away from new ways of thought and new steps in experience.* Freer airs blow for many men and women in their later years. The stakes are less and intimidating jailers are gone. The steady process of maturing may have brought a courageous wisdom, a courageous compassion. One of the loveliest features of the later years is the affinity that many older adults develop for the causes and crusades of the young.

Thus the creative life is not only as possible for men and women in the later years as when they were much younger, but in important respects often *more* possible. Nor does lack of money, nor chronic ill health, nor lack of family and friends remove these advantageous conditions for creativity in many older adult lives. They are still present even when one is naked on the shore.

However, at all ages the creative life has to be purchased by an effort of the will and by the adoption of a certain lifestyle. Obsolescence of mind and spirit waits for those who think that creativity in the later years descends like manna from the sky. To grow and create, to bring into actuality the unique space-time intersection that is our life, requires exertion of the self—exertion undertaken with love, faith, and hope.

Part of this process of self-actualization with a view to creativity in the later years is the sharpening of the senses. It is incredible that so little attention is paid to the deeper world of the senses. For surely to "see" and to "hear" is a process immensely greater than the physical act. I recall a conversation a few years ago with a group of men at a luncheon where two brothers, both friends of some members of the group, were under discussion. One brother was blind. However, in the rapid exchange of conversation, when one person suggested Bob, the sighted brother, for a committee job, another man cut in quickly: "No. I suggest Jim—he sees things so much more clearly than Bob." At the remark, which nearly everyone at once agreed to, delighted smiles spread among the group. The paradox was true, and the instinctive reference was beautiful.

For purposes of the creative life, there is not much advantage in having 20/20 vision if one really does not "see" very much. In fact, few of us, in the later years or at any time in the life drama, have developed our ability to "see" as we should. The point is developed extensively in a fine book by Ross Parmenter, *The Awakened Eye*. Parmenter was a

---

*A friend of mine in her 60s tells me that one day, lonely and reflective, it occurred to her that she had never set foot in a temple, synagogue, or mosque. When she put on her coat to do so, a voice from her "Board of Directors" (loved and lost), remarked in her mind, "But in our family we don't do such a thing." She paused. Then "giving herself permission" ("But I am 63!"), she went on to the symbolic act that has enriched her late religious life—her sense of the cosmos.

journalist and music editor of the *New York Times* until 1964 when he "retired" in his late 50s to travel and write, and to bring out four years later his book on the awakening of the deeper vision. Parmenter identifies three categories of "seeing" beyond ordinary vision. The first degree above the ordinary he calls *sharpened vision*, as for example, the astonishing array of things in a pack of face cards which ordinary vision never notices, even though one may play bridge for years on end. The next stage he terms *heightened vision* where symbolism is perceived. In heightened vision the candle on a red-checked café table becomes a symbol of the idealism of man; a wider context appears than simply the candle seen at the moment with the physical eye.

The highest category is *transfigured vision*, and Parmenter illustrates this at length with the description of an episode in 1949 which occurred on the road from California to Colorado when he was driving a 79-year-old retired school-teacher, Thyrza Cohen, to her sister's home in Denver. Parmenter became lost among primitive roads and mountain passes in the area of the Great Divide. He realized bleakly that the car, a 1932 four-cylinder Plymouth sedan, was very old, that his gas supply was giving out, and that they had little food. Then suddenly the canyon walls fell away and they could see, beyond green fields, the town they had sought for the night.

Parmenter describes the euphoria that seized him at the sight. He and Thyrza Cohen had been obsessed with the need of food, of gasoline, of shelter. Now in the ecstasy of relief, Parmenter "saw" what later turned out to be a dingy enough row of houses and filling stations as a Tunisian scene, bathed "in magical light"—the light of the afternoon sun. The owner of the run-down service station, although "in reality" simply a good-humored obliging auto mechanic of considerable skill, seemed transfigured into man as the universal helper of man.

Parmenter asks how it is possible that we can live so close for so long beside human beings to whom we relate, and so rarely see them with the insights and perspectives of the awakened eye. He gives many instances of the awakening power, sometimes the wonder-working power, of sharpened, heightened, and transfigured vision. He speaks of a "looking gear" into which one has to shift out of ordinary seeing. And Parmenter suggests a host of games that one can play to come alive and to gain joy by using the marvelous gift of sight.

Closely allied to the zone of new powers of physical vision is a whole world of creative potentiality made available by the imaginative play of the mind, fantasy, the intersection of opposites, the inversion of conventional viewpoints, and mind-storming. Here we are usually at opposite poles from the staid, carefully sanctified protocols of unexamined routines of thought—the "normal," "natural," "safe" scenarios that are the maps of the life of Total Expectedness. To all adults, of course, exotic and exciting ideas can arise from the unconscious. However, others will come innumerable times because summoned by techniques of the applied imagination.

Thus, Bonnie Cashin tells us that in the early process of opening her mind to daring new ideas in fashion design she will take a whole lot of dresses from the rack in her bedroom and throw them in wild confusion throughout the room. Sometimes she will hang or wear gowns and coats upside down, or in bizarre positions, so that from this riotous and colorful disorder new fashion concepts may leap into her mind.

It is not surprising that when testers of creativity in adults approach subjects in their 50s (and older) to find out how they react to well-known proverbs, too many men and women react with interpretations that are lifeless and, in fact, mummified. We need to be roused from the self-inflicted (and society-inflicted) torpor that engulfs much of our mental "set" in attacking problems. In many adults, their creative potentials are not dead, but only asleep.

In an effort to stimulate fresher, more original approaches to problems, a Toronto consultant, Savo Bojicic, invented a small (3½ pounds) inexpensive "Think Tank," which was used in a game of putting the imagination to work on new paths. Explaining why he spent over $100,000 developing his little Think Tank, Bojicic said "I want to help people to think properly, to widen their potential as human beings, to teach people how to learn again. Thinking skills will become more important as more and more people need to be retrained." Manuel Escot in *The Canadian Magazine* for June 8, 1974, described how this little machine could be used by someone, perhaps an adult in late middle age, to help save his marriage. Suppose the five words produced by manipulating the knobs of the tank come up as WOLF, MIMICRY, CONFETTI, VIRGINITY, and BULLDOZER. Let the mind move, really *move*, imaginatively on these words (I have space for only two here, the two most seemingly incongruous perhaps): MIMICRY: Acting, artificiality. Be natural, be human. Distortion, arguments. End this, and abandon pettiness. BULLDOZER: Power. Stop overpowering her. Don't tell her she's stupid. Level up, smooth the edges of our relationship. Demolish, rebuild. Start from the beginning, remember the things that used to give pleasure and repeat them.

In Synectics, a transactional idea-gathering technique that operates best with seven or eight people, an exercise occurs that really astonishes people new to the technique. It derives from Charles S. Whiting, and is called the Forced Fit. Suppose the group is struggling with the problem of inventing a more efficient hairdryer, one that will be almost silent. The manager of the discussion will ask the group members to choose an object as wildly different from the still-uninvented hairdryer as possible. Someone suggests the Taj Mahal! This is accepted, and members of the group strain to find analogies that might confer new attributes upon the proposed dryer, and open up new approaches for a creative invention.

Too fantastic? Too absurd? Yet this technique for stimulating the adult imagination has worked well enough, long enough, in Synectics groups to be retained to stimulate creative power. Synectics also employs the "excursion," which I find virtually the same as mind-storming. In this, members of a group are invited to release their imaginations freely for solutions, and not to worry about the cost. Two benefits occur. For one thing, the air can become electric with ideas—many seeming to be "bizarre," "far-out," "absurd," but often rich with original solutions. Every excursion like this is a stretching exercise to get rid of mental inertia.

The second benefit is that immense questions, and certain seemingly fantastic ideas developed within their larger-than-lifesize dreaming, can often be reduced to the small canvas of the problem in such a way as to provide the solution. For example, the immense question, posed in a group: "How can we get the United Nations to work better?" can be reduced to a manageable, still fascinating query: "How can an older adult become a citizen of the world?"

It is crucial, of course, that all ideas in enclave mind-storming discussions be at first accepted and posted. In these sessions, without putdowns, highly workable ideas will emerge and get everybody's recognition. There is no room, however, for the "little killer ideas," as Alex Osborn used to call them: "We tried that last year"; "We are too small for that"; "It isn't worth doing"; "It won't work"; "It costs too much"; or, as recorded at an engineering deans' conference when they were looking at needs and solutions: "Are you serious?"; "You must be joking"; "I've got a better idea"; "It's too early"; "It's too late"; "Nobody would agree to that."

In fact, there is an interesting folder available called *The Absurd Dictionary*, which lists 500 ways of saying "No" to a new idea! (It's published as a service to the creative process by IBM Corporation.)

Astonishing and unusual ideas and approaches can ensue from group sessions. Thus, the designer Victor Papanek of the Department of Creative Arts at Purdue University reported in 1969 to a national seminar on creativity* that he and his students had been able to originate more than 800 ideas that could contribute to the solution of social problems across the world.

Papanek reported some devices and toys invented by him and student associates in Finland for partly disabled children:

> A 24-square-meter exercising environment for children with cerebral palsy was designed and built in Finland. This environment has built-in toys. It folds up into a two-meter-square cube which, in turn, breaks into two parts to make it transportable through revolving doors or in a microbus. Most clinics in Finland and

*Sponsored by the Thomas Alva Edison Foundation, the Institute for Development for Educational Activities, and The Johnson Foundation.

Sweden do not have the necessary equipment for these children; so this cube is now taken from town to town.

A second cube of this type has just been completed at Purdue University and is designed for use by mongoloids, cretins, and children with other disabilities. In this environment, there are quiet corners in which the children can hide. Other areas are so very, very soft that the children can jump headfirst from the top of the six-foot rack and land enveloped by the extra-soft pillows on the floor. These low-cost cubes were designed, built, and completed in 42 hours. They will soon be made available to clinics in the United States.

One of the students working with Papanek in Finland found that when he took a rubber ball, put wooden pegs into it, and then pressed on them, the pegs would spring back. This made an excellent toy for children suffering from paraplegia, quadriplegia, cerebral palsy, and other disabling diseases.

Papanek calls the key to his and his students' success their "wealth of enthusiasm"—exactly the commodity that is so often in short supply among many otherwise well-equipped adults in their later years.

So far the discussion here has concentrated on older adults in idea-arousing groups. Yet there is wide scope in developing one's imaginative gifts as an individual, not least for many older adults who find themselves frequently or constantly alone and lonely.

The report of one creativity conference invites the individual reader to try a number of small creative exercises devised to help develop creativity among schoolchildren through the magic of words. One of these asks, "Which is bigger, a pain or a pickle?"* The editor of the report remarks:

Dead silence is exactly how most adults respond, but children in the elementary age group do not hesitate a minute. One says, "A pain, because you feel it all over." Another answers, "A pickle, because it is big and long, while a pain is sort of shrimpy." Such questions do not seem nonsensical to them as they do to most adults; youngsters are attuned to questions like this.

Nonsensical? But without some element of the nonsensical in our lives, the drying-up process begins. Fantasy also: the bubbling cataract that can irrigate the drying soil of our imagination. We know very little about how much people fantasize in their ordinary lives. How many Walter Mittys are there? And where does simple wishing break off and fantasy begin?

Great are the uses of fantasy, and never more so than in the later years of life. Alan Lakein, the management consultant, suggests that fantasies are good in coping with life and trying to plan one's years pro-

*From *Making It Strange*, by E. Paul Torrance.

ductively, but that people tend to censor even their fantasy life, and that in fact "there's nothing wrong with uncensored fantasies." And he goes on: "Don't be afraid to include such far-out wishes as climbing the Matterhorn, going to a group-sex party, eating a whole cheesecake, taking the year off, building a retirement home in Italy, chartering a yacht, adopting triplets, and losing 40 pounds by jogging an hour a day." The world of fantasy can be the individual adult's "excursion." In that world the rules of routine life that inhibit us should be suspended during the game.

Unleash the mind! From such liberation comes most of our prose fiction, our poetry, our plays, our music and ballet, much of our art and architecture; all our utopias, and many of our utopian ideas (children's villages, literacy villages, Pugwash-type conferences); many medical breakthroughs, space adventures, astonishing yet seemingly "simple" inventions, and some of our finest breakthroughs in interpersonal relations.

Fantasy can be the generator of real adventures. If you can maintain the fantasy of going "on the stage," you may, years late, enroll in an amateur company and begin the adventure. At the least, you may take part in the production side of plays. If you can continue to imagine yourself as a painter, even though like Clementine Hunter everything interferes, the chances are high that, like her, you will one day apply oil to canvas, or hand to clay. However, you must have the will to ultimately make real the fantasy on whatever terms.

And especially should we in our middle and later years train ourselves to turn concepts upside down; intersect opposites; challenge conventionalities; look at the kitchen at home or the park around the corner from the retirement home as arenas for the game of "Why and Why not?" and the game of "How?"

In our time, in a society that deluges the TV screens and living rooms with canned emotions; in the society of the nuclear family and the insatiable computer, where real death and illness and old age are as deftly hidden as possible, people not only "lose touch" but lose the sense and consolation of physical touch.

A good side of our age is its willingness to accept the fact that there is a threshold of isolation in the individual life beyond which the estranged or grieving self must call out for counsel or comradeship. Hence the appearance of sensitivity groups, T-groups, encounter weekends, Primal Therapy sessions where adults may regain both the ecstasy of actually being touched by others, and the therapy of being able to bring into the open among hopefully sympathetic companions, old traumatic wounds and crippling or inhibiting hangups.

In North America there is a continent-wide network of therapy groups, producing finally the scenario so vividly described by Jane Howard in the pages of *Please Touch*. Jane Howard did more than simply visit representative groups practising celebrated techniques and interview their high priests. She often participated in the exercises, and cogently described her personal reactions as an experimental subject.

Those who do read *Please Touch* may, however, be struck by the impression that there is little room for older adults in sensitivity and release sessions. Is it widely supposed that there is a cut-off point on the life journey, say age 60, where it no longer matters whether people are sensitized or not? That perhaps—as it is said in law enforcement circles that elderly criminals are rare—so also the therapy world of *Please Touch* is for the young, the aggressive careerists not yet past early middle age, and the affluent couples whose marriages are falling apart or who are simply bored to death? Many advertisements of encounter groups across the continent specify age: not over 45, interested people 20 to 40, and so on. What is the rationale here? That older adults lack funds? That they lack the energy? That they are "past all that"?

There is another explanation. Some encounter experiences can be demanding and abrasive. Organizers of the groups, in addition to fearing that the gap between youngest and oldest may be too great, may also have a conception of later adults as too conservative, too rigid, and too respectable to be good subjects for the demands (in some cases, actual rigors and grotesqueries) of the encounter situations. At all events, few older adults appear, least of all the ill and the impoverished.

Yet a frequent phenomenon among people from their mid-50s on, and notably in their 70s and older, is that like Gide they feel themselves to be far younger than their years. The 80-year-old widow of a famous American judge whom I once met in Vancouver felt herself to be inwardly as young as when she was a girl at college; small and slight, even physically she showed much of the *joie de vivre* of a far younger woman. And a Canadian woman, Olive MacKay Petersen, writing about her reactions to her age in the Toronto *Globe and Mail* states, "I turned 65 last year—and on a good day feel about 25." Thus in spirit and mind many older adults are equipped to respond to the best of the sensitivity groups.

In addition, there are great numbers of men and women in their later years who have carried all their lives secret fears and feelings of sorrow and guilt. Simply because they are now 65 or 75 or older does not mean that these feelings have got up and gone away. Of course in many cases they have been assuaged or compensated for, or in some instances actually outlived—but many in the later years are suffering from personal deficits, anxieties, and open wounds. And what about the large company described by Erikson who end their lives in "disgust and despair"? They are surely as entitled to the consolations and support of touch therapy and transactional empathy as the anxious and disquieted young. It is hard to deny that for many older adults the techniques of some of the encounter groups might indeed be distasteful or ineffective—perhaps injurious. Many, however, would thrive and grow with them.

The later years also offer another exciting potentiality—the possibility of participating on one of the new frontiers of experimentation with the beneficent effect of brain waves—what Maya Pines well calls the "beautiful world" of bio-feedback.[1] Pines documents the advances made in the study of the rhythm of our brain waves: the discoveries that not only mental but also physical states may be transformed by the individual's learning to recognize under guidance the varying waves of the brain—called alpha, beta, theta, and delta—and to employ his or her concentration in such a way as to obtain therapeutic benefits from the alpha states; also to generate from the low-alpha or theta rhythms the kind of reverie that often delivers breakthroughs and production.

The extraordinary Swami Rama, a noted yogi from India who astonished the experimenters at the Menninger Foundation by being able in effect to stop his heart (that is, to create a beat so rapid that it could no longer pump blood) for 17 seconds, was 45, and approaching the Ulyssean gates. Scientists like Neal Miller, Barbara Brown, Joe Kamiya, and Elmer and Alyce Green have no inhibitions about the age of their subjects. As is so often the case, it is the self-image that older adults have of themselves, and nothing else, that admits or bars them to the new and beautiful worlds of transcendental meditation, touch therapies, and bio-feedback.

Many men and women whose image of themselves lowers their confidence and joy of living can find new pride and happiness even in very late years by improving body and spirit. Programs such as those sponsored by the SAGE organization (Senior Actualization and Growth Explorations) and those of the TELOS Group in Bellevue, Washington, introduce adults over 60 to the wonderful worlds of body rhythm, musical exercises, self-awareness "games," and mind healing. Marie Paulyn's Stepping Stones Centre where adults feeling at the end of their tether can be renewed through sauna, voluntary exercises, massage, meditation, delicious but healthful diet, and nonintrusive group companionship, is still another example of resources for renewal.

There is clearly a need for the development of new kinds of groups in which older adults can talk out their deeper fears and anxieties and find the therapy for remorse that is sometimes provided among sympathetic companions—companions, moreover, whose role in the sessions is that of peers, not gods or high priests. How these newer-style groups might come into being, and what their processes might be, would be excellent target questions for mind-storming among enclaves of interested older adults. One approach would be to use E. L. Thorndike's questionnaire on the learning and unlearning of attitudes among adults for the initial thrust.

Obviously, Ulyssean voyages can be undertaken not only in the physical world but in the inner world of the self. Once again, in a number of currently popular cults, the attention is focused on the young. Yet in large cities, at least, many opportunities exist for older adults to find their horizons widening through exploration of mystic lore derived from man's ancient encounters with the mysteries of the universe. Nor does this fresh search for old and new wisdom necessarily require abandonment of your own long-held faith (a common fear).

Two hungers are typical of many older adults who give serious thought to what their whole life has been about. One hunger is the desire to know more about the supernatural world, or even to establish once and for all whether it exists. Usually they look in vain to the orthodox religions for illumination or certainty in this field. Many conventional clergy are very quiet or evasive about it, because they themselves are doubtful or insecure. Some adopt exaggerated social concerns as a substitute for faith in supernatural things.

The second hunger is for the availability of every power that will aid the feeling of integration of the self: that you are a unique being, spiritual as well as physical, and—in spite of the terrible enigma of unexplainable evil—part of an essentially harmonious universe. The healing power, therefore, of meditative religions, yoga, and beneficent occult studies can be very great. Orthodox religions have beautiful things to contribute to those willing to make the real effort to grasp them.* However, in the meditative and occult groups at their best the seeker can find a beauty drawn from the universe, its winds, stars, and flowers which can enrich and help integrate the self; the best of the white occult is one example. If older men and women find all these stimuli and consolations in orthodox religions alone, or in humanism or atheism alone, well and good; but if not, why do so few investigate the potentialities of the less conventional faiths and philosophies? To do so is to engage in a Ulyssean adventure, although your may not travel more than 15 miles from your home. On the other hand, the search may take you late in life across continents and seas, among strange peoples and to distant cities you never dreamed to see except in fantasy.†

There is another way, often neglected, to explore and actualize the unique inner self. This is through the medium of the personal journal. The most typical record book of our society is probably the office calendar—certainly it is the most prestigious. Here are entered the hundreds, finally thousands, of interview engagements, luncheons,

*The churches are already contributing to the new field of successful aging through such organizations as the ecumenical Canadian Institute for Religion and Gerontology founded by the remarkable Ulyssean nun, Sister St. Michael Guinan, and the international society *Opera Pieta* founded by Monsignor Alcido da Filippo, representative of the Holy See at the United Nations.
†Robert Munroe, a California businessman who is also a serious student of psychic phenomena, and author of *Journeys Out of the Body*, has helped prepare a number of dying people for the next stage of their cosmic journey. Indeed, why not?

committee meetings, and other supports and impediments of the busy executive. "Impediments," because often in his 50s or early 60s he feels the weight upon him of a succession of days already given away to innumerable meetings, however seemingly important; "supports," because so long as the office calender is filled, he can feel that his existence is justified. It is a testimonial of his identity.

Many women, and some men, keep a diary of events attended, items bought, and other daily happenings, usually recorded in skeleton form. The value of this is obvious—not least for later years when you can check back to revive memories or ascertain when certain personal things occurred. Even so meager a record helps to break the gray anonymity of days that otherwise stream past, soon lost in limbo. Even if you keep a personal journal, there is merit in reserving the very top of the page for jotting down succinctly the day's events.

But nothing can equal or replace the personal journal as the sphere of action for a special kind of Ulyssean journey—the continuing quest of the self, seen in the light of events experienced and books and people encountered. The journal is the record of one's reactions to life and to the fascinating thrust and play of the self. As such, it involves both mind and emotions; and it is usually written in the illusion or with the profession that no one is going to read the entries except oneself. For exactly these reasons, the journals of the very young—mid-adolescents, for example—are usually tiresome to read on the rare occasions when they are made available. They are important documents for insight into the writer and, of course, for his or her insight into the self. However, the emotions are usually too heavy and melodramatic for older adult readers (usually yourself, years later!), and the words are too self-conscious and postured.

These are not usually the faults of personal journals kept by adults in their later years. Why, therefore, has the journal as an art form had so little attention in North America and so much in England and Europe? One obvious answer may be that in older cultures mature men and women have learned to look inwardly into their reactions to life much more than have adults in a largely externalized, volatile society. At all events, it is so—but it need not always be so.

In the office calendar, the personal self never enters at all: "At 3 P.M. Mr. Herbert Cloke, National Elevator Company"—what does this tell us later about Mr. Cloke or the person who is going to interview him?

The little daily diary of events does better, a good deal better:

May 14, 1981 (Thursday).
Got up at 8 A.M.
Cleaned house, had coffee with Mary.
3 P.M. Paid plumber for fixing drain ($15).
Mary picking up Bobby at school.

I stayed in with the baby and Bobby at night, and reread *The French Lieutenant's Woman*, by John Fowles. Baby fretful (caught cold Sunday?).
To bed at 11 p.m. Must check on supplementary pension cheque tomorrow.

This clears away the gray anonymity of the days, but it provides little insight into the interesting, and often enchanting, journey of the self. The personal journal is light years in advance of this, and I give a fictional example: (a brief summary of the day's events has already been listed in the upper right-hand margin of the journal):

Tuesday, August 25, 1981. A beautiful morning. Sky banked with clouds, light sweet wind. I went for a stroll in the fields behind the house. Startled a snake which went gliding off down the path and into the deep grass. Also startled me. How can a 60-year-old-man and a veteran of 40 air missions over Europe still be chilled by a harmless snake? Where did this fear come from? Mother, perhaps: she also feared insects. No—both parents. Can you unlearn a fear of snakes? At the campus in the city last week, a notice up inviting "adult subjects" to volunteer for a course on getting rid of fear of water, reptiles, etc.

At suppertime, delegation from the town to ask me to run for mayor. I offered coffee and said No. They pressed pretty hard—they are dear people, and hard to refuse. I reminded them that I had twice before run for mayor and been defeated, admittedly by narrow margins. Marge Kelly said, "Mark, everybody loves you but everybody doesn't vote for you," and Doug Ogilvie said, "You're our Adlai Stevenson."

Picked up at random after supper O'Connor's book on the sinking of the *Titanic (Down to Eternity)*. Wonderful things turn up: like the bravery of the 50 young bellboys and messengers who spent the last hours "joking with the passengers, with that sparrow-like impudence of the young Cockney." Not one of them tried to get into the lifeboats. Likewise, the members of the ship's band. Marvelous quality of the so-called "little" people. And the so-called "great"?

Near midnight I turn on the FM. Surprised by a flute concerto by Mozart. The solo flute is about at the bottom of my list, still I listen spellbound. I wonder, is the flute the oldest of wind instruments? shepherd boy on Greek hill, etc.? Feel as always how quiet the house is. It is almost a year. Somehow the flute concerto keeps returning to my mind, and also that group of people from town. A sort of festival?

It is so late. I will look at this in the morning.

This entry has a number of the qualities of the personal journal: insight, reporting to oneself, restrained emotion, the birth of creative ideas. Typical of many journal entries is the switch to the present tense at some point in the entry, sometimes through the whole entry—it has the advantage of bringing an episode back more intensely. Aside from all its other advantages, the personal journal can provide a sustained dialogue for many older adults who feel that they can never seem to find anyone with whom to exchange their many reflections.

One objection to keeping such a journal may be that it takes too much time. "I'm just too busy." But "too busy" doing what? Alan Lekein urges all of us to analyze our use of time—watch ourselves for a week, for example. The journal entry above might take the writer about three-quarters of an hour, far less than a situation comedy program on TV; and whereas the program leaves those who watch with a rather flat feeling of temporary risibility, the journal provides an experience in reflection, imagination, and the intimate sense of one's own life. Another objection may be that a journal entry like the foregoing is too close to a literary exercise, although presumably it would be natural enough to many well-read adults. But in any case, the personal journal still functions well on a simpler level:

Saturday, June 13, 1981. Not knowing what else to do today, I cleaned my room, and went out to the Zoo in the park. It was cloudy but it didn't rain, and afterward the sun came out. I've been going to the Zoo off and on for years, and then today I had a funny reaction.

I was watching the children looking in at the cages and pits and then running away laughing and shouting, and suddenly it didn't seem to me right that animals should be closed up all the time like that, and everybody else should be free. I actually wondered if it meant anything to the animals that the children could run and jump and be free. I think I would rather go to a safari park such as they write about in the weekend paper where at least the animals can run free. Maybe I know something about being in a cage, when I think of it. Still I can go free in a way they can't.

I loved the children today. I love them anyway. I don't mind their noise—I wouldn't want to be isolated from them. I was thinking this afternoon, my grandmother never seemed to like children. We were always kept in corners, etc. I wonder why she was like that? Something in her own childhood, perhaps?

At 5 P.M. I found a new little teahouse two blocks over near the subway stop. They have Twinings Tea—Earl Grey tea! And not very expensive, and the service is so friendly and nice. I haven't much, but I have enough to be able to go a couple times a week to that teashop. For the company. And the tea. Also, of course, I can buy some Twinings tea bags, when I think of it, and invite in two or three women here who've probably never heard of it.

I have two books here from the library. One I can't read—a story with characters that could never live on land or sea. I don't often pick lemons like that. But the other one I can hardly put down. It's about a women in her 70s who makes economy trips all over the world. I don't exactly envy her, still I would like to do it. You never can tell. Anyway, I realize today that I've been overlooking the big travel section. One of the girls said to me today, "If you can't go to the world, you can bring the world to you." She tells me they have free travel movies every Wednesday night, and why don't I come? Maybe I will.

When we are feeling tired or flat, we may be stimulated in making journal entries by a few questions kept at hand. For example: How did I react to the weather today? Has it been, all in all, a "great" day, "ordinary" day, "dead loss" day—and why? Who was the most interesting person I met today (or this week)? What was the most interesting conversation I had today (or this week)? What was the most interesting dream or fantasy? What was the item in the papers or magazines, or on TV or radio, that most widened my horizons? What book, film, or play most intrigued, informed, and moved me? What was my most frustrating experience today (this week)? When did I feel myself to be most real today? (I am indebted to June O'Reilly for adapting these questions from my self-actualization seminars for use in journal-keeping.)

A little book and pens, costing altogether five to ten dollars a year, does not seem too high a toll to pay for the entrance to what may become across the later years a personal Ulyssean journey, freshening your mind, reinforcing and illuminating your identity, helping heal and integrate the self, and stimulating creativity in your later years.

An excellent way to enter the Ulyssean life in later adulthood is to become devoted, even passionately committed, to social causes. Even Simone de Beauvoir sees light pouring from and around such social crusaders as Voltaire, Zola, and Bertrand Russell. Few older adults are placed in the limelight of history as these Ulyssean figures were; but scaling down the dimension of the enterprise in no way weakens its power for the person whose mind and spirit have been captivated by what he conceives to be a first-rate cause. However, to produce rich benefits for the self, the commitment must be real. It must not be a flight from the self by a feverish round of activity, but a stimulating investment of heart and mind in promoting or supporting human causes—with comrades or alone. Of course a later life of social commitment need not exclude journal-keeping or the quiet seeking of inner self-journeys.

What the true exercise does is to enrich the self by experiences in social comradeship, which help to teach it new insights while also testing the strength and variety of its inner resources. And all too few older adults do this. Where are all the people, especially age 65-plus, well enough equipped with time, money, and health—where are they in the ranks of the adults in our society who are pitting often slender resources against what they conceive to be the powers of darkness?

Causes come in little packages and big packages, in permanent exercises and temporary exercises. A permanent exercise, for example, is standing watch on the kind of soulless developer who will conduct an endless King Kong expedition through still-undestroyed inner-city areas unless someone stands up to him. A temporary exercise might be mobilizing public opinion in one of the frequent cases where locked-together groups of management and union disputants callously expose whole populations to the discomforts of stalled transportation systems, immobilized hospitals, reeking jungles of garbage, and undelivered mail.

Situations like these call for pressure groups, confrontations, representations through newspapers, radio, and television outlets, and similar techniques. The antagonists have their rights and needs; so has the public; so—very much so—have the older adults. How is it possible for a transit strike, for example, to freeze the public arteries of a great city for a month and, in effect, imprison great numbers of elderly people who have no cars within the tiny orbits of their normal walking range—and for days to pass with no letters of protest, no telegrams, no blocked switchboards at municipal and other government offices or corporation or union headquarters?

"But I keep informed." Many older men and women take a certain pride in the fact that they are well informed about the issues and crises of the day, including those occurring in their midst—and this is a just pride. It is important for anyone who has some thought of being actualized by outside human events to read the newspapers regularly; also to evaluate issues, tune in to press conferences and issues-and-answers programs, and monitor live telecasts and broadcasts of controversial events. Useful, too, to make telephone calls to informed or, even better, uninformed friends about these crises and issues.

It is important—but it is not really a Ulyssean exercise. The Ulyssean adult is the one who, like the Toronto architect Eric Arthur at the age of 70, sets up a hue and cry about some encroachment on human rights that otherwise will go by unnoticed—in some cases hardly noticed by the encroachers themselves. Arthur organized vigorous opposition to the development plans of a giant merchandising firm that would have destroyed the historic and still-beautiful Old City Hall of Toronto. In nearly all great cities there are now groups that keep watch over the historical heritage and beauty of the city. Other groups—all of them low in funds and membership—try to keep a city's or county's conscience awake to the need to guard against unnecessary destruction of homes. There is a whole domain of good development, but still *ad hoc* groups are needed to protect a lake, a park, a settlement of cottages, a street, or a whole neighborhood or area.

Few of these active groups seem to include older adults. Incredibly enough, even the desperately needed movement to reform the scandalous conditions in many nursing homes throughout North America has enlisted little active support from the huge population of older adults. Passive support? "I keep informed"? What can passive support accomplish?

The most searing book, and a deeply moving one, about the neglect of the friendless and helpless old in North America, *Nobody Ever Died of Old Age*, was published in 1970 by a young American woman, aged 32. Likewise, Josephine Lawrence was in her 30s in 1934 when she wrote the powerful and heartbreaking novel, *Years Are So Long*, describing the desolation of an elderly couple who thought they could depend on their family. Jan de Hartog was middle-aged (about 50) when in 1964 he wrote *Hospital*, one of the most chilling documentary accounts ever written, about the terrifying conditions in a huge municipal hospital for blacks and poor whites, many of them old people, in Texas. De Hartog was inspired to write the book by his experience as a volunteer hospital assistant while he and his wife were on a visit to Texas. It was not even their country! And still, millions of older adults listen nightly to vapid remarks passing for humor from television talk-show guests about all those oil-rich Texans.

Where is everybody? It is not just Texas—Texas is no worse and no better than anywhere else: it is the human condition, the outcry of the needs of all the world. "My life has been governed," said Bertrand Russell in his 80s, "by. . .an unbearable pity for the sufferings of mankind." Yet, as already indicated, Russell brought joy wherever he went. In the process of losing himself in causes he found himself more and more. Beauvoir tells with obvious pleasure of the aged and infirm Voltaire, routing himself out of his comfortable chateau where he still enjoyed the varied delights of love, to go great distances in bone-shaking coaches, and insistently pestering the king of France until a terrible wrong to a young man had been righted. Is it a coincidence that everyone speaks of Voltaire's joyousness of spirit in his old age?

The point here is the self-actualizing power of the enterprises, not the exploits themselves. The size of the enterprise is immaterial, so long as the involvement of the person concerned is one of devotion, of losing-one's-self in participation, which in turn enriches and further activates the self and establishes around it the continuing climate of creativity. Almost nothing can hinder older men and women from engaging in some kind of active role in meeting human needs or preserving beauty except actual physical immobilization, and often not even that. One immobilized man, then 76, proved this to me by dictating letters to the newspapers which were published from time to time and were full of good sense, wit, and some creative ideas.

To run for political office after, say, age 60 can be a big and authentic Ulyssean adventure. Fewer and fewer older adults seem to do it, partly because of the expense, which can be high; but more because there is an evident trend in North America toward the nomination of younger candidates. The real problem is the silent disqualification of themselves by men and women 60,70, and older because, as usual, though perhaps splendidly qualified, they think of themselves as "too old". Why too old?—if they are physically vigorous, mentally alert, rich with experience, open to new ideas, and devoted to the good of community or nation?

A congenial arena for older Ulysseans to enter is municipal government. Perhaps this is largely due to the absence of party machinery and power cliques. Local or regional communities are natural stages for the nonpartisan man or woman. At all events, in city and county and village councils, older adults who have the energy and guts to do so frequently become mayors, controllers, aldermen, and councillors. (I speak chiefly here of Canada. Gus Harris, 73, mayor of Scarborough, Ontario, is a good example.)

Much more of this could be true of provincial, state, and federal politics if later-age adults had more faith in themselves. These political arenas need more models of attractive, well-performing, dedicated older adults. And this may indeed ensue as the political "clout" of the 60-plus group increases with the shift in population figures. Meanwhile, at the very least, older adults can do what the splendid Canadian Ulyssean, Dr. Hans Blumenthal, recently did, when in 1979, at age 84, he ran as his own man in the Canadian federal election because he believed enough in his principles to do so. He garnered a very small vote (his cause was control over nuclear arms) but he found an excellent way of spreading his ideas; he also gave a fine model of a vigorous, intelligent, dedicated citizen in his 80s, meeting people at parties, gatherings, and at their doorsteps, and speaking on radio and TV. With a major party behind him, it is safe to say that he might have won. His performance made his age irrelevant.*

For many adults, not politics "as such" but "passionate causes" become their concern—that is, human causes where personal emotion fortifies that commitment. Three useful examples, among many options, are Amnesty International, Civil Liberties, and movements to reduce the the cruelty of world hunger and medical deprivation. Such causes evidently arouse little more than mild or nominal commitment from most adults, although even this is a gain. They periodically arouse personal anger in the minority of committed Ulyssean people. Perhaps

*A charming Press Gallery story tells of a candidate in a backwoods constituency who was accused by his opponent of being a sexagenarian. He could not deny it!—and lost, thus reinforcing one of two wrong stereotypes about age, morals, and politics.

this arousal of anger is one reason why such great causes have so few backers from the passive armies of middle and later adults. Many people fear anger—fear their own even more than others'! Anger, after all, is a powerful emotion. "What will people think if I seem too emotional?" etc.

Yet anger can be a cleansing and self-actualizing emotion. I refer here, so to speak, to the "big" angers, but there are also hundreds of justifiable little angers, such as that of Artur Rubinstein when he arrived late and chilled one night in Montreal after some abominable mismanagements in plane schedules. The pianist, who was 87 at the time, remarked heatedly to the music critic Jacob Siskind that "the amazing thing is that no one complained. People just accept these things without protesting. I was furious. . .You can quote me. They the airline personnel are liars. They have no right to treat people in such cavalier fashion!" Siskind reported that Rubinstein's face was slightly flushed by the excitement; but then he had got it off his chest, and "soon we were back to the Old Rubinstein."

Anger is therapeutic when used like this; bitterness and frustrating cynicism are not. It can channel off tensions and self-pity; explode frustrations; bring a certain glow to body and spirit; and promote the zest for life and the active rather than reactive attitude toward the human scene out of which creativity can be born.

The symbol of people creatively involved in social causes in their later years is not that of the woman of whom it was said that "she went through life asking for the manager." On the contrary, it is the happy warrior, whose spirit and thrust the years have not weakened.

Another form of "social cause" is individual service to others in need. Many large cities in North America now have "volunteer bureaus" where men and women who choose to do so can find many avenues to service. The process of enrolling is simple. You go to a central office (where you will be warmly welcomed), and are invited to select from a very large circular file of people in need of the special contribution you want to make: read to a blind person? Visit a lonely shut-in? Drive a "meals-on-wheels" car? Act as a foster grandparent? Teach a skill to a group of older (or younger) people? The opportunities seem endless because the offers to help never match the needs.

To follow the Ulyssean way is to accept the reality of change, not to accept all change passively and reactively, but to negotiate it imaginatively and dynamically for yourself and your society, and to create change.

There are hundreds of ways, small and large, of breaking the cast of routines that otherwise gradually hardens about one until the drying process has desiccated vision, originality, spontaneous responses, and the reflexes of change. Even physical posture and style of dress begin to reflect the aridity of old ideas. For example, elderly men who invariably choose drab colors, dispiriting suits, and squarely placed hats to match funereal faces betray their rigidity of response. If, as is usually the case, these physically dried-out and mournful attributes are accompanied by moribund attitudes toward the self and life, then potential creativity dies. Better by far to put on a colorful pullover, buy a beret (cheaper than a hat), pick up an outrageous paperback, and go out to a café to sip the espresso coffee or the capuccino never tasted in all one's 53 or 75 years. Better to haunt for an hour or two each week the gourmet section of a supermarket and try out Burgundy snails and octopus.

Not many of us follow Colette and turn a dignified procession through a garden into a child's excursion, breaking and smelling petals, tasting and crumbling, stroking the backs of inquisitive insects—but we are the losers. Better, instead of endlessly deploring marijuana from reading about it in the newspapers, and listening to "informed opinions" on the radio and television, to talk with young people who have actually smoked it or, if opportunity offers, smoke a marijuana cigarette oneself. If you have never in your whole abstaining life allowed alcohol to pass your lips, drink a glass or two of wine; if you enjoy wine and for years have castigated abstainers as living drab lives, try going without for two weeks to see if any joy remains in life. Better—to quote one of the most perceptive men I have known, Kenneth Norris—to break the unvarying routine of moderation by doing something too much: "Once in a while eat too much, drink too much, love too much, spend too much, play too much. . . ." "Everything in moderation," said Oscar Wilde, "even moderation."

What holds us back from the small creative adventures that, as they multiply, fill life with a certain verve, small exhilarations that build the climate for larger odysseys? The self-image of what we think we ought to be and ought to do. Men and women who would not now hesitate to attend a Billy Graham rally for interest's sake, because that has long since become a respectable enterprise, will not set foot inside a local Buddhist temple or attend an open and introductory session on yoga or transcendental meditation—not because they are not interested, even fascinated (they have "read a lot about it")—but because it is too heterodox for their idea of what older adults ought to do.

Little evidence exists as to whether adults in their 50s, 60s, and later years can successfully learn to play an instrument. The actor Barry Fitzgerald learned to play the organ at 53, but then organs have some sort of sanctified connection with *The Messiah*, hard-working church choirs, and Easter services. It may be that numbers of adults in the 50-plus years have mastered the guitar and the accordion, but if so we never hear of it. Yet even limited mastery induces growth and generates energy in the whole self.

Arthur Ingham of Niagara Falls took up golf when he was about 75, surely a rather rare phenomenon; and other features of his late life were strong indications of a self-actualizing personality. Thus, Ingham was not only still driving at 91, but the car he chose was a red convertible runabout, a dashing choice for an "old gentleman." When he was 90 he went on a two-month cruise to Fiji, New Zealand, Australia, Manila, Hong Kong, Guam, and Singapore. Jack Marks, who interviewed Ingham, observed that he was "chipper and cheery, walking sprightly and swiftly. He talks and acts the same way."*

The study of another language and its culture can throw open windows of the mind to a whole flood of new concepts and knowledge. André Gide never mastered Latin, yet he was working happily at it the day he died at 81: the process helped keep him young, and filled part of his days with pleasure. Yet few older adults commence language study, although perhaps the problem here is the lack of a powerful motive and lack of confidence.

The extent to which older adults can learn another language after 40 if they set their minds to it is shown by a preliminary study (1975) of the performance of a large sample of 862 men and women who took the Canadian civil service training programs in learning French. The study, by Thérèse Sibiga and associates, shows that about 30 percent of students age 50 and over obtained A or B standing; as against about 33 percent of those 40 to 49; about 42 percent for those 30 to 39; and 42 percent for those 20 to 29. It is a fact that in achievement of A standing alone the two younger categories clearly outstripped the students 40 and over, but not in the B classification.[2]

One of the best, and neglected, reasons for studying a language in later years is that the study itself stimulates mind and imagination. Besides, knowing the Ulysseans, one can just conceive of a few of them setting out to show that experimental new methods of learning a language may be efficient. As volunteers, and with little to lose, these pioneers could, for example, undertake studies under the so-called Lazonov or suggestology technique, based on the theory of suggestion, devised by Georgi Lazonov of the Institute of Suggestology and Parapsychology at Sofia. Lazonov contended in a series of lectures given at universities throughout the United States and Canada in 1971 and 1975 that adults could become proficient in, say, French or English as a second language in a matter of 20 days. Lazonov's interest in the subject came out of his training and practice in psychiatry. The method was born from his own experiences in psychotherapy, and does not employ hypnosis.

Three of Lazonov's dicta relate to the whole subject of the fears that hold adults back from new adventures in languages, and other fields of learning. With this technique, he claims, "no longer is a person limited by believing that learning is unpleasant; that what he learns today he will forget tomorrow; that learning deteriorates with age." (Lazonov

*Lady Maud Robinson of Toronto, at 84, and with a severe hearing handicap, flew off to the Magnetic Pole, and developed a fascinated interest in the myths and habits of the northern musk oxen.

himself is now 54.) And he adds: "The whole of life is learning—not only in school. I believe that developing this high motivation—which comes through the technique—can be of the greatest importance to humanity." For an older adult to volunteer for language learning under this technique would be a small but immensely valuable Ulyssean act. Even more so would be to hazard a second career by becoming a teacher in the technique, trained in the Sofia institute.

The way in which explorations of a more self-creative lifestyle frequently lead on to superb Ulyssean adventures is also exciting. For example, a professional man, a 67-year-old widower, "adopts" a young Greek boy under the Foster Parents Plan. His connection with the lad, which will be officially terminated when the boy reaches 16, is maintained by occasional visits to Greece. In the course of their nine-year relationship, the foster father becomes deeply interested in modern Greek culture, especially the language and the music: he learns Greek moderately well and develops a deep affection for the bouzouki. He also visits the Greek Islands every other year. Finally, as the years pass, he becomes deeply interested in Ulysses and in the modern locations of the voyages, and proficient enough in the subject to be invited to lecture on it in summer courses.

Two women, a nurse and a teacher, both in their late 50s, and friends for several years, decide to give up motoring for cycling, partly as a result of new convictions about the automobile as an environmental pollutant. They take an extension course at a community college in the efficient handling and maintenance of bikes, and thus meet two or three people devoted to hosteling as a way of travel life. The two women become keen hostelers—they had always supposed that hostels were only for very young people. In the course of time, their interest in both travel by bike and hosteling takes them through Europe, and to international meetings of hostelers at Stockholm, Paris, Vienna, and Rome. And they become the co-authors of a useful guidebook on hosteling for older adults.

A 61-year-old bachelor taxi driver in Syracuse, New York, living a lonely life in a rooming-house, has had a very limited education. Quite late in life, however, he develops two passions: to listen as often as possible to experts on the radio and at library extension meetings talking on all kinds of subjects, and to listen to folk music—an interest roused by coming to know a Yugoslavian woman at his rooming-house who belongs to a folk-dancing group. He also develops a liking for ballet music and for Schubert and Dvorak. Concertos begin to fascinate him, first because the solo players seem to him comparable to the great lonely heroes of certain sports—then their music captivates him. He has saved a good deal of money, but he has no special interest in business; he is limited in manners and in the use of English. This has contributed to his loneliness; only a few perceptive people see his quality. He decides to take two months off every summer and visit the great music festivals and centres in North America. He begins what develops into a series of annual odysseys driving to many musical events in different parts of the country. When I met him he was developing a package of creative plans to stimulate interest in classical music among elderly people and meet their needs through cheaper and more accessible festivals.

The role of the will in later-life creativeness is paramount.[3] However, the will does not alone produce the way. The word "will" is defined as: "energy of intention"; not merely the intentions that traditionally pave the roads to both heaven and hell, but the energy to enforce the intention, to transform it into action. Physical energy is exactly the commodity that seems to be in diminishing supply among many older adults. Some commentators on the productivity of creative people attribute their later failure to produce, not to incapacity of mind and talent, but to increasing deficits of will and physical energy. But the greater factor may be loss of psychic energy: caused by the ever-deepening and darkening sense that one has become locked into unchangeable ways, or, in the words of Shakespeare's Richard II, "I wasted time, and now doth time waste me." *Lack of confidence:* this is almost the summation of the matter.

How is the older adult to break free from the immobilizing encirclement of these blocking forces: increasing physical inertia, psychic despair, and failure of nerve and confidence? The answers are not easy, because each individual self has its own complex personal history, often calling for the therapies of love and understanding; for the therapy of individual self-forgiveness; and occasionally for the therapy of extraordinarily sensitive psychoanalysis. Nonetheless, later adults can take important decisions and actions that will help them re-establish or maintain and expand their creative powers.

The first act is one of *acceptance.* This means not to mourn the past fruitlessly, not to sit immobilized by thoughts of how one is situated on entering the last years of life. Rather: greet the day lovingly, and live its precious hours as though yesterday's sorrows and tomorrow's hazards were what they mostly are—chimeras luring us from the day-by-day actualization of the self.

The second act is one of *recognition,* the acknowledgment that high potentiality remains to human beings in later life.

"But how do I start to live the creative and Ulyssean life after years of passiveness, or while in the throes of terrible self-doubts about being able to carry through?" The answer, strange though it may seem, is not unlike the first actions to set in order a disordered and dust-laden house. However, you must start where you are, in a relaxed mood of friendship with your self and with acceptance of the human comedy of which we are all a part, and begin with some simple action of clearing and remaking. It is a holy moment: "the journey of a thousand miles begins with the first step."

So simple an action as reaching for a dictionary can be the start—the dictionary that may have sat neglected for many months, even years, except for sporadic and hurried uses. Language is the stimulator of thought, and is an important channel to creativity. "Language," Peter Abelard insisted, "is generated by the intellect, and it generates intellect." In the mysterious process known to writers, thoughts are many times clearly summoned by some evocative or nostalgic word, some image-making or image-summoning word. All good writers are vocabulary builders; they have learned how traffic flows from words to concepts and images, and back again. They have also learned how to throw English vocabulary into new combinations that are not only delightful but idea-making. The same processes work to awaken the powers of older adults who are not writers at all—simply intelligent readers and seekers.

Vocabulary building is one of the least expensive and most stimulating of sports. Dictionaries provide wonderful opportunities for detective work on the derivations of words we have used without thought all our lives. Also, a considerable number of delightful paperback books are available such as Maxwell Nurnberg's *Word Play*, which uses dozens of games not only to tease and test adult readers but also to delight and educate them well—to make them grow. A deeper book and no less entertaining is Nurnberg's and Morris Rosenblum's *All About Words;* and all the paperbacks of Norman Lewis are energizing and growth-producing.

Every so often in stations, libraries, office waiting rooms, or even on subway trains, the crossword puzzle addict can be seen totally absorbed in the latest teaser. At its best, this is an admirable exercise, and if somewhere some ancient man or woman has fallen into what is euphemistically known as their "last sleep" while trying to find words to fit blanks, it will have been a worthy final curtain. This exercise has some resemblance to the creative process: problem-solving, the mental quest, some limited but real imaginative leaping. The game should, however, lead on to the richer personal arena described above: the enchanting search to enliven and enrich one's vocabulary, and through new words to open windows to new concepts.

Hundreds of little odysseys, any one of which may become a larger one, present themselves to the older man or woman who adopts an attitude of curiosity to the great world.[4] Clipping items of unusual interest from the pages of the newspaper remote from the tiresome cavalcade of front-page events can be a vital exercise. In time, and with a lively will, some of these items can be collated steadily into new worlds of interest and inquiry, even of expertise. But why do we confine ourselves to one or two local newspapers and perhaps two or three familiar magazines, when we can explore new worlds in papers and journals published in far-off places? Consider a fascinating newspaper like the *Straits Times* or the *Bangkok Post*, bringing packets of news often exotic to North

Americans and keeping the imagination supple and alive. Older adults also should break the pattern of their walks, of their drives, of their weekend excursions by bus or foot. Of course, thousands more should bicycle again, try hosteling even on a small scale, find a way of going by boat along a network of canals, make new coastal steamer trips, climb in the summer and rest on the sides of mountains or hills that have been within easy reach of life and limbs for unused years.*

What is needed is a new *set:* the "set" which demands that you put a quota on the destructive indulgence of tired drifting of thoughts, or of nostalgic sorrow for the dead days beyond recall, and of resigned refuge in the routine. To experience recurrent periods of sadness is only proof that you have depth as a human being. It is beautiful to light candles in hospitable churches for people you love and have loved. Nor is a creative life nourished by a stagnant lifestyle. A terrifying phrase that has destroyed more creative impulses than any other is "if only"—"if only I had done (or not done). . ." To dwell upon missed opportunities is to blaspheme the Sacred Present, and to miss new opportunities to live creatively. For example, there is something intensely moving and renewing in watching a younger middle-aged couple, as I have, who lost their only son, a handsome, laughing, brilliantly talented boy of 14, and a year later adopted a little deserted girl of two, naming her, significantly, Dawn.

Why do so few older adults become protectors and friends of desolate and deserted young people and children? Because older men and women have their own grandchildren? Is this a sufficient rationale for creative and compassionate people? And what of the several million reasonably well-off single adults—well enough off to have some money to spare—single by reason of choice or of death of a life partner? Is there no creative exercise by which they can match themselves with the millions of lonely young who also inwardly ache to resolve the enigma of personal isolation and alienation? I came to know an unmarried woman in her 70s whose love of young people takes the form of turning up at free concerts and plays, where attendance is often all too slight, and applauding and encouraging young musical performers and actors. "It's a great function," my own mother used to say, "to clap your hands for somebody else"—and this she did with loving interest and zest until her death at age 84. (This is what Robert Peck meant when he spoke of *ego-transcendence* in the later years.)

Thus the creative lifestyle for middle and later adulthood comes in power from looking life in the face, from *acting*, not simply mourning and brooding. But another important approach to gaining and increasing creativeness is to turn much of life and thought into problem seeking: not to be the eternal receiver, the droning echoer (which so many

*A popular sea coastal trip is the voyage from New York via the Panama Canal to Chile, and also the trips by barge through the canals of France.

older adults become), but the active questioner, the zestful attacker of hundreds of riddles that life delivers to us, and the joyous redesigner of trite things and shapes.

A problem, the *Concise Oxford Dictionary* remarks mournfully, is a "doubtful or difficult question." For example, "how to prevent it is a problem," or "problem child (difficult to control, unruly)." How dour all this is! And how much this point of view is driven home to everyone in Western society by the thousands of solemn panels wrestling, unfortunately often all too fuzzily, with "social problems, family problems, business problems, health problems," and so on and so on. Just at the end of its list of definitions, the *Concise Oxford* discovers the word "challenge": as, for example, "in chess." Then a different air enters, bracing, tonic—the air of creativity. Then problems become challenges to the applied imagination, and vivid contributors to the creative "set" of older adults.

To be specific: a small enclave of men and women, meeting to stimulate one another's creative zest and skills, can find enormous pleasure and motivation from such challenging exercises as these (those asterisked are drawn from Alex Osborn; the rest, except the first, are mine):

1. List all the unusual uses you can think of for empty cardboard boxes. (Resist the temptation to simply keep filling the box!)

*2. Men's canes have gone out of style. What would you do to try to repopularize them?

*3. Name five practical inventions that the world could use to advantage that have not yet been invented.

4. If you were deeded $300,000 to open a new store or enterprise on the major commercial street nearest your home, on condition that it must present something uniquely creative among all the tired commercial ideas—what three proposals could you make?

*5. List ten unexplored uses for Scotch Tape.

6. Think of three places commonly in use in the routine of one's progress through life that either stifle you with boredom or cause you vague feelings of dread, and describe how you would remove from them the curses of boredom and gloom.

7. Your college-age son, interested in the occult, has persuaded you to provide housing for a few delegates to the witches' convention. How do you explain their presence to your son's no-nonsense, fabulously wealthy Presbyterian great-aunt who has simultaneously decided to honor you with her presence on the same weekend?

*8. Devise three ways to adapt an old snare drum to other uses.

*9. Describe the most annoying habit of a person close to you in work or in life. Think up six tactics to get that person to change that habit for the better.

10. Take two objects as bizarrely different as possible—for example, a wrench and a brown trout, and see how far you can draw from them analogies, creative ideas, or new concepts filled with productivity for other beings or things.

11. "Your mind is like a parachute; it's no use unless it's open." To a similar result, complete the following: "Life is like a Bible;——"; "Love is like a flying saucer;——"; "Love is like Grandma's spectacles;——". (Creative exercise from the *London Spectator*.)

12. Describe an idea for a thoroughly new television show.

13. Suggest your choice of two, three, or four historical people whose meetings beyond time and space would create (a) bizarre, ludicrous, or comical conversation; (b) a highly creative situation.

14. How do you estimate another person's creativity? Write down your criteria.

14. What uses could be made of a silk top hat other than as a head covering?

Exercises like these are particularly successful in group meetings because members of the group can often hitch a ride on the ideas of others to produce additional ideas, and, of course, a certain creative excitement is generated by a mind-storming group. Individuals, however, working alone can also find immense pleasure and stimulus from these problems.

Ideas, as Alex Osborn says, are burning embers; judgment is cold water. There is a time and a place for judgments, but ideas must first have their day, and in the later years of adulthood, after most of us have spent a lifetime growing gray in the process of issuing and receiving judgments, usually the only hope we have that we can glow again with creativity is that we can now think of "problems" as challenging games, and then let our mind roam and play in the wonderful country of the unusual and the absurd.

Inevitably there are objections: good-humored, courteous, filled with good will, but objections nonetheless. *Objection One:* "Very interesting, no doubt, but I am a practical person. I'm not really interested in hypothetical situations." *Response:* But is there anything more practical really than nourishing and extending our creative powers? And do the routines of your practical life provide this? *They do?* Then yours is an exceptional case. The problem of many 60-year-olds, comments a brilliantly creative older adult, the editor Aron Mathieu, is that they already know from long experience that the thing can't be done. The 30-year-old doesn't know it can't be done, and frequently does it. This, Mathieu, goes on, is what it means to become dated—that the practical man or woman, in later maturity, has stopped looking at the exotic, the off-beat, the simply different.

Objection Two: "But I'm quite an ordinary person who's lived an ordinary life. I haven't traveled much, seen much, read all that much. I'm just out of my depth." *Response:* If that is true, that is one of the situations that does seem to affect creative performance. Of course it helps to have filled one's mind with experiences that extend the reservoir of the unconscious: this is perhaps one application of Christ's parable of the talents. Still, the great world is all about us, waiting to be explored. To be human is to possess the potentiality of creativity, and an expert witness is that extraordinary Ulyssean who has spent most of his life among workers at docks and in casual labor, Eric Hoffer, the writer of *The True Believer.* Calvin Tomkins, in his portrait of Hoffer when he was about age 66, cites Hoffer's continual astonishment at the variety and originality of the many hundreds of laborers he worked among—men unknown to the world, usually uneducated in any extensive or higher academic sense.

Finally, and in complete reverse: *Objection Three:* "I understand and appreciate what you are talking about. However, I have made it a point for years to develop ways and means of keeping creative, and following up any further suggestions in my case would just be overloading the circuits." *Response:* Beautiful. However, perhaps you would take a few minutes to check this list of facilitating the creative process derived from this book and from other writers and creative people:

1. Look at life with fresh wonderment, as though you were a child—and in fact, whenever possible, stay in the presence of young children and listen uncondescendingly and attentively to the cascades of original reactions and verbal expressions with which they color drab reality. Note some of them down: they evaporate like raindrops in the sun!

2. Seek to generate new ideas by upsetting the neat, tired order of your thoughts and throwing them in temporary disarray so that new shapes and images may appear from the creative confusion. For example, mentally rearrange your local park at which you may have stood thousands of times waiting for the undeviating bus manned by the automaton driver.

3. Read, view, and react with an active learning "set," to break the passivity that otherwise stifles new opportunities for learning. Keep at hand, unobtrusively but invariably, a notebook

and pencil with which to record striking reactions, questions, later brief reflections.

4. Keep a notebook and pen beside your bed so that, when awake, you can enter fragments of poetry and dreams; ideas that arise unbidden from the unconscious mind, and which once lost may not reappear; and concepts and plans developed by the restless mind during periods of sleeplessness. This "idea trap" can serve both day and night.

5. Keep a journal not merely of events concisely noted, but of personal thoughts roused by certain books and films, by contacts with people who have stirred your curiosity, pity, admiration, amused anger, or whatever. Reflect in it that part of the cosmos which happens to have been reflected in the tiny comprehensive mirror of your own life. Simple or complex, well or not-very-well written, the entries bear the accumulating colors of your unique self—a life mosaic.

6. Pile up your fresh and strange ideas and points of view, good and bad, so that you may stimulate the practice of the free flow of ideas, and prove what is most certainly true—that continuously advancing years need by no means inhibit the creative potentiality of men and women. Judgments—the choice of the best and most workable ideas—can come later.

7. Keep *a changing* list of everyday examples of the ways in which new situations or new products might be made out of different elements that are combined, adapted, or multiplied, magnified, and minified, put to other uses, eliminated, reversed, substituted. Do this as an exercise to keep the mind alert and tuned to change, and thus stimulate what Alex Osborn calls "applied imagination." Here are a few samples to start you off:

Combine products and functions into new relationships: combine long and short lenses in bifocals; combine skis with small motorized vehicles to make snowmobiles; combine kitchen implements in a single tool; place stereo on city buses; switch land-based conferences to shipboard voyages; provide cocktail service on skates; combine a little library with a hotel bar; combine television, tapes, correspondence materials, tutors, seminars, libraries, and summer schools in a single extension service for adults; combine young singers and guitarists with the Catholic mass to form the folk Mass.

Adapt and substitute: place arbors and gardens inside otherwise sterile inner-city business skyscrapers; put the telephone to uses never seen in earlier years—for 24-hour distress centres, for inspirational messages, for long-distance small conference "round-ups", for wake-up services, for widely separated chess opponents; convert light bulbs to germicidal lamps; send audio and video tapes of seminars on new legal issues to thousands of lawyers throughout the United States; provide a dial-a-diagnosis network for isolated physicians; video-tape laboratory demonstrations and make them available on need to college students; use electric beams for supermarket doors.

Gain new uses by magnifying, minifying, or multiplying products and functions: invent the jumbo jet (and advertise for staff trained in hotel administration); multiply benefits in insurance policies and doubling compensations, e.g., "double your money back"; produce handy miniatures of standard products: the tiny portable radio and tape-recorder, the telescoped umbrella, the TV dinner package (note that lists like this cite applied ideas only, without evaluating them!), miniature golf; and miniature time—e.g. the three-minute sermon, the mini-lecture in universities (the students have the text), and the fascinating little book of sixty one-minute "whodunits."

Seek ways to rearrange, to reverse: engage in role-playing to gain appreciation of other people's feelings and points of view; have visitors to a science centre actually play and do things rather than simply observe; build a skyscraper on the site of an old church, and put the church on the seventeenth floor; place the eye of the needle of the sewing machine at the point, as Howe did, instead of at the other end; sell flowers in book stores, books in flower stores, and both in cafés; rearrange rigid bus schedules to meet dial-a-bus needs; turn zoo animals loose on huge public estates, take a restaurant into a woods, and grow trees in a restaurant.

8. Actually use "the unforgiving minute." Creativity has everything to do with making the most of time—not in frantic pacing but by creating a kind of private peace in which productive time comes alive—rescuing our mind from the long wasteful rambles it too often makes at the expense of enriching, creative thinking.

What use can be made of the often bored and idle periods that clutter many of our days? If the brain chatter will not be still, try using a "mantra" at various times during the day which stills its triviality—for example; repeat often: "Love, Laugh, Learn, Heal, Create," and see how the mind recovers both poise and purpose.

And there is that decaying network of people to be written to, or otherwise contacted, or that journal entry to make— it is a matter of *will*. What hinders us? A ready excuse is that we have no note-paper handy, no acceptable envelope, no stamp, and of course, no time. Some noted actualizers of friendship circles use the back of small slips of paper or folders, circulars, or other odd pieces of paper, and send off cheerful fragments of news or messages, or better, one idea jotted down but personal to the receiver. Cheap envelopes are everywhere, and so are stamps. Pre-prepared envelopes are an incentive.

To perform these small acts of love and will, to do them now, is to maintain the climate of creative "set"—to be more self-actualized indeed, but also to be readier for the creative life. Creativity is not, as some maintain, a matter of choice between living in solitude and living in the world, but a matter of judiciously living in the best of both.

To gain entry to the country and the company of the Ulyssean people no passport is required. No restrictions exist as to race, class, religion, political ideology, or education—just the reverse. The Ulyssean country is an open commonwealth of older adults of every racial group under the sun; its membership includes every degree of wealth and non-wealth, every level of education, every form of belief and nonbelief. Membership has nothing to do with whether one is physically well or dogged by ill health, whether one is personable or plain, well traveled or confined to a limited area. No period of years of residence is required for citizenship—citizenship exists, but it is not a static thing, conferred at a ceremony. It is a process, not a state; a process of *becoming*, and great practitioners of the Ulyssean way would certainly describe themselves as voyagers, not inhabitants.

These are the attitudes toward life and the later years that are typical of Ulysseans: that life is a process of continuous growth, as much through the later and very late years as in any earlier period; that the capacity to learn is fully operative among human beings across the entire span of life, and that a seeker-adult simply goes ahead and learns, and grows; that human creativity comprises, apart from the splendors of genius, thousands of manifestations of the mind and imagination that transform an individual's own self or his or her environment at any age; that creativity cannot be taught and learned like a language—but that certain conditions, all of them potentially available in the later years, can be fostered so that the creative attitude and powers, on whatever scale, can be liberated. The most important of these conditions are maintenance of a sense of wonder toward life, openness to experience, the sense of search, faith in one's powers, and the summoning of will and psychic energy.

I emphasize that these conditions are *potentially* available, because in our society millions of older adults enter the later decades with such conventional lifestyles and attitudes, their individual identity so diffused or confused, and their powers of creativity so unused and rusted, that only by a gradual process or by the intervention of some revolutionizing event in their lives can new capacities for growth and creativity emerge and begin a transforming process. This is not even a situation of "us" and "them"—few of us are home free. It takes sustained imagination, will, courage, and love to live the later years as Ulyssean adults, to maintain our own identity on our own terms.

We are dealing, after all, with a human journey, not an air-regulated shelter. Everything we know of Ulyssean adults tells us that they are total human beings. They are quite aware that in the important domain of physical powers they no longer possess the prowess they had when young, nor the unbounded physical energy that among many young adults surges beautifully but unproductively. Ulyssean people know that advancing years bring hazards, and they know that either their own misjudgments or external fate, or both, may bring them for a time naked on the shore.

But either because of their nature or from their experience, they look into the face of life, not away from it. They cultivate the high art of looking at both the human comedy and the drama of the mysterious universe with intense interest and wonder. They use the remarkable brain-and-mind that is their heritage without fretting about supposed declines and deficits, knowing that there is an abundance of power there, knowing it will serve them well. And day by day they renew in themselves the springs that nurture creativity: freshness of outlook, spontaneity of feelings, acceptance of the constructive disorder of change, loving review of the past but with the eye of interpretation and growth, and the sense of life's adventure, its unexpectedness, its marvelous "you never can tell."

Thus Ulyssean adults maintain and develop their own real identities, quicken the pulses of creative growth in themselves and in the people around them. They enjoy the harvest, but they keep the winds of spring and its seed-time blowing through their lives.

HOW TO FORM A ULYSSEAN SOCIETY

When *The Ulyssean Adult* appeared in 1976, there was no Ulyssean Society. In fact, the book referred in its closing pages to Ulyssean people as an unorganized world community of middle- and later-life seekers and creators who contained in their ranks men and women of every color, creed, income group, and physical type who were members of a kind of society having no cards, rituals, membership fees, or constitution.

However, *The Ulyssean Adult* also urged the importance of "enclaves" for those adults who still wish in their middle and later years to maintain and extend their powers to learn, produce, and create (see also Chapter 6 of the present book). An enclave can be defined as a cultural group surrounded by, if not a hostile population, at least one that lacks understanding or sympathy. The value of the enclave group is that it reinforces the sustained objectives and personal independence of its members. It also makes possible the beaming-out of the message or good news of its cultural philosophy. It is a kind of lighthouse or glowing centre that can attract the attention of adults to the Ulyssean philosophy.

Such an enclave is The Ulyssean Society, founded in December, 1977, and which obtained a Canadian charter in 1979. The Society was formed by a group of former students from John McLeish's seminars on creativity and aging at the School of Continuing Studies, University of Toronto, and also included some readers who had enjoyed and benefitted from The Ulyssean Adult. The Society has at present approximately 200 members in the city of Toronto, and since inquiries continue to be received from widely distributed points on the continent as to how similar Ulyssean groups might be formed elsewhere, the following description of the Society may prove useful.

The Creed of the Society, which is printed on the reverse side of the membership cards, is as follows:

As a Companion of THE ULYSSEAN SOCIETY, I am committed to the noble concept and the provable fact that men and women in the middle and later years can, if they choose to do so, richly maintain the powers to produce, to learn, and to create, until the very end of the life journey.

The Society was formed as a result of a number of small supper circles called by John McLeish during 1977, followed by a founding meeting of 17 men and women on Sunday afternoon, December 4, 1977, at a downtown Toronto hotel. At this meeting the general shape of the Society's organization and program was confirmed, and the first of what, by August, 1982, had become 55 consecutive monthly general program meetings was held in the beautiful Music Room of Hart House, University of Toronto.

Members of the Ulyssean Society are called Companions, and a new member or Companion of the Society finds the following features of its life when he or she joins:

General Program Meetings: These are held monthly, with central themes of great diversity (see later sample list). They are designed to provide intellectual stimulus and to indicate channels of creative action.

These meetings are held on every month of the year, on the second Sunday of each month, from 2:30 to 5 P.M. sharp.

The meeting opens with the lighting of the Ulyssean flame, a huge candle that burns symbolically throughout the meeting at the President's table, and the reading of the Ulyssean Creed. These functions are performed at each meeting by a different member of the Society.

The meeting is divided at 3:30, after a first presentation by the guest speaker or panel, by the *Conversazione,* a half-hour period of refreshments and social exchange, a joyous interlude in which members are asked to occupy the first few minutes in talking with some Companion or visitor hitherto unknown or little known to them. When the meeting reconvenes at 4 P.M. either the first speaker or panel have a period for further comments and questions with the audience, or a second speaker and topic is occasionally introduced. Some meetings are turned over to short descriptions by various members of Ulyssean adventures-in-progress. Occasionally a chapter from *The Ulyssean Adult* is reviewed and discussed. At all general program meetings, either Ulyssean people in the community—writers, singers, athletes, travelers, inventors, craftspeople, artists, and others—are personally introduced, or recent achievements of Ulyssean men and women far and near are reported in a 20-minute period called "Ulysseans in Action."

The meeting typically closes with two or three appropriate readings by the President and other Companions, followed by the Ulyssean Benediction, read by the President:

> May the zest for learning
>   And the renewing power of seeking,
> May the healing joy of laughter
>   And the redeeming power of serving,

> May devotion to passionate causes
> And the transforming actions of love:
> Be with us and enlighten our ways
> Throughout the Ulyssean life voyage.

The new member of the Society also finds that a newsletter, *The Ulyssean,* bearing not only news about the Society, but also book reviews, contributions by members, excerpts from journals and news reports, and poems, arrives monthly.

A number of interest groups are available, as well:

The Armchair Travel Group: makes available speakers (often members of the Society just returned from some trip to distant or exotic places), films, color slides, often with music, refreshments, and discussion.

The Music Appreciation Group: makes available the opportunity to listen to fine classical and other recordings on stereo, with discussion and refreshments.

The Playreading Group: offers the opportunity for any Companion to join in reading plays by Chekov, Shaw, Ibsen, Williams, Maugham, Wilde, Sheridan, and others. Closes with discussion about future choices of plays, and refreshments.

The Cosmic Trails Group: provides a little forum for discussion of some of the religious and philosophical concepts outside the great conventional religions (e.g., reincarnation, the concepts of Gurdjieff, Ouspensky, and Steiner, Eckankar, transcendental meditation, creative dreaming, etc.) Closes with extended discussion and refreshments.

The Tai-Chi Group: makes available to any member the chance to learn the Chinese rhythmic exercises called Tai-Chi, which combine in a unique way the beauty of movement and the promotion of physical suppleness. Tai-Chi is practised by adults of all ages, and is remarkable in the way that it can accommodate both younger adults and men and women of advanced years and with at times arthritic conditions. Group sessions close with refreshments.

The SCAHN (Social Concerns and Human Needs) Group: has the special role of reporting back to the general Ulyssean Society on social issues and public causes relating to injustice, human need, and social change that may call for individual enlistment by Companions of the Society on behalf of the cause or need. The one prohibition in the Society is any discussion involving party politics. Closes with discussion and refreshments.

The Creative Potentials Group: makes available the opportunity to practise some of the exercises in creativity described in *The Ulyssean Adult* (and now, *The Challenge of Aging*). Meets in small "workshops," quarterly. Rich in discussion techniques. Closes with refreshments.

The President's Open Circle: is an informal meeting of some Companions with their friends, to chat between meetings with the President of the Society on a Saturday afternoon (monthly) in the relaxed atmosphere of a downtown café.

Cultural Trips: The "Cultural Attaché" of the Society arranges special group trips to theatres, concerts, sometimes trips to outside points (conservancy centres, e.g.). Also keeps members posted on cultural events.

Volunteer Services: Although not a group, this aspect of the Society's life makes possible to the Companions a channel (through a Ulyssean Society adviser) to the Volunteer Centre of Metropolitan Toronto.

The interest groups meet in the homes of convenors (except for SCAHN and the Open Circle) in some cases monthly, in all cases at least six times a year. Note that the General Program Meetings of the Society always take place monthly, on the second Sunday afternoon—one exception annually is the Easter month meeting, which occasionally is held on the third Sunday. The December meeting annually is always devoted to a wholly musical program, and is the only general meeting that closes with refreshments, rather than the usual mid-program *Conversazione*.

Direction of the Society: The Executive Committee of The Ulyssean Society consists of 13 Companions, elected annually, who in turn elect the officers of the Society: a President, Vice-President, Secretary, and Treasurer. This executive group, which bears the name Steering Committee (a colorful attribution to the Ulyssean world!) meets approximately ten times a year, and appoints appropriate working committees, such as the Program Committee.

Membership in the Society: is open to all "mature adults," since the founders did not wish to specify precise chronological ages. No inhibitions whatsoever exist as to age, color, creed, racial group, educational standards, etc. Members are expected to adhere to the statement of the Ulyssean Creed. Membership in the Toronto founding chapter of the Society is heavily distributed across the years 50 to 80, with a considerable number below and above these age lines.

Membership dues: are based on a donation system. It is suggested that annual donations to the Society be in the range $15 to $60 (as of 1982). Obviously, larger donations are welcome, and lesser donations where there is need are acceptable. (All interest groups are open to members, plus *The Ulyssean* newsletter.)

15 PROGRAM TITLES FROM ULYSSEAN SOCIETY GENERAL PROGRAMS, 1978-82:

1. Physical Renewal and Prowess after 50.

2. Ulyssean Vacations.

3. Creativity, Aging, and the Arts.

4. Where Is the Computer Taking Us?

5. The Mysterious World of E.S.P.

6. Injured Giants: Achievements Among the Disabled.

7. Civil Liberties and Human Rights.

8. Bioenergetics: the Language of the Body.

9. Lifelong Learning: Successful Strategies and Resources.

10. Keeping the Personal Journal: Adventures in Selfhood.

11. The Roles of Humor in Living and Healing.

12. The Four Channels of Love: Agape, Eros, Platonic Love, and Friendship.

13. Dreams and Dreaming, and the Secret Self.

14. Low Moods and Healing Strategies.

15. The Ancient Mystery of the Temple of Ephesus: a Ulyssean Search.

Much of the Society's programming has developed from ten objectives for the Ulyssean life presented in John McLeish's seminars:

TEN CHANNELS TO THE ULYSSEAN LIFE

1. To understand the myths of aging, and to reject, on the basis of reason and experience, their blocks and defeatism.

2. To believe in one's inherent value as a unique human being, and as an aid to this, to keep a personal reflective journal.

3. To "give oneself permission" in the middle and later years to seek, to explore, to experiment, to learn, and to create.

4. To invest one's interests and talents widely, but not to dissipate one's strength and powers.

5. To seek for and see the comedy always present in human affairs, and to believe in the healing power of laughter.

6. To keep in view a private "pantheon" of Ulysseans to serve as models, and steadily to add to it.

7. To endorse, and engage in, "passionate causes" (many of them neglected and undermanned), thus helping diminish "man's inhu-

manity to man." Also to engage in some way in "the redeeming power of serving."

8. To seek and see the wonder of the world—to maintain the spirit and freshness of the "child within": not least by participating in the many worlds of the arts.

9. To accept, and to use creatively, necessary loneliness and depression; to learn to match low moods with healing strategies.

10. To keep learning, by oneself and with the stimulus of others, until one's last day on Spaceship Earth.

Readers who seek more information about The Ulyssean Society are invited to write to:

> Mrs. Daniel Krangle
> Secretary, The Ulyssean Society
> 215 Richview Avenue
> Toronto, Canada
> M5P 3G2

APPENDIX I

60 WAYS TO BE YOUNGER THAN YOU ARE

(Adapted from an article by Barbara Crost in *Chatelaine*,
August, 1964. Reprinted by permission).

1. Collect something—wild flowers, coins, book matches, souvenir spoons.

2. Enroll in a night-school course: a new language, music appreciation, history, a new skill.

3. Buy a copy of a magazine you've never read before.

4. See a foreign movie at least once a month.

5. Make an effort to meet someone you don't know at church or club.

6. Follow your bus route to the end of the line.

7. Shop at a different store once a week.

8. Track down full titles of 'initials' organizations (NATO, SEATO, SAC, FAO, etc.) and find out what they do.

9. Get curious about mythology (*The Age of Fable*, by Bulfinch; *The Heroes*, by Kingsley; *Myths to Live By*, by Joseph Campbell).

10. Try one new recipe every week.

11. Track down the origin of 20 words on this page.

12. Pick a book 'blind' from your library shelves every month.

13. Go for a walk at 5 A.M. on a summer Sunday.

14. Dig out the fascinating early history of pharmacy, architecture, astronomy.

15. Try a new food from the gourmet shelf every week.

16. Pick a country and read everything you can about it and its culture.

17. Buy a frivolous hat or a pair of shoes.

18. Read up on one specific subject—shells, heraldry, quilt-making.

19. Write for travel folders and plan your dream trip.

20. Track down and write the history of your local church, city hall, oldest building—or your own family.

21. Choose an unfamiliar TV or radio program once a week and jot down your reaction as a critic.

22. Make your home a pickup point for old magazines, for hospitals and overseas.

23. Volunteer for the next church or club job to come up.

24. Learn to identify breeds of dogs, names of flowers, trees.

25. Revive an early interest—piano, ballet, poetry, dress-designing.

26. Start a neighborhood magazine.

27. Leaf through one volume of a good encyclopedia once a week.

28. Learn a new card game (*Hoyle Up-To-Date* will help you).

29. Study flower arranging.

30. Make a miniature garden in a pie plate, or a dwarf Japanese garden in a tray (query your library or the Japanese Embassy).

31. Furnish an orange-crate doll's house from anything handy—buttons, boxes, ribbons, popsicle sticks.

32. Do odd jobs at a service club—chauffeuring, stuffing envelopes, rolling bandages.

33. Join a drama group: act, take tickets, write programs.

34. Go to a city council meeting.

35. Find pen pals in many countries.

36. Dine at a different restaurant once a month.

37. Try making something by hand—candies, embroidery, origami (Japanese paper-folding).

38. Find out who the best current opera singers are.

39. Draw a floor plan of your ideal house and pick color schemes and furniture from catalogues.

40. Read some copies of any monthly magazine of 50 years ago (in your library).

41. Grow plants from orange pips, sweet potatoes, avocado seeds, carrot tops.

42. Read Malory's *Morte d'Arthur* and dig into the Arthurian legend.

43. Try one new household hint from every magazine you see.

44. List the 20 things you're most interested in.

45. See if you can form a group to share your greatest interest.

46. Collect cartoons.

47. Pick out a civic project and go after it: skating rink, larger library, save-a-historic-site.

48. Get to know a city you've never visited—London, New York, Moscow—from street maps, pictures, books.

49. Have lunch weekly with one of your neighbors.

50. Find out what Stonehenge is, and its story; or the story of a local historical site.

51. Take a course in wood-carving, puppet-making, or sewing.

52. Serve a formal dinner (candles, flowers, best china) for the family only.

53. Plan a "family surprise dinner" once a month (fancy-dress costumes, ornate centrepiece, buffet meal, hidden favors in food).

54. Visit one "shut-in" a week, or take someone out for an outing.

55. Plan a "Creativity Centre" to stimulate adults to want to keep being creative.

56. Join a group demonstrating for a good cause.

57. Make up a home-grown film festival with a few friends, visiting several movies in one week-end; or watch free movies from distributors.

58. Write "A Letter to the Editor" (brief and readable) quite often. They'll print some!

59. Go to school and community concerts and become a fan. Good for them, great for you! Enjoy!

60. Keep a little journal of what you've learned today, and what you plan to learn tomorrow.

THE CONTINUING HIGH CREATIVITY OF SCIENTISTS THROUGH THE MIDDLE AND LATER YEARS

In opposition to H. C. Lehman, who asserts that scientists normally attain a peak of creativity in their late 20s and their 30s and then decline, and advancing beyond Wayne Dennis, who shows the continued productivity of scientists but is not concerned with their creativity as such, *The Challenge of Aging* contends that scientific creativity should not be evaluated solely by the criterion of productivity, and that it is naive to identify a scientist's "peak of creativity" as the occasion where he made his supposedly "most important" discovery.

The creative process is not a simple rising-and-falling curve to and from a supposed single peak; the whole creative life of scientists must be reviewed—scientists active in many fields and roles who have continued to make investigations in enterprises of the first order throughout their 40s, 50s, and 60s, and even in numerous cases into the later years.

For my own interest, although I recognized its serious limitations, I made a study, somewhat Lehman-style, of a large number, chosen at random, of the lengthy abbreviated biographies of scientists no longer living, in the excellent, multi-volume *Dictionary of Scientific Biography* published by Charles Scribner's Sons commencing in 1970. Even in this exercise, I had no difficulty identifying a large group of scientists who had continuously creative lives. (I propose an extended study of this subject, The Ulyssean Scientist, for later publication.) Readers interested in the subject of scientific creativity will find it a challenging but rewarding project to do a similar exercise.

CREATIVE SCIENTISTS THROUGHOUT LIFE: A REPRESENTATIVE GROUP

PIETRO D'ABANO, 1257-1315 (medicine, natural history, philosophy); JOHN JACOB ABEL, 1857-1938 (pharmacology biochemistry); ERIK ACHARIUS, 1757-1819 (botany); FRANK DAWSON ADAMS, 1859-1942 (geology); THOMAS ADDISON, 1793-1860 (medicine); JACOB GEORGE AGARDH, 1813-1901 (botany); ROBERT

GRANT AITKEN, 1864-1951 (astronomy); HANS BERGER, 1873-1941 (psychiatry, electro-encephalography); HENRI BERGSON, 1859-1941 (philosophy, encompassing fields of science); JOHANN I. BERNOULLI, 1667-1748 (mathematics); PAUL BERT, 1833-1886 (physiology, comparative anatomy, natural history); ENRICO BETTI, 1823-1892 (mathematics), NIELS HENRIK DAVID BOHR, 1885-1962 (atomic and nuclear physics, epistemology); BERNARD BOLZANO, 1781-1848 (philosophy, mathematics, logic); GIOVANNI ALFONSO BORELLI, 1608-1679 (astronomy, epidemiology, mathematics, physics, physiology); WILLIAM HENRY BRAGG, 1862-1942 (physics); FEDOR ALEKSANDROVICH BREDIKHIN, 1831-1904 (astronomy); ALEXANDRE BRONGNIART, 1770-1847 (geology); ROBERT BROOM, 1866-1951 (palaeontology); FRANZ BOAS, 1858-1942 (anthropology); HENRY CAVENDISH, 1731-1810 (natural philosophy; notably mathematics, optics, magnetism, and geology); AUGUSTIN-LOUIS CAUCHY, 1787-1857 (mathematics, mathematical physics, celestial mechanics); JOHN HENRY COMSTOCK, 1849-1931 (entomology); CHARLES AUGUSTIN COULOMB, 1736-1806 (physics, applied mechanics); PAFNUTY LVOVICH CHEBYSHEV, 1821-1894 (mathematics); FERDINAND JULIUS COHN, 1828-1898 (botany, bacteriology); WILLIAM CROOKES, 1832-1919 (chemistry, physics); PETER JOSEPH WILLIAM DEBYE, 1884-1966 (chemical physics); JULIUS WILHELM DEDEKIND, 1831-1916 (mathematics); LEE DE FOREST, 1873-1961 (electronics); GIRARD DESARGUES, 1591-1661 (geometry, perspective); JAMES DEWAR, 1842-1954 (organic chemistry); DIETRICH VON FREIBERG, 1250-1310 (optics, natural philosophy); HUGO ALBERT EMIL HARMANN DINGLER, 1881-1954 (philosophy); CORNELIO AUGUST SEVERINUS DOELTER, 1850-1930 (chemical mineralogy); PIERRE-MAURICE-MARIE DUHEM, 1861-1916 (physics, rational mechanics, physical chemistry, history of science, philosophy of science); RENE-JOACHIM-HENRI DUTROCHET, 1776-1847 (animal and plant physiology, embryology, physics, phonetics); ARTHUR STANLEY EDDINGTON, 1882-1944 (astronomy, relativity); LUTHER PEAHLER EISENHART 1876-1965 (mathematics); JOHANN PHILIPP ELSTER, 1854-1920 (experimental physics); JOSEPH ERLANGER, 1874-1965 (physiology); LEONHARD EULER, 1707-1783 (mathematics, mechanics, astronomy, physics). GIROLAMO FABRICI, 1533-1619 (anatomy, physiology, embryology, surgery); MICHAEL FARADAY, 1791-1867 (chemistry, physics); ALEXEI YEVGRAFOVITCH FAVORSKY, 1860-1945 (chemistry); GUSTAV THEODOR FECHNER, 1801-1887 (psychology: psychophysics); LEONARDO FIBONACCI, or LEONARDO OF PISA, 1170-1240 (mathematics); ADOLF EUGEN FICK, 1829-1901 (physiology, physical medicine); HOWARD WALTER FLOREY, 1898-1968 (pathology); AUGUST FOPPL, 1854-1924 (engineering, physics); JOHAN GEORG FORCHHAMMER, 1874-1965 (geology, oceanography, chemistry); FERDINAND ANDRE FOUQUE, 1828-1904 (geology, mineralogy); GIROLAMO FRACASTORO, 1478-1553 (medicine, philosophy); JAMES FRANCK, 1882-1964 (physics); BERNARD FRENICLE DE BESSY, 1605-1675 (mathematics, physics, astronomy); GEORGES FRIEDEL, 1865-1933 (crystallography); KARL FRIEDRICH VON GAERTNER, 1772-1850 (botany); GALILEO GALILEI, 1564-1642 (physics, astronomy); FRANZ JOSEPH GALL, 1758-1828 (neuroanatomy, psychology); LUIGI GALVANI, 1737-1798 (anatomy, physiology, physics); GEORGE GAMOW, 1904-1968 (physics); JOHN PETER GASSIOT, 1797-1877 (electricity); ALBERT JEAN GAUDRY, 1827-1908 (palaeontology); JOHN SCOTT HALDANE, 1860-1936 (physiology); GEORGE ELLERY HALE, 1868-1938 (astrophysics); STEPHEN HALES, 1677-1761 (physiology, public health); ASAPH HALL, 1829-1907 (astronomy); MARSHALL HALL, 1790-1857 (physiology, clinical medicine); ARTHUR RUDOLF HANTZSCH, 1857-1935 (chemistry); CHARLES HERMITE, 1822-1901 (mathematics); WILLIAM HERSCHEL, 1738-1822 (astronomy); ALEXANDER VON HUMBOLDT, 1769-1859 (cosmology); JOHN NEWPORT LANGLEY, 1852-1925 (physiology, histology); IRVING LANGMUIR, 1881-1957 (chemistry, physics); ANDREW COOPER LAWSON, 1861-1952 (geology); ANTONI VAN LEEUWENHOCK, 1632-1723 (natural sciences, microscopy); ADRIEN-MARIE LEGENDRE, 1752-1833 (mathematics); GOTTFRIED WILHELM LEIBNITZ, 1646-1716 (mathematics, philosophy, metaphysics); LEONARDO DA VINCI, 1452-1519 (anatomy, technology, mechanics, mathematics, geology); DOMINIQUE-AUGUST LEREBOULLET, 1804-1865 (zoology, embryology); FRANZ YULEVICH LEVINSON-LESSING, 1861-1939 (geology, petrography); GILBERT NEWTON LEWIS, 1875-1946 (chemistry); LEONID SAMUILOVICH LEYBENZON, 1879-1951 (mechanical engineering, geophysics); FRANK RATTRAY LILLIE, 1870-1947 (embryology, zoology); OTTO LOEWI, 1873-1961 (pharmacology, physiology); HEINZ LONDON, 1907-1970 (physics); ALEKSANDR MIKHAILOVICH LYAPUNOV, 1857-1918 (mathematics, mechanics); CHARLES LYELL, 1797-1875 (geology, evolutionary biology). MARCELLO MALPIGHI, 1628-1694 (medicine, microscopic and comparative anatomy, embryology); PATRICK MANSON, 1844-1922 (tropical medicine); ANDREAS SIGISMUND MARGGRAF, 1709-1782 (chemistry); ANDREI ANDREEVICH MARKOV, 1856-1922 (mathematics); GERARDUS MERCATOR, 1512-1594 (geography, cartography); MARIN MERSENNE, 1588-1648 (natural philosophy, acoustics, music, mechanics, optics); JOHN MICHELL, 1724-1793 (astronomy); GUSTAV MIE, 1868-1957 (physics); WILLIAM MILLER, 1817-1870 (chemistry, spectroscopy, astronomy); WILLIAM HOBSON MILLS, 1873-1959 (organic chemistry); CHARLES

FRANCOIS BRISSEAU DE MIRBEL, 1776-1854 (botany); AUGUST FERDINAND MOBIUS, 1790-1868 (mathematics, astronomy); ANDRIJA MOHOROVICIC, 1857-1936 (meteorology, seismology); ABRAHAM DE MOIVRE, 1667-1754 (probability theory); GIOVANNI BATTISTA MORGAGNI, 1682-1771 (pathological anatomy); THOMAS BURR OSBORNE, 1859-1929 (protein chemistry); GUISEPPE PIAZZI, 1746-1826 (astronomy); MUHYI AL-DIN PIRI RAIS, 1470-1554 (geography, cartography); GEORGE NICHOLAS PAPANICOLAOU, 1883-1962 (anatomy); ALPHEUS SPRING PACKARD, JR., 1839-1905 (entomology); LOUIS PASTEUR, 1822-1895 (crystallography, chemistry, microbiology, immunology); KARL PEARSON, 1857-1936 (applied mathematics, biometry, statistics); IVAN PETROVICH PAVLOV, 1849-1936 (physiology, psychology); JAMES PARKINSON, 1755-1824 (medicine, palaeontology); JOSEPH PLATEAU, 1801-1883 (mechanics). CHANDRASEKHARA VENKATA RAMAN, 1888-1970 (physics, physical theory, physiology of vision); SANTIAGO RAMON Y CAJAL, 1852-1934 (neuroanatomy, neurohistology); OWEN WILLANS RICHARDSON, 1879-1959 (physics, electronics, thermionics); GUSTAV ROSE, 1798-1873 (mineralogy, crystallography); ANGELO RUFFINI, 1864-1929 (histology, embryology); GIOVANNI VIRGINIO SCHIAPARELLI, 1835-1910 (astronomy); LUDWIG SCHLAFLI, 1814-1895 (mathematics); HEINRICH SCHLIEMANN, 1822-1890 (archeology); Erwin Schrodinger, 1887-1961 (theoretical physics); CHARLES SCHUCHERT, 1858-1942 (palaeontology); DUKINFIELD HENRY SCOTT, 1854-1934 (botany, paleobotany); JOHANNES JAKOB SEDERHOLM, 1863-1934 (geology, petrology); FRANCESCO SEVERI, 1879-1961 (mathematics); ALEKSEY NIKOLAEVICH SEVERTSOV, 1866-1936 (comparative anatomy, evolutionary morphology); SHEN KUA, 1031-1095 (polymathy, astronomy); IVAN IVANOVICH SHMALHAUZEN, 1884-1963 (biology); NEVIL VINCENT SIDGWICK, 1873-1952 (chemistry); THEOBALD SMITH, 1859-1934 (bacteriology, animal pathology); LAZZARO SPALLANZANI, 1729-1799 (natural history, biology, physiology); HERMAN STAUDINGER, 1881-1965 (organic and macromolecular chemistry); JOHN WILLIAM STRUTT, 3rd Baron Rayleigh, 1842-1919 (physics, natural philosophy); EDUARD SUESS, 1831-1914 (geology); NILS EBERHARD SVEDELIUS, 1873-1960 (psychology); JAMES JOSEPH SYLVESTER, 1814-1897 (mathematics); PIERRE TEILHARD DE CHARDIN, 1881-1955 (palaeontology, geology); WILLIAM THOMSON, Baron Kelvin of Largs, 1824-1907 (physics); GAVRIL ADRIANOVICH TIKHOV, 1875-1960 (astrophysics, astrobotany); KONSTANTIN EDUARDOVICH TSIOLKOVSKY, 1857-1935 (mechanics, aeronautics, astronautics); LEON-LOUIS VAILLANT, 1834-1914 (ichthyology, herpetology); GABRIEL GUSTAV VALENTIN, 1810-1883 (embryology, anatomy, physiology); MAR-

CUS TERENTIUS VARRO, 116 B.C.-27 B.C. (encyclopedism, polymathy, biology); EMIL GABRIEL WARBURG, 1846-1931 (physics); WILHELM EDUARD WEBER, 1804-1891 (physics); QUTB AL-DIN AL-SHIRAZI, 1236-1311 (optics, astronomy, medicine, philosophy); CHARLES THOMSON REES WILSON, 1869-1959 (atomic physics, meteorological physics); EDMUND BEECHER WILSON, 1856-1939 (cytology, embryology, heredity); CHARLES LEONARD WOOLEY, 1880-1960 (archaeology); CHARLES-ADOLPHE WURTZ, 1817-1884 (chemistry); NIKOLAY DMITRIEVICH ZELINSKY, 1861-1953 (chemistry); NIKOLAY NIKOLAEVICH ZUBOV, 1885-1960 (oceanography).

CHAPTER NOTES

CHAPTER 2

1. Calvin Taylor and J. Holland, in an important study (1964) of possible predictors of creative performance, observe: "There is some evidence that creative persons are more autonomous than others, more self-sufficient, more independent in judgment, more open to the irrational in themselves, more stable, more feminine in interests and characteristics (especially in awareness of their impulses), more dominant and self-assertive, more complex, more self-accepting, more resourceful and adventurous, more radical (the old word was Bohemian), more self-controlled, possibly more emotionally sensitive, more introverted but also more bold." I suggest in my University of Michigan paper (October, 1980), however, that we must also be on guard to think of adults as "most creative" and "more creative" rather than dividing them simply into "creative" or "noncreative".

2. The creativity of humor—through helping shape the tone and thrust of a lifestyle—seems clearly related to physical and mental healing as well.

This relationship was dramatically brought home to the general public by Norman Cousins' widely published article from the *New England Journal of Medicine* (December 1976), subsequently enlarged and republished as the best-selling book, *Anatomy of an Illness* (Norton, 1979). Cousins attributes his recovery from a dangerous and crippling illness substantially to the healing powers of deliberately invoked laughter.

"I have learned," Norman Cousins writes, "never to underestimate the capacity of the human mind and body to regenerate, even when the prospects seem most wretched." (This is precisely why the morbid term, "terminally ill" should never be used, even though, of course, many battles are lost.)

Another writer who merits careful attention is the physician Dr. Raymond Moody, whose book *Laugh After Laugh* was published in 1978 by Headwaters Press. Like Cousins, he links humor to important therapeutic releases of tension and to generating the will to live. A practitioner, he cites many cases in which laughter has aided healing—both physical and emotional. "In the deepest sense," Moody writes, "humor works by rallying, and by being a manifestation of, the will to live."

And both Cousins and Moody from their fields join Roberto Assagioli in his: that we are only beginning to tap the mystery and the resources of the human will.

CHAPTER 3

1. The word "role" is a much more sophisticated word than it appears in this useful listing. We all—except the most brainwashed of our generation—have hidden roles and hidden agendas. We often live actual sublives or other-lives, which usually escape the inquiring mind and the eager pen of the social psychologist. And some of us live fantasy lives that, in some cases, have a power, and a hidden governing force that appear, disappear, and reappear at different stages of the life drama. Some of these hidden lives, roles, fantasies, and agendas work beneficially for the adult wayfarer. Some, as Cyril Connolly vividly portrays them in *Enemies of Promise*, work against the humanity and the creativity of the adult. Connolly's title is thought- provoking. What elements are there in our "system of selfs" that release us or block and defeat us as time goes on?

2. Take one example: the ebullience common to many in their 30s, as contrasted with the detachment and retrospection typical of many adults in their 60s and 70s. My own mother, when about 68 and widowed for several years, was once present with me at the successful live studio production of a Home and School broadcast. The volunteer producer, a young public relations man, and two or three teacher colleagues, all in their 30s, had expanded as much energy and excited concern on this show as though it was a major network program. Watching them quietly, my mother, who was what the older North American idiom used to call a "booster," or in the British idiom, a "well-wisher," was expected as usual to add her warm and happy congratulations. Indeed she did this, but before the production ended she turned to me and said with an expression of indescribable sadness, "When I see the work that Gerald and his friends are putting into this, and all it means to them, I think of how your Dad and I used to plan and dream, how excited we used to get." Her comment astonished me. I was not insensitive—I was simply age 35, and was myself in the throes of the ebullient decade. This charming and life-loving woman, who turned out to be a Ulyssean herself, had simply a greater perspective from the further heights of the life journey.

3. Klemme called the point of migration between young and mature adulthood, the 'mid-life crisis," and found that it seems to arise at approximately the end of the period roughly from ages 21 to 35, i.e. the period which David L. Gutmann of the University of Michigan has named the phase of "alloplastic mastery" in which young adults try to achieve mastery over the external world, seeking material gain and the approval of others. (Gutmann's interesting version of the life drama includes two other major phases: "autoplastic mastery," the period from about 35 to 60, and 'omniplastic mastery," the period from age 60 on, when the person who has successfully met the tests of earlier periods often turns his or her attention to broader concerns.)

4. Readers interested in the development of "life stage theory" will find informative studies in Gould, Levinson, Sheehy, Vaillant, and Osherson (see Bibliography for recommended titles). A fine summation of the first four investigators as well as certain other researchers can be found in Chapter 3 of Douglas C. Kimmel's text, *Adulthood and Aging: an Interdisciplinary Development View*, which is indispensable for the lay reader for its scope and depth in treating the subject.

The writers and researchers named above are engaged in valuable work, and write with perception and compassion about aspects of the human life journey before or approaching the period I have generally identified as the beginning of "Ulyssean adulthood". However, specifics of adult "transitions" remain unproved, outside of what can be generally accepted as "the human condition". So far, current commentators are overly preoccupied with precisely identified transition points; their samples are very limited in scope as to income group, sex, education, and radical culture; and thus far they seem to have only scratched the surface of not only the complex nature but the multiplex nature of the human adult life. Kimmel's warning is useful that too naïve acceptance of suggested development "crisis" points can be self-fulfilling for certain adults.

Still, as these studies advance and others like them appear, two benefits may be seen. Great numbers of adults, not least in the earlier middle years, may be induced to think actively about the nature of the human life journey; and specifically, they may reflect more perceptively and creatively on their own life's meaning and direction.

5. The powerful thrust that adult human beings ordinarily have toward some kind of self-actualization of the mind is borne out in many ways. The studies of the Canadian adult educator Allen Tough, dealing with why adults learn and the ways in which they try to learn, have lighted up a much neglected fact: that a great number of people throughout much of their adult lives are engaged in one or more learning projects, often virtually unaware that they could be described in these terms, and with their activities unknown to most or all of their friends. Tough's formal writing has little to say about adults in their later years, but one of my students, who was captivated by the idea of this unseen learning, went through her apartment building in Toronto interviewing a number of people of all ages, and found fascinating verification of Tough's theme. The fact, incidentally, that many of these learning experiences are so-called "temporary systems"—that is, experiences and decision-making exercises that "have their day and cease to be" (a jury at a murder trial, or an abortive attempt of six weeks' duration of a 40-year-old man to teach himself the guitar)—does not destroy their interest or validity.

CHAPTER 5

1. The best refutation of the myths about memory and aging is found in a superb chapter (Chapter 3) of Morton Hunt's recent (1982) study, *The Universe Within* (Simon and Schuster). Among many references, Hunt quotes Marion Perlmutter, a researcher on memory efficiency in both young (20s) and older (60s) adults. Perlmutter agrees that in general people in their 60s and older 'definitely recall and recognize lists of words less well than people in their 20s but, interestingly, they recall and recognize facts better". Thus Perlmutter concludes: "if, in fact, the memory task is not a rote one but a real-life one, involving a well-stocked mind, older people definitely perform better than young people.

2. Some intriguing oddities turned up among these early investigations. The psychologist E. J. Swift had decided that, if medical researchers could experiment on themselves, surely psychological inquirers could do the same. At age

43 he submitted himself to two self-administered exercises. He practiced typewriting by the sight method for an hour a day for 50 days, steadily improving and finally attaining the not very stunning rate of 171/2 words a minute. Then this intrepid pre-Ulyssean studied shorthand for 68 days for an hour and a half a day, writing (was this done ironically?) William James's *Talks to Teachers* from dictation and reading back copy taken down ten or more days earlier. Within two months (he was also doing the many other things his daily work required), he had raised his speed of reception and transcription so that his score climbed by 500 percent. Swift's curiosity about himself, his precision in trying to measure his achievements, and his gutsy self-disciplining until the exercise was completed still could be emulated in our time by adults of all ages who want to change themselves from dilettantes to productive learners.

3. After all these years, one feels the gusto of an investigator who can write: "We considered making up for our experimental work a brief intellectual system wholly independent of any of the existing sciences, of which all learners would have little and equal knowledge at the start, and in learning which very little of the stock varieties of human knowledge would be of specific help. A system of ethics from the point of view of the domestic cat or an artificial agglutinative language using nothing of Indo-European syntax or vocabulary are samples of the sort of material contemplated. But on the whole it seemed better to use Esperanto."

4. In reviewing Theta Wolf's life of Alfred Binet (1973), Read Tuddenham was struck with the fact that the great father of testing had himself some very strong reservations about what one might describe as no-nonsense definitions of intelligence. Noting the neglect and the distortions that have been Binet's lot ever since he and Simon devised their famous intelligence scale, Tuddenham remarks: "Those who would suppress such tests in the service of egalitarianism may be surprised to learn that Binet declined to define intelligence lest he foreclose its exploration, that he specifically believed in the power of training to increase it, that he invariably used the phrase 'mental level' (*niveau*) to avoid the connotations of 'mental age', and would certainly have objected violently to calculating the IQ (Simon called the IQ a betrayal!)."

Two great problems were bound up with the concept of the IQ from its earliest years. The first problem was, as already indicated, that the attempt to sum up the "intelligence" of a complex human being in a single box score was too naïve. The second, that it became evident as the years passed that the IQ (whatever it was) was anything but a fixed entity. The tests were saturated with the culture attitudes and knowledges of the testers. Thus, if you retested a young person after a period of improved environmental conditions and better training in language, the IQ increased—in some cases by as many as 20 points.

Since the IQ, the most primitive way of defining an individual's intelligence, was essentially a label for schoolchildren, its application had little to do with adults and the life-cycle until industry adopted testing on an enormous scale for the assessment of young adults seeking to enter commercial and industrial life. For that purpose, much of the testing is invalid. The applicant may have taken heaps of tests, often the same ones, in a three-month search for work among various firms, and under very uneven conditions of administration. No matter: there must be scores in the dossier, from which the solemn sub-priests will try to construct his competence and his suitability. Sometimes the material is highly personal and is a flagrant invasion of his rights as a private person. Older adults have become involved as job mobility has become a major phenomenon and as large numbers of women, after a period of marriage, have returned to work that involves retraining or new training. Besides, the increasing vogue for "mature matriculation" at universities has increased the trend to test the mental abilities of adults especially in the age range 25-50.

CHAPTER 6

1. An interesting example of the 'network' effect of Ulyssean learning adventures is seen in the case of Donald Love, a retired Toronto businessman, who in the course of assiduous visiting with his wife Edna of museums in Cairo and the Near East found himself facing a long-standing mystery: What was the actual appearance of the ancient Temple of Diana in Ephesus, one of the Seven Wonders of the World? In pursuit of this, Love visited numerous centers and authorities, and from his studies was able to derive a highly possible design. He has reported to the Ulyssean Society that one of his discoveries was the approachability of really great scholars!

2. How did people respond to the Open University network when it began operations in January, 1971? When the university opened its list for applicants in the spring of 1970, more than 40,000 adult Britons applied; of these, 24,000 students provisionally registered in January, 1971, for the first three months of the year, and in April, 1971, some 19,500 students finally registered. By 1980 the number of people studying for credit under the Open University system was 42,000 and there was an enormous waiting list.

How many older adults have participated, that is, people over 55? This is, for our purpose, a rather crucial question! The percentages supplied by the Open University are: 6 percent aged 50-54; 3 percent aged 55-59; 1 percent aged 60-64; and about 1 percent 65 or older.

How do the Open University students perform in their course examinations? It must be remembered that many have not studied for years, and that many have no formal qualifications for regular university study. In spite of the insistence of the university on maintaining the equivalent of academic standards elsewhere, no less than 70 percent of the students throughout the British Isles have passed their courses.

CHAPTER 9

1. Pines describes a successful experiment in which she herself took part at the Menninger Foundation under the tutelage of Elmer and Alyce Green—a preliminary exercise in feedback training intended to demonstrate how one could by mental concentration make one's hands get warmer and one's forehead cooler. She remarks that after emerging with an effort from a highly successful small experiment, she "glanced at my partner, an elderly, retired businessman. He was smiling." Precisely: this man was in fact a Ulyssean person engaged in helping create new knowledge about the conquest of mind over body.

2. A fine monograph by Professor H. H. Stern (1982), which reviews the most recent research on the topic of age and language learning, first dispels the myth, promoted by earlier concepts of Wilder Penfield and others, that "the

plasticity of the young brain" gives children an advantage over adults. And he quotes in summary S. D. Krashen (1973 and 1981) as concluding his views on the neurolinguistic debate as follows: "While child-adult differences in second language acquisition potential do exist, the evidence for a biological barrier to successful adult acquisition is lacking." (My italics.) Stern, although showing a scholar's caution throughout his monograph, goes on, however, to provide much further evidence that no one age or stage on development grounds stands out as optimal or critical. He asks the question, "At what age can language teaching be started?" and responds tersely, "At any age."

3. The modern psychotherapist who has written most richly and most creatively about "the human will" is Roberto Assagioli, who by the time of his death in 1974 at a very late age had established important training centres for the comprehensive or holistic psychology that he called psychosynthesis.

Any reader of *The Challenge of Aging* who has wanted to perform some creative act but was too inert to do it, and now can only watch with exasperation or melancholy the flow of unused time, will find Assagioli's *The Act of Will* healing and bracing. Assagioli, a true Ulyssean who wrote both of his major books cited in the Bibliography when past 80, appeals vividly to both mind and emotions as he indicates paths of escape and achievement from the inert self.

4. Many older adults are finding fresh Ulyssean paths in "the lively arts" in our times through programs that are all too little known despite their immense potential.

Projects include orchestras, drama groups, film-production groups, and varied craft groups for participants active in the community. Especially new and creative are projects using teacher poets and teacher artists who regularly give classes in certain retirement and nursing homes (including classes for disabled adults), to stimulate latent talent among older people—to awaken sleeping interests and talents.

A splendid brochure, rich with program descriptions, *Older Ameicans and the Arts*, by Jacqueline Tippett Sunderland, was published by the National Center on the Arts and Aging, Washington, D.C. in October, 1976, and reprinted. It is of equal interest to Canadians and those of other societies.

Learning to Be: the great life art that Erich Fromm celebrated in one of his books *To Have or To Be?* (Bantam, 1976) is realizable even into the very latest years. To dance, to paint, to act, to write, to sculpt, to design, to play—the arts are always waiting with their renewal powers.

SELECT BIBLIOGRAPHY

Allport, Gordon. *Becoming*. New Haven: Yale University Press, 1954.

_____. *Pattern and Growth in Personality*. New York: Holt, Rinehart, and Winston, 1961.

Anderson, Harold H., ed. *Creativity and Its Cultivation*. New York: Harper and Row, 1959.

Anderson, J. R. L. *The Ulysses Factor, the Exploring Instinct in Man*. London: Hodder and Stoughton, 1970.

Arasteh, A. Reza. *Final Integration in the Adult Personality: A Measure for Health, Social Change and Leadership*. Leyden: E. J. Brill, 1965.

Arieti, Silvano. *Creativity, The Magic Synthesis*. New York: Basic Books, 1976.

Assagioli, Roberto. *Psychosynthesis: a Manual of Principles and Techniques*. London: Penguin, 1974.

_____. *The Act of Will*. London: Penguin, 1974.

Bardwick, Judith. *Psychology of Women*. New York: Harper and Row, 1971.

Barell, J. *Playground of Our Minds*. New York: TCP, 1980.

Barron, Frank. *Creativity and Psychological Health*. New York: Van Nostrand, 1963.

Beauvoir, Simone de. *The Coming of Age*. New York: Putnam, 1972.

_____. *The Second Sex*. New York: Putnam, 1968.

Berdiaev, N. A. *The Meaning of the Creative Act*. New York: Harper, 1955.

Berenson, Bernard. *Sunset and Twilight*. New York: Harcourt Brace, 1963.

Beresford-Howe, Constance. *The Book of Eve*. Toronto: Avon, 1973.

Berne, Eric. *Games People Play*. New York: Bantam Books, 1964.

_____. *What Do You Say After You Say Hello?* New York: Bantam Books, 1973.

Birren, James E. *The Psychology of Aging*. Englewood Cliffs: Prentice-Hall, 1964.

_____. and K. Warner Schaie. *Handbook of the Psychology of Aging*. New York: Van Nostrand Reinhold, 1977.

Bischof, L. J. *Adult Psychology*. New York: Harper and Row, 1969.

Blakeslee, T. R. *The Right Brain*. New York: Anchor/Doubleday, 1980.

Block, J. *Lives Through Time*. Berkeley, Calif.: Bancroft, 1976.

Bode, Carl, ed. *The Selected Journals of Henry David Thoreau*. New York: New American Library, 1967.

Bolles, Richard N. *The Three Boxes of Life and How to Get Out of Them*. Berkeley, Calif.: Ten Speed Press, 1978.

Borden, Charles A. *Sea Quest: Global Blue-Water Adventuring in Small Craft*. Philadelphia: Macrae Smith, 1967.

Botwinick, J. *Aging and Behavior*. New York: Springer, 1973.

Bradford, Leland. *Retirement: Coping with Emotional Upheavals*. New York: Nelson-Hall, 1979.

Brooks, Van Wyck. *Helen Keller: Sketch for a Portrait*. New York: Dutton, 1956.

Brundage, Donald H., and Dorothy MacKeracher. *Adult Learning Principles*. Toronto: OISE, 1979.

Buber, Martin. *I and Thou*. Trans. W. Kaufmann. New York: Scribner's, 1972.

Buhler, Charlotte, and Fred Massarik, eds. *The Course of Human Life*. New York: Springer, 1968.

Burgess, E. W., ed. *Aging in Western Societies*. Chicago: University of Chicago Press, 1960.

Burnshaw, Stanley. *The Seamless Web*. New York: Braziller, 1970.

Butcher, H. J. *Human Intelligence, Its Nature and Assessment*. London: Methuen, 1968.

Butler, Robert N. *Why Survive? Being Old in America*. New York: Harper and Row, 1975.

_____. with Myrna I. Lewis. *Sex After Sixty*. New York: Harper and Row, 1976.

Campbell, Joseph. *Myths to Live By*. New York: Viking, 1972.

_____. *The Masks of God: Creative Mythology*. New York and London: Penguin, 1976.

Caprio, Frank S. *Add Life to Your Years*. New York: Citadel Press, 1975.

Cattell, R. B., and H. J. Butcher. *The Prediction of Achievement and Creativity*. Indianapolis: Bobbs-Merrill, 1968.

Chevalier, Maurice. *I Remember It Well*. New York: Macmillan, 1970.

Chew, Peter. *The Inner World of the Middle-Aged Man*. New York: Macmillan, 1976.

Clausen, J. 'The Life Course of Individuals' in *Aging and Society*, Vol. 3, *The Sociology of Age Satisfaction*. Riley, M. W. et al. New York: Russell Sage Foundation, 1972.

Clements, Robert J. *Michelangelo, a Self Portrait*. New York: Prentice-Hall, 1963.

Coles, Robert. *Women of Crisis: Lives of Struggle and Hope*. New York: Delacorte, 1978.

_____. *Lives of Work and Dreams*. New York, Delacorte, 1980.

Colette (Sidonie Gabrielle Claudine). *The Evening Star*. London: Peter Owen, 1973.

Comfort, Alex. *A Good Age*. New York: Crown, 1976.

_____. *The Anxiety Makers: Some Curious Preoccupations of the Medical Profession*. London: Pantheon Books, 1968.

Confucius. *The Analects*. Trans. D. L. Lau. London: Penguin, 1979.

Connolly, Cyril. *Enemies of Promise*. London: Deutsch, 1973.

Cousins, Norman. *Anatomy of an Illness*, New York and London: W. W. Norton, 1979.

Cowley, M. *The View from 80*. New York: Viking, 1980.

Craft, Robert. Stravinsky: *Chronicle of a Friendship*, 1948-71. New York: A. A. Knopf, 1972.

Creativity: the State of the Art, Report of a National Seminar (Undated). Racine, Wisconsin: The Thomas Alva Edison Foundation, the Johnson Foundation, and the Institute for Development of Educational Activities, 1970.

Cross, Milton, and David Ewen. *Encyclopedia of Great Composers*. New York: Doubleday, 1970. 2 vols.

Crowther, J. G. *British Scientists of the 19th Century*. London: Penguin Books, 1940. 2 vols.

_____. *Famous American Men of Science*. London: Secker and Warburg, 1937.

Crystal, John C., and Richard N. Bolles. *Where Do I Go From Here With My Life?* New York: The Seabury Press, 1974.

Cumming, Elaine, and W. E. Henry. *Growing Old: the process of disengagement*. New York: Basic Books, 1961.

Curtin, Sharon. *Nobody Ever Died of Old Age*. Boston: Atlantic Monthly Press, 1973.

Cushing, Harvey. *Sir William Osler*. New York: Oxford, 1940.

Czaky, Mick, ed. *How Does It Feel? Exploring the World of Your Senses*. London: Thames and Hudson, 1979.

Dangott, L. R., and R. A. Kalish. *A Time to Enjoy: the Pleasures of Aging*. New York: Prentice-Hall, 1978.

Dante Alighieri. *The Divine Comedy*. Trans. Charles S. Singleton. Princeton, N. J.: Princeton University Press, 1970.

Davies, David. *The Centenarians of the Andes*. London: Barrie and Jenkins, 1975.

Davis, Mary A., and Joseph Scott. *Training Creative Thinking*. New York: Holt, Reinhart, and Winston, 1976.

De Ropp, Robert S. *The Master Game*. New York: Delta, 1968.

Dictionary of Scientific Biography. New York: Charles Scribner's Sons, 1970. + 10 vols.

Di Lampedusa, Giuseppe. *Two Stories and a Memory*. Trans. Alexander Colquhoun. London: Collins and Harwill, 1962.

Dixon, W. MacNeile. *The Human Situation*. London: Penguin, 1958.

Donahue, Wilma, and Clark Tibbits. *The New Frontiers of Aging*. Ann Arbor: University of Michigan Press, 1957.

Douglas, A. Vibert. *The Life of Arthur Stanley Eddington*. London: Nelson, 1956.

Dru, Alexander, ed. and trans. *The Journals of Soren Kierkegaard, 1834-1854*. London: Collins/Fontana, 1958.

Durant, Will and Ariel. *A Dual Autobiography*. New York: Simon and Schuster, 1977.

Eccles, John C. *The Understanding of the Brain*. New York: McGraw-Hill, 1973.

Eckerman, J. P. *Conversations with Goethe*. London: J. M. Dent., 1935.

Edwards, M., and E. Hoover. *The Challenge of Being Single*. New York: Signet Books, 1974.

Ellison, Jerome. *Life's Second Half: The Pleasures of Aging*. New York: Devin-Adair, 1978.

Erikson, Erik H., ed. *Adulthood*. New York: W. W. Norton, 1978.

_____. *Childhood and Society*. New York: W. W. Norton, 1964.

_____. *Identity and the Life Cycle*. Psychological Issues. Monograph L, 1959.

Fair, Charles M. *The Dying Self*. Middletown, Conn.: Wesleyan University Press, 1969.

Fine, Benjamin. *The Stranglehold of the I.Q.* New York: Doubleday, 1975.

Fisher, Welthy Honsinger. *To Light a Candle*. New York: McGraw-Hill, 1962.

Flach, Frederic F. *The Secret Strength of Depression*. New York: Bantam Books, 1975.

Foss, J. O. *Ralph Vaughan Williams:* A Study. London: Harrap, 1952.

Frankl, Victor E. *From Death Camp to Existentialism*. Boston: Beacon Press, 1959.

Fromm, Erich. *The Art of Loving*. New York: Bantam Books, 1970.

_____. *The Heart of Man*. New York: Harper and Row, 1968.

Fuchs, Estelle. *The Second Season: Life, Love and Sex for Women in the Middle Years*. New York: Anchor/Doubleday, 1977.

Fulton, E., ed. *Death and Identity*. New York: John Wiley, 1965.

Galton, Lawrence. *Don't Give Up on an Aging Parent*. New York: Crown Publishers, 1975.

Gardner, John. *Self-Renewal: the Individual and the Innovative*. New York: Harper, 1964.

Gary, Romain. *Promise at Dawn*. London: Sphere Books Ltd., 1971.

Ghiselin, Brewster. *The Creative Process*. New York: New American Library, 1952.

Gide, André. *Journals*. New York: Vintage Books, 1956.

Goble, Frank. *The Third Force: the Psychology of Abraham Maslow*. New York: Simon and Schuster, 1971.

Goffman, Erving. The *Presentation of Self in Everyday Life*. New York: Doubleday, 1959.

Gordon, William J. J. *Synectics, the Development of Creative Capacity*. New York: Harper and Row, 1961.

Goudeket, Maurice. *The Delights of Growing Old*. New York: Farrar, Straus, and Giroux, 1966.

Gould, Roger. *Transformations*. New York: Simon and Schuster, 1978.

Graham, Sheila. *College of One*. New York: Viking Press, 1967.

Gregory, J. C. *The Nature of Laughter*. London: Kegan Paul, 1924.

Groch, Judith. *The Right to Create*. Boston: Little, Brown, 1969.

Gross, Martin L. *The Brain Watchers*. New York: Random House, 1962.

Gross, Ronald. *The Lifelong Learner*. New York: Simon and Schuster, 1977.

_____. *The New Old: Struggling for Decent Aging.* New York: Anchor/-Doubleday, 1978.

Haefele, J. W. *Creativity and Innovation.* New York: Reinhold, 1962.

Hagberg, Janet. *The Inventurers: Excursions in Life and Career Renewal.* Reading, Mass.: Addison-Wesley, 1978.

Hall, Edward T. *The Hidden Dimension.* New York: Doubleday, 1966.

_____. *The Silent Language.* New York: Fawcett, 1959.

Harding, James. *Saint-Saëns and His Circle.* London: Chapman and Hall, 1965.

Harris, Irving, D. *Emotional Blocks to Learning.* New York: Free Press of Glencoe, 1961.

Harris, Janet. *The Prime of Ms. America: The American Woman at 40.* New York: Putnam, 1975.

Harris, Thomas A. *I'm OK—You're OK.* New York: Avon, 1973.

Hartog, Jan de. *Hospital.* New York: Atheneum, 1964.

Havighurst, Robert J. *Developmental Tasks and Education.* Toronto: Longman's Green, 1960.

Henig, Robin M. *The Myth of Senility: Misconceptions About Aging.* New York: Anchor/Doubleday, 1981.

Hesse, Hermann. *Steppenwolf.* New York: Holt, Rinehart and Winston, 1963.

Hiestand, Dale L. *Changing Careers After 35.* New York: Columbia University Press, 1971.

Hodin, J. P. *Kokoschka, the Artist and His Time.* Greenwich, Conn.: New York Graphic Society, 1966.

Hoffmann, Banesh. *The Tyranny of Testing.* New York: Collier-Macmillan, 1964.

Horney, Karen. *The Neurotic Personality of Our Time.* New York: W. W. Norton, 1937.

Houle, Cyril. *The Inquiring Mind.* Madison: University of Wisconsin Press, 1961.

Howard, Jane. *Please Touch.* New York: McGraw-Hill, 1970.

Hunt, Morton. *The Universe Within.* New York: Simon and Schuster, 1982.

Ibsen, Henrik. *Peer Gynt.* Trans. Michael Meyer. London: Hart-Davis, 1963.

Jacobs, Jane. *The Death and Life of Great American Cities.* New York: Random House-Knopf, 1961.

Jarvik, L. F., ed. *Aging Into the 21st Century: Middle-Agers To-day.* New York: Gardner Press, 1978.

Johnston, Priscilla W., ed. *Perspectives on Aging: Exploding the Myths.* Cambridge, Mass.: Ballinger/Harper and Row, 1981.

Johnston, William. *Silent Music: The Science of Meditation.* New York: Harper and Row, 1974.

Jonas, Doris and David. *Young Till We Die.* New York: Coward, McCann, Geoghegan, 1973.

Jourard, Sidney M. *The Transparent Self.* New York: Van Nostrand, 1964.

Jung, C. G. *Memories, Dreams, and Reflections.* New York, Pantheon, 1963.

_____. *Man and His Symbols.* New York: Doubleday, 1964.

_____. "The Stages of Life" in *The Collected Works of C. G. Jung,* Vol. 8. Princeton, N. J.: Princeton University Press, 1960.

Kanin, Garson. *It Takes a Long Time to Become Young.* New York: Doubleday, 1980.

Karlsson, Jon-L. *Inheritance of Creative Intelligence.* New York: Nelson-Hall, 1978.

Katz, Robert L. *Empathy.* New York: Free Press of Glencoe, 1963.

Kazantzakis, Nikos. *Report to Greco.* New York: Bantam, 1966.

Kidd, J. Roby. *How Adults Learn.* New York: Association Press, 1973.

Kierkegaard, Soren. *Journals, 1834-1854.* London: Collins Fontana, 1958.

Kimmel, Douglass C. *Adulthood and Aging: An Interdisciplinary, Developmental View.* New York: Wiley, 1980.

Kneller, George F. *The Art and Science of Creativity.* New York: Holt, Rinehart, and Winston, 1965.

Knopf, Olga. *Successful Aging.* New York: Viking Press, 1975.

Knott, James E. *Career Opportunities in the International Field.* Washington, D.C.: Georgetown University Press, 1977.

Koestler, Arthur. *The Act of Creation.* London: Hutchinson, 1964.

_____. *The Ghost in the Machine.* London: Hutchinson, 1967.

Krantz, D. *Radical Career Change.* New York: The Free Press, 1978.

Kresh, Paul. *Isaac Bashevis Singer.* New York: Dial Press, 1979.

Kronenberger, Louis, ed. *Atlantic Brief Lives: A Biographical Companion to the Arts.* Boston: Little, Brown, 1965.

Kubie, L. S. *Neurotic Distortion of the Creative Process.* New York: Noonday Press, 1965.

Kubler-Ross, Elizabeth. *On Death and Dying.* New York: Macmillan, 1969.

Kutner, B., D. Fanshel, A. M. Togo, and T. S. Langner. *Five Hundred over Sixty*. New York: Russell Sage Foundation, 1956.

Lakein, Alan. *How to Get Control of Your Time and Your Life*. New York: New American Library, 1974.

Lasson, Frans, ed. *The Life and Destiny of Isak Dinesen*. Text by Clara Svendsen. New York: Random House, 1970.

Lawrence, Josephine. *Years Are So Long*. New York: Grosset and Dunlap, 1924.

Lehman, H. C. *Age and Achievement*. Princeton, N. J.: Princeton University Press, 1953.

LeShan, Edna. *The Wonderful Crisis of Middle Age*. New York: Warner, 1974.

LeShan, Lawrence. *How to Meditate*. Boston: Little, Brown, 1974.

————. *You Can Fight For Your Life*. New York: M. Evans, 1977.

Levinson, Daniel, et al. *The Seasons of a Man's Life*. New York: A. A. Knopf, 1978.

Liberman, Alexander. *The Artist in His Studio*. New York: Viking, 1960.

Lilly, John and Antonietta. *The Dyadic Cyclone: The Autobiography of a Couple*. New York: Simon and Schuster, 1976.

Liss, Jerome. *Free to Feel: Finding Your Way Through the New Therapies*. New York: Praeger, 1974.

Livesey, H. B. *Second Chance: How to Change Your Career in Mid-Life*. New York: Signet, 1977.

Loevinger, J. *Ego Development*. San Francisco: Jassey-Bass, 1976.

Lorge, Irving, et al. *Psychology of Adults*. Washington, D.C.: Adult Education Association of the USA, 1963.

Losey, Frederick D. *The Kingsway Shakespeare*. London: George G. Harrap, 1927.

Lowen, Alexander. *Bioenergetics*. London: Penguin, 1976.

Lowes, J. L. *The Road to Xanadu*. Boston: Houghton-Mifflin, 1940.

Luce, Gay Gaer. *Your Second Life*. New York: Delta, 1979.

Lynch, James J. *The Broken Heart*. New York: Basic Books, 1977.

Maas, Henry S., and Joseph A. Kuypers. *From Thirty to Seventy*. San Francisco: Jassey-Bass, 1974.

MacGregor, Frances Cooke. *Transformation and Identity, The Face and Plastic Surgery*. New York: Quadrangle/The New York Times Book Company, 1974.

Mariano, Nicky. *Forty Years with Berenson*. London: Hamish Hamilton, 1966.

Maritain, Jacques. *Creative Intuition in Art and Poetry*. New York: Pantheon Books, 1953.

Marshall, Victor. *Aging in Canada*. Toronto: Fitzhenry and Whiteside, 1980.

Maslow, Abraham H. *Motivation and Personality*. New York: Harper and Row, 1970.

————. *Toward a Psychology of Being*. New York: Van Nostrand Reinhold, 1968.

Mathieu, Aron, ed. *The Creative Writer*. Cincinnati: Writer's Digest, 1961.

May, Rollo. *The Courage to Create*. New York: W. W. Norton, 1975.

————. *Man's Search for Himself*. New York: Signet, 1953.

————. *Love and Will*. New York: W. W. Norton, 1969.

Mayer, Nancy. *The Male Mid-Life Crisis: Fresh Starts After 40*. New York: New American Library, 1978.

McCay, James T. *The Management of Time*. Englewood Cliffs, N.J.: Prentice-Hall, 1959.

McCoy, V. R., Colleen Ryan, and J. W. Lichtenberg. *The Adult Life Cycle*. Lawrence, Kansas: University of Kansas Press, 1978.

McGill, M. E. *The 40-60 Male*. New York: Simon and Schuster, 1980.

McLeish, John A. B. *September Gale, The Life of Arthur Lismer*. Toronto: J. M. Dent, 1973.

————. *A Canadian for All Seasons*. Toronto: Lester and Orpen, 1978.

McLeish, Minnie Buchanan. *They Also Lived*. Ottawa: Runge Press, 1962.

McMorrow, F. *Midolescence: The Dangerous Years*. New York: Quadrangle, 1974.

Menninger, Karl. *Love Against Hate*. New York: Harcourt, Brace, 1942.

Migel, Parmenia. Titania, *The Biography of Isak Dinesen*. New York: Random House, 1967.

Monroe, Robert A. *Journeys Out of the Body*. New York: Anchor/Doubleday, 1973.

Mooney, Ross L. *Explorations in Creativity*. New York: Harper and Row, 1967.

Morris, Peter. *Loss and Change*. London: Routledge and Kegan Paul, 1974.

Moustakas, Clark, ed. *The Self: Explorations in Personal Growth*. New York: Harper and Row, 1956.

_____. *Creative Life*. New York: Van Nostrand Reinhold, 1977.

_____. *Loneliness*. Englewood Cliffs, N. J.: Prentice-Hall, 1961.

Muggeridge, Malcolm. *Something Beautiful for God, Mother Teresa of Calcutta*. London: Collins, 1971.

Neugarten, Beatrice L., ed. *Middle Age and Aging*. Chicago: University of Chicago Press, 1968.

Nin, Anais. *Diary of Anais Nin*. New York: Harcourt, Brace, Jovanovich, and London: Peter Owen, 1978. 7 vols.

Olney, James. *Metaphors of Self, the meaning of autobiography*. Princeton, N.J.: Princeton University Press, 1972.

O'Neill, Barbara Powell. *Careers for Women After Marriage and Children*. New York: Macmillan, 1965.

Ornstein, Jack H. *The Mind and The Brain*. The Hague: Martinus Nijhoff, 1972.

Ornstein, Robert E. *The Psychology of Consciousness*. London: Penguin, 1972.

Osborn, Alex F. *Applied Imagination*. New York: Scribner's, 1963.

Osherson, Samuel D. *Holding On or Letting Go: Men and Career Change at Midlife*. London: The Free Press, 1980.

Parker, Elizabeth. *The Seven Ages of Women*. Baltimore: The Johns Hopkins Press, 1960.

Parkes, C. M. *Bereavement: Studies of Grief in Adult Life*. New York: International University Press, 1972.

Parmenter, Ross. *The Awakened Eye*. Middletown: Wesleyan University Press, 1968.

Parnes, Sidney J. *Creative Behaviour Workbook*. New York: Scribner's, 1967.

Percy, Charles H. *Growing Old in the Country of the Young*. New York: McGraw-Hill, 1974.

Perry, Bliss. *The Heart of Emerson's Journals*. Boston: Houghton-Mifflin, 1926.

Peterson, James A., and Barbara Payne. *Love in the Later Years*. New York: Association Press, 1975.

Peterson, R. E., et. al. *Adult Education Opportunities in Nine Industrial Countries*, Vol. 1. Princeton, N.J.: ETS, 1980.

Pines, Maya. *The Brain Changers, Scientists and the New Mind Control*. New York: New American Library, 1975.

Powell, John. *Fully Human, Fully Alive*. Niles, Ill.: Argus, 1976.

Price, Lucian. *The Dialogues of Alfred North Whitehead*. New York: Mentor, 1954.

Prince, Gilbert. *The Practice of Creativity*. New York: Harper and Row, 1970.

Progoff, Ira. *At a Journal Workshop*. New York: Dialogue House, 1975.

Puner, Morton. *Getting the Most Out of Your 50s*. New York: Crown, 1977.

Quennell, Peter. *Samuel Johnson, his Friends and Enemies*. London: Weidenfeld and Nicolson, 1972.

Reich, Charles. *The Sorcerer of Bolinas Reef*. New York: Random House, 1976.

Reichard, S., F. Livson, and P. G. Peterson. *Aging and Personality, a Study of Eighty-Seven Older Men*. New York: Arno Press, 1980.

Reid, Doris. *Edith Hamilton, an Intimate Portrait*. New York: W. W. Norton, 1967.

Renoir, Jean. *Renoir, My Father*. Boston: Little, Brown, 1958.

Restak, Richard M. *The Brain: the Last Frontier*. New York: Doubleday, 1979.

Rieu, E. V., translator. *Homer: The Odyssey*. London: Penguin, 1946.

Riley, Matilda W. *Aging from Birth to Death: Interdisciplinary Perspectives*. Boulder, Colo.: Westview Press, 1979.

Rogers, Dorothy. *The Adult Years: an Introduction to Aging*. Englewood Cliffs, N.J.: Prentice-Hall, 1979.

Rosner, Stanley, and Lawrence Abt, eds. *The Creative Experience*. New York: Grossman, 1970.

Rothenberg, A. *The Emerging Goddess*. Chicago: University of Chicago Press, 1979.

Russ, Lavinia. *A High Old Time: How to Enjoy Being a Woman Over 60*. New York: Saturday Review Press, 1971.

Russell, Bertrand. *Autobiography*. New York: Simon and Schuster, 1969.

Samuels, Ernest. *Bernard Berenson: The Making of a Connoisseur*. Cambridge, Mass: Belknap and Harvard University Press, 1979.

Samuels, Mike, and Nancy Samuels. *Seeing With The Mind's Eye*. New York: Random House, 1975.

Scarf, Maggie. *Unfinished Business: Pressure Points in the Lives of Women*. New York: Doubleday, 1980.

Schnell, Maxine. *Limits: A Search for New Values*. New York: Clarkson N. Potter, 1981.

Schutz, William C. *Joy: Expanding Human Awareness*. New York: Grove Press, 1967.

Seamon, John G. *Memory and Cognition: an Introduction*. New York: Oxford, 1980.

Selye, Hans. *The Stress of Life*. New York: McGraw-Hill, 1956.

————. *Stress Without Distress*. Toronto: McClelland and Stewart, 1974.

Seskin, Jane. *More than Mere Survival. Conversations with Women Over 65*. New York: Newsweek Books, 1980.

————. and Bette Ziegler. *Older Women/Younger Men*. New York: Anchor/Doubleday, 1979.

Sheehy, Gail. *Passages: Predictable Crises of Adult Life*. New York: Dutton, 1975.

Silverstein, Alvin. *Conquest of Death*. New York and London: Macmillan, 1979.

Simon, Anne W. *The New Years, a New Middle Age*. New York: Knopf, 1968.

Smelser, Neil J., and Erik H. Erikson. *Themes of Love and Work in Adulthood*. Cambridge, Mass.: Harvard University Press, 1980.

Smith, Constance Babington. *Rose Macaulay*. London: Collins, 1972.

Smith, Ethel Sabin. *Passports at Seventy*. New York: W. W. Norton, 1961.

Stainesby, Charles, ed. *Strip Jack Naked*. London: Marshall Cavendish Publications, 1971.

Stein, Mauria R., A. J. Vidich, and D. M. White, eds. *Identity and Anxiety*. New York: The Free Press, 1960.

Stern, E. M., and E. Ross. *You and Your Aging Parents*. New York: Harper and Row, 1968.

Stern, Karl. *The Pillar of Fire*. New York: Doubleday, 1956.

————. *The Flight from Woman*. New York: The Noonday Press, 1965.

Stetson, Damon. *Starting Over*. New York: Macmillan, 1971.

Stevenson, Joanne S. *Issues and Crises During Middlescence*. New York: Appleton-Century-Crofts, 1977.

Still, Henry. *Surviving the Male Mid-Life Crisis*. New York: Crowell, 1977.

Storr, Anthony. *The Dynamics of Creation*. London: Secker and Warburg, 1972.

Strachey, Lytton. *Eminent Victorians*. New York: Harcourt Brace and Jovanovich, 1969.

Strindberg, August. *Inferno, Alone*. New York: Doubleday, 1968.

Tanner, Ira J. *Loneliness: The Fear of Love*. New York: Harper and Row, 1973.

_____. *The Gift of Grief*. New York: Hawthorne Books, 1976.

Taylor, C. W. *Creativity, Progress, and Potential*. New York: McGraw-Hill, 1964.

Tettemer, John. *I Was a Monk*. New York: A. A. Knopf, 1951.

Thorndike, Edward L. et al. *Adult Learning*. New York: Macmillan, 1928.

Toffler, Alven. *The Third Wave*. New York: Morrow, 1980.

Tolson, A. *The Limits of Masculinity*. London: Tavistock, 1977.

Tomkins, Calvin. *Eric Hoffer, an American Odyssey*. New York: E. P. Dutton, 1968.

Torrance, E. P. *Education and the Creative Potential*. Minneapolis: University of Minnesota Press, 1963.

Tough, Allen. *The Adult's Learning Projects*. Toronto: OISE, 1972.

Truman, Margaret. *Harry S. Truman*. San Diego: Morren Publications, 1973.

Unterecker, John. *Yeats*. Englewoods Cliffs, N.J.: Prentice-Hall, 1963.

Vaillant, George E. *Adaptation to Life*. Boston: Little, Brown, 1977.

Vasari's Lives of the Artists. Abridged and edited by Betty Burroughs. New York: Simon and Schuster, 1946.

Vernon, P. E., ed. *Creativity*. London: Penguin, 1970.

Volin, Michael. *Challenging the Years*. New York: Harper and Row, 1979.

_____. *The Quiet Hour*. London: Pelham Books, 1980.

Vorres, Ian. *The Last Grand Duchess*. London: Hutchinson, 1964.

Watson, Lyall. *Supernature*. New York: Anchor/Doubleday, 1973.

Wechsler, David. *The Measurement and Appraisal of Adult Intelligence*. Baltimore: Williams and Wilkins, 1958.

Whitbourne, S. K., and C. S. Weinstock. *Adult Development: the Differentiation of Experience*. New York: Holt, Rinehart, and Winston, 1979.

White, Robert W. *Lives in Progress*. New York: Holt, Rinehart, and Winston, 1966.

_____. *The Study of Lives*. New York: Atherton, 1966.

Widening Horizons in Creativity. Proceedings of the Fifth University Research Conference, University of Utah, C. W. Taylor, ed. New York: John Wiley and Sons, 1964.

Wiggam, Albert Edward. *The Marks of an Educated Man*. Indianapolis: Bobbs-Merrill, 1930.

Williams, R., and Claudine G. Wirths. *Lives Through the Years*. New York: Atherton Press, 1965.

Williams, Robin. *American Society*. New York: A. A. Knopf, 1970.

Wolf, Theta Holmes. *Alfred Binet*. Chicago: University of Chicago Press, 1973.

Yourcenar, Marguerite. *Memoirs of Hadrian*. New York: Farrar, Straus and Giroux, 1954.

INDEX

Eliot, T.S.,   17

ENCLAVES:
    defined by Houle,   116
    examples of,   116-117
    uses for older adults,   116,
        189
Enemies of Promise,   221
Erikson, Erik,   3, 46, 47, 52, 57,
    182
Escott, Manuel,   178
"essential energy,"   78
Everlasting Mercy, The,   58

F

Fairley, Barker,   140, 141
Far Pavilions, The,   36
Fels Institute,   101
Fields, Gracie,   81
Finch, Edith,   145
Finch, Peter,   42
Finch, Robert,   140
Finch-Hatton, Denys,   158, 159
Fisher, Mary,   168
Fisher, Welthy,   136, 137, 138
Fitzgerald, Barry,   193
Flaccorio,   171
flexible life scheduling,   52
Flight of the Firecrest,   127
Forty Days of Musa Dagh, The,
    46-47
Frampton, R.G. (Dick),   119
Franck, César,   15
Frankl, Viktor,   45, 46
Franklin, Benjamin,   116
Franzen, Ulrich,   28
Freud, Sigmund,   9, 28, 102
Friedman, A.S.,   101
Fromm, Erich,   23, 24, 225
Fromm-Reichmann, Frieda,   47
Frost, Robert,   17, 28
Fuller, Buckminster,   15, 117
Fully Human, Fully Alive,   58

G

Galileo,   109
Galton, Lawrence,   88

Gandhi, Mahatma,   138
Gary, Romain,   31, 169
Gayn, Mark,   147
Gerbault, Alain,   126
Ghiselli, E.E.,   101
Giacometti, Alberto,   16
Gibson, Mary,   142
Gide, André,   72, 73, 81, 82
Goethe, J.W. von,   34, 140
Goetzke, John,   128
Goldstein, Kurt,   58
Gonzales, Pancho,   76
Goudeket, Maurice,   134, 135
Graham, Martha,   139, 140
Granick, Samuel,   101, 102
Grappelli, Stephane,   17
Graves, A.F.,   169
Greek Way, The,   8
Green, Alyce,   183
Green, Elmer,   183
Guilford, J.P.,   96
Guinan, Sister St. Michael,   184
Gutmann, D.L.,   221

H

Haefele, J.W.,   25
Hamilton, Edith,   8, 9
Handel, G.F.,   15, 160, 161
Hardy, Thomas,   17
Harris, Gus,   191
Harwood, E.,   102
Havighurst, Robert,   49, 50
Haydn, Joseph,   15
Healing Power of Laughter,   220
Hebb, D.O.,   96, 97
Henry, W.E.,   50
Herbert, Martin,   41
Hermippus,   92
Hess, Hella,   136
Hiestand, Dale,   118
*History of the Church in
    England*,   87
*History of the French
    Revolution*,   163
Hoffer, Eric,   201
Holland, J.,   220

A graduate of McGill (M.A.) and Cornell (Ph.D.) universities, with postdoctoral studies at Harvard, John McLeish has been a university teacher, faculty dean, writer, and consultant on adult life and learning for over 30 years. During his career he has counselled several thousand men and women of all ages.

He has given seminars, workshops, and papers on the modern adult and the creative process at numerous campuses and congresses throughout North America, and in 1980 he received the Citation of the School of Continuing Studies, University of Toronto, for outstanding performance in the field of university continuing education. He has also appeared from time to time on network and local television and radio programs.

Professor McLeish's range of interests is wide. He is a member of Amnesty International, the Writers' Union of Canada, the Canadian Civil Liberties Association, and the Foster Parents' Plan; and he has been a director of the Canadian Mental Health Association (Toronto.) His personal avocations include devoted attention to the arts, especially music and cinema, interest in the new athleticism of older adults, fiction and poetry writing, and a passion for talking with people, especially in late evening coffee-houses.